# TRANSPORTATION PLANNING AND POLICY DECISION MAKING

# TRANSPORTATION PLANNING AND POLICY DECISION MAKING

## Behavioral Science Contributions

edited by
# Richard M. Michaels

PRAEGER

PRAEGER SPECIAL STUDIES • PRAEGER SCIENTIFIC

**Library of Congress Cataloging in Publication Data**

Main entry under title:

Transportation planning and policy decision making.

   Papers and summaries of workshops from a
conference held in late 1978.
   Bibliography:  p.
   1.  Transportation planning--Psychological
aspects.  2.  Transportation and state--United
States--Congresses.  I.  Michaels, Richard M.
HE193.T65      380.5'01'9      79-24820
ISBN 0-03-055786-0

Published in 1980 by Praeger Publishers
CBS Educational and Professional Publishing
A Division of CBS, Inc.
521 Fifth Avenue, New York, New York 10017 U.S.A.

© 1980 by Praeger Publishers

# PREFACE

This book contains the proceedings of a conference on the application of behavioral science to transportation held in Charleston, South Carolina, October 31 to November 2, 1978. This conference was sponsored by the office of the Secretary of Transportation through its Office of University Research under a contract with the Urban Systems Laboratory of the University of Illinois at Chicago Circle. The views expressed in this book are those of the authors and do not reflect those of the U.S. Department of Transportation.

The purpose of this conference was to bring together a broad spectrum of transportation planners and policy makers with behavioral scientists. Its purpose was to expose both groups to the problems in transportation and the possibilities for the behavioral sciences to deal with critical aspects of these problems. It was, in essence, an attempt to initiate a broad-based dialogue and to expand channels of communication between the two groups. Doing this is essential now because of the fundamental changes that must be made in transportation, especially in policy and planning. These changes are a product of the changes in social, economic, and functional requirements for mobility in American society. Many, if not most, of these requirements depend critically on behavioral considerations that are not well understood and that have not been attacked using modern behavioral science and technology.

The conference itself was the product of a group effort. A steering committee was established in July 1977 to help develop its philosophy and organization. This committee was composed of Ricardo Dobson, Charles River Associates, Boston, Mass.; David N. Goss, Greater Cleveland RTA; David Hartgen, New York Department of Transportation; Robert Paaswell, SUNY-Buffalo; George Wickstrom, Metropolitan Washington Council of Government; and Richard Worrall, Peat, Marwick and Mitchell & Co., Washington, D.C. The editor wishes to express his thanks to the members of this group for their consistent support and insights. The editor also wishes to thank Mary Lynn Tischer, the project manager for the Department of Transportation. Her direct assistance, patience, and continuous constructive suggestions were invaluable in developing the conference and this volume.

Finally, the author wishes to express special appreciation to Patricia Lane. She was responsible for all the administrative arrangements for the conference. That the operation of the conference was as effective as it was is due to her efforts. She has played a major role in the editorial work in the preparation of the manuscript. This book is as much hers as it is the editor's and the participants'.

# CONTENTS

# LIST OF TABLES

# TRANSPORTATION PLANNING AND POLICY DECISION MAKING

# 1
## INTRODUCTION

### Richard M. Michaels

Transportation systems are the essential technologies for linking people with goods and services produced by the society. In essence, the social systems that determine the net quality of life provided to society's members require means of access for people and for the distribution of services. The properties of those means are themselves critical determinants of the ultimate quality of life available to the members of the society. It is obvious, therefore, that there is a direct connection between the characteristics of transportation and social organization. Equally, the way in which transportation is used, market shares among alternatives, and the time-space distribution of travel reflect trade-offs people make in their individual and collective actions to achieve their personal goals. Transportation may then be viewed as mediating between needs and their sources of satisfaction. In this sense, transportation is a generic cost that people must pay—in the physical, economic, and psychological areas—to satisfy their needs. Conversely, transportation systems reflect a cost that the society as a whole must bear to insure its viability. Although the costs of transport are distributed between the public and private sectors, the public role has been, and is, critical to the planning, organization, and operation of these systems.

Transportation systems are technologies that have evolved largely by trial and error and remain constrained by available technological and engineering capability. In this context, traveler behavior has been a second-order concern in the design and operation of these systems. Urban rail transit, for example, was attractive at the time of highly concentrated urban form because it provided an extremely high capacity system at low cost per passenger mile.

Although elemental human factors were considered in the design (for example, maximum acceleration), the fundamental decisions were based on maximizing aggregate accessibility within the structure of distributed origins and destinations. Operating strategies were determined largely by the characteristics of the technologies and by the economics of supply and demand that inhered in the technologies themselves. The consequences, direct and indirect, on social organization and performance were rarely considered systematically. The objective was to implement a technology and satisfy its operational requirements. Users were required to adapt to those requirements and adjust their needs to them.

The evolution of transport technology was, well into the twentieth century, a process of innovation to more efficient mobility. Progress from canal systems to railroads, from horse-drawn vehicles to electrified railways reflected major improvements in capacity and performance. These major innovations significantly improved the mobility of goods and people. They were rapidly adopted with direct and indirect support from all levels of government as well as with private capital investment.

As it turned out, these transportation innovations also brought about radical changes in demography, geographic form, and social organization. Few of these changes were clearly recognized at the time. In an earlier review (Michaels 1967) the major positive and negative effects of existing modes of transportation were summarized, and both classes of impacts have been profound. It appears clear that transportation technology has been a basic determinant of the social and cultural, as well as economic, development of the country. It is equally clear that major changes in transportation, which are bound to occur, will product significant social changes.

Transportation systems planning and design have evolved with limited understanding of social and behavioral consequences. Only elemental analysis was ever done on the use and operation of the systems or their impacts on social or physical environments. Traffic accidents were categorized as human error rather than system design error. Land taken for facilities was rarely surveyed in terms of effects on individuals or neighborhoods, but rather in terms of the "greater good." Designs considered system users only in terms of a narrow statistical range. Consequently, the very young, elderly, handicapped, and economically disadvantaged have been mobility limited because of transportation system design.

Development and expansion of highway transportation was crucial in making single family home ownership feasible, but suburbanization, as it affected cities' population distribution and changed requirements for social services, was not anticipated, nor the consequences estimated. The emergence of energy constraints, in highway transportation in particular, now poses a severe threat to the dispersed social structure that this mode of transportation was instrumental in creating. The social and behavioral implications of energy shortages are not now predictable, either on people's immediate responses or on the political and economic structure of the society as a whole.

In essence, transportation design, planning, operations, and management have been guided by technological and economic concerns, with secondary concern for the behavioral considerations or consequences. This is not to suggest that social and behavioral techniques have not been used in transportation research and practice. They have, but generally for specific operational purposes, in support of developing particular modes. However, until recently, the behavioral sciences have not been used as part of the policy and planning process, especially for evaluation and impact analysis.

In part, the failure to use the behavioral sciences as an integral part of any comprehensive transportation planning and policy system can be traced to the focus of transportation on the hard technological and economic issues that inhere in the development of such massive systems. There has been a social organization with its own power structure, in which psychological and social issues were of marginal concern. For example, the then Bureau of Public Roads, whose formal existence can be dated from the Federal Highway Act of 1916, had no behavioral scientist in a staff position until 1958. (This is not to say that the agency did not support behavioral science research. It has done so since the 1930s.)

It is instructive here to examine the history of the highway planning process. In this area, the primary concern has been predicting the use of and demand for facilities. Since finding out who wanted highways and why and how they were used is primarily a behavioral question, it might be expected that planning methodology would involve significant applications of behavioral science. Actually, until the past five years, it has not. This has been due partly to a concentration on planning for work-trip travel. Since all transportation systems are capacity constrained, it is peak hour demand that has been the major determinant of facility needs. Although work hours are a socially determined process, planning has simply accepted them as immutable fact and modeled the demand process accordingly.

Given this framework, the planning process reduces to a straightforward (albeit complex) mechanical operation in which manifest behavior is relevant. From each household a certain number of trips will be generated, depending upon socioeconomic status. Assuming homogeneity within class, a certain number of work trips will occur within that zone. Given that number, these trips are distributed among a set of employment or activity sites on the basis of some distance-minimizing or attractiveness-maximizing criterion or both. These criteria must be behaviorally based, but the models in use are derived empirically from historical patterns of trip making. Once the origin-destination pattern and qualities are determined, they are assigned to a facilities network according to a behavioral assumption: travelers will always seek the minimum time path to their destination. This is clearly questionable on perceptual and cognitive grounds, but leads to an elegant algorithm. The process produces an output, a demand distribution over space, which, in time, brings to light corridors requiring new facilities. Finally, if we estimate the changes in population, residence, and employment location for some time in the future, it is possible to project requirements for new transport facilities. Again, the assumption underlying these projections is behavioral; in this case, it is that people's attitudes, values, and goals will not change.

It is obvious from this discussion that the field of planning has used a series of very simple behavioral assumptions to create a process for making long-term transport investment decisions. It is a process that has never worked very well; it predicts poorly and the models are not generalizable. This does not surprise any behavioral scientist who has studied planning models. The assumptions are behaviorally naive. The fact that the models work as well as they do is a measure of how constrained work-trip travel has been and of the perseverence of planners in manipulating the models.

It should also be noted that the limited use of behavioral science, especially in transportation planning and policy, is as much a failure of the behavioral sciences as of the transportation field itself. Much of behavioral science has had an academic base detached from application. There has been little interest on the part of theoretical and academic sociologists and psychologists in larger sociotechnical systems like transportation. One important consequence has been the negligible diffusion of behavioral science and technology into transportation. The diffusion process is, of course, essential if any cohesive social institution is to incorporate new science or technology. In fact, transportation system planners and engineers have been unaware of most of the advances in the behavioral sciences and have seen little relevance in what they have been exposed to, generally in diluted form via mass media.

The lack of transaction between transportation planning and systems design and the behavioral sciences stands in stark contrast to the sophisticated transactions in aerospace and military systems. Early in the 1950s in these areas there developed a strong base of support for a broad range of cooperation between behavioral science and technology. Ranging over the spectrum from perception to small group dynamics to management systems, this work is now an integral part of the design, development, and deployment of tactical systems.

Major changes in consensus in transportation began around the end of the 1960s and have led to greater sensitivity to the behavioral sciences. One change was the emergence of environmental quality concerns and requirements for social and environmental impact evaluation. The other was the major shift to interest in public transportation. Both involve major behavioral science considerations.

The latter is the most instructive. Essentially, if it is a policy goal to increase the use of public transportation in competition with the private automobile, two major behavioral issues emerge. One is the basic question of how people make choices among competing modes. The other is how public transport can or should be marketed to increase its market share. The first question, that of choice behavior, is a theoretical issue with important implications for urban transportation planning. Using utility models such as Luce's (Stopher and Meyburg (1975), it has been possible to develop behavioral models of mode choice for work-trip travel that, in practice, are quite reliable. Although a variety of important issues in these models are unsettled, they do represent a major example of behavioral science application to transportation.

The marketing question has led to a substantial investment in behavioral science research on the attributes of modes and modal alternatives. To a significant degree, this work has drawn on modern scaling theory and consumer psychology. It is now possible, to a first approximation, at least, to define qualitative and operational attributes that significantly determine traveler perceptions of transportation. This work provides a basis for evaluating existing modes of transportation and also for analyzing the potential of new technology. In sum, the mode choice area has been perceived as a behavioral science area, and sophisticated behavioral science techniques have been applied to it, drawing on much of the theor~
attitudes and behavior developed in academic psych~'
past 30 or more years. This movement h~~
basic behavioral issues previously ~
tem planning design, operations,

In the last five or so years,
have changed. Until the 1970s, nat
concerned primarily with technologi
and air transportation and, more rec
were promoted as the means of satisf
mobility. For highway and air transp(
every evidence that the growth in these

to growth in the gross national product. When to this was added the redistribution of population to lower residential and employment densities, the projected demand for transportation dictated continuing transport investment, especially in highways.

The particular policies that were supported by these projections led to three major social problems. The first was a series of direct and indirect effects on the urban environment. The second was the effect on the mobility limited. The third was the change in the resource supply, mainly energy, and its effect on transportation.

The growth in highway transport supported the flight of the middle class out of the cities. Industry followed that out-migration, so that the resources available to cities to meet their needs was markedly reduced. In addition, although less traffic was bound to the city itself, much of that traffic had to pass through the city and its road network. This increasing congestion, and its consequent effects on the environment, was borne by the cities. This was an inequity that raised serious political as well as economic conflicts.

The diffusion of employment sites, as well as social, recreation, and consumption locations, generated problems for the mobility limited. The economically disadvantaged, the physically handicapped, and the elderly—always limited in their capacity to travel—had their opportunities reduced even more by the "metropolitanization" process. The issues were raised at a sociopolitical level, leading to regulations that mainly impacted mass transit. However, the problem of the mobility limited is a complex one involving the definition of the groups and their transportation needs, the quantitative distribution of both, and the design requirements for systems adequate to meet their needs. These elements are implicitly a series of behavioral science questions. They must be answered if cost-effective solutions to the transportation needs of neglected groups are to be developed.

The third problem was the emergence of energy resources constraints. The social and economic developments of the post-World War II era were predicated on the assumption of cheap and available energy. The pattern of residential and industrial diffusion was supported and driven by that assumption. Half the petroleum energy budget of the United States is now expended in transportation, mainly on highways. Over the short run, supply constraints are likely to continue, and energy conservation, especially in highway transport, has become a major national policy. This has led to a s of alternative strategies, ranging from more energy-efficient biles to reducing auto use and increasing vehicle occupancy. energy savings from all combinations of these strategies, ental problem is how and whether travelers will adopt ly these are all behavioral science questions. Further, these policy changes have significant consequences for the social, political, and economic organization of metropolitan regions. For example, how will transport energy constraints affect housing and industry location decisions? What are the social organization consequences of limitations in personal mobility?

What has happened in the decade of the 1970s has been a major breakdown in the assumptions that for a half century underlay the development of transportation. Since transportation is crucial for sustaining the pattern of social, economic, and political development of American society, the failure of these assumptions raises serious questions about society's future stability. Essentially, transportation investment has been based on the notion of satisfying a demand derived from the expressed desires of the majority of the population. In so doing, our society has committed itself to technologies that are energy inefficient, expensive, and ill-suited to the needs of many segments of the population.

The old assumptions, if no longer valid, lead to a series of short- and long-term questions, as well as to direct and indirect effects of major proportions. All these questions must lead to modifications of attitudes, values, and behavior and to modifications in transportation policy, planning, and technology.

The current and emerging issues in transportation lead to a wide range of behavioral science requirements for their reevaluation. The ultimate question is whether the state of the art of behavioral science and technology is sufficient to meet these requirements. Are the theory and techniques in human factors, psychometrics, decision making, cognitive behavior, organization development, consumer behavior, and learning sufficient to deal with the transportation process problems that currently face the society? The answer, of course, is not unequivocal. But, in general, the capabilities of modern behavioral science are far more well developed than the transportation community generally recognizes. The major outstanding problem is not behavioral science capability, but rather whether the organization and the sophistication exist to utilize it effectively. If the transportation policy or planning community states inappropriate or trivial behavioral questions, the behavioral science product will be of negligible value. Conversely, if the behavioral science community focuses only on descriptive or abstract considerations, its product will also be of negligible value. To solve the difficult issues in a critical component of this society now requires a sophisticated multidisciplinary effort.

It was out of these considerations that the conference, which this volume records, was conceived. To begin a dialogue among behavioral scientists and transportation planners and policy makers, the conference was designed to provide an overview of the needs of current transportation and the current thinking in the behavioral sciences. The chapters by Brand, Parsons, Hartgen, Michaels, and Klausner provide this background.

In addition, the conference was designed to extend the dialogue to four specific and currently critical issues in transportation: energy conservation, transportation for the mobility limited, social and environmental impact analysis, and transportation systems management. In each case, a group composed of transportation specialists and behavioral scientists attempted to identify the issues and aspects in which behavioral science and technology were critical for understanding and problem resolution. The summaries of these dialogues are contained in Chapter 7. Finally, there is an interpretive summary of the process provided by Klausner. Thus, this volume reflects a directed attempt to provide an overall frame of reference for defining the ways in which the behavioral sciences can be drawn into transportation and employed in specific areas and, generally, in constructive support of transportation policy, planning, design, and operation.

REFERENCES

R. M. Michaels. 1967. "Transportation Technology and Its Effects on the Human Environment." In Transportation and the Changing South, edited by T. E. Nichols. North Carolina State University.

Stopher, P. R., and A. H. Meyburg. 1975. Urban Transportation and Modelling. Lexington, Mass.: Lexington.

# 2

# TRANSPORTATION POLICIES AND PROBLEMS FOR STUDY IN THE BEHAVIORAL SCIENCES

## Daniel Brand

## INTRODUCTION

This paper presents a decision maker's perspective on transportation policy issues, problem areas, and behaviors in transportation worthy of study by behavioral scientists. The intent is to trigger ideas on approaches and solutions to the many problems and issues raised here. The paper covers topics in each of the conference's four workshop areas (transportation for the elderly and handicapped, energy, environmental and social impact analysis, and short-range transit operations and alternatives analysis). Many other issues and problems that place the four workshop areas in some perspective are also raised.

In writing this paper, I will pose not as a researcher or problem solver, which I am at heart, but as a hard-bitten local official, in this case, a state official. Between 1975 and 1977, before joining Charles River Associates, I was undersecretary of the Massachusetts State Department of Transportation. In this position I had the opportunity to deal with all the major actors in transportation decision making, including the legislature, the bureaucracy, and the few key actors in the executive branch interested in transportation. On the judicial side, I attempted to reorganize the state transportation regulatory agency and have been an expert witness in federal court.

I am too much of a realist to put priorities on the many policy issues raised in this paper. The importance of any issue is too much a function of the immediate context or controversy to set priorities at this time. Also, like a good decision maker, I do not make a decision unless it is required.

However, priorities will emerge for you as researchers. There is a stimulus-response or supply-demand behavior in the conduct of research, as in any other behavior. There is a good

9

supply of research findings and approaches that may have gone begging because the demands were not known. This paper gives some perspective on the demands of the marketplace, with the intent of stimulating behavioral science applications.

First, let me lay out a set of values: that of the state and local official in transportation. Transportation facilities are built and operated at the state and local level. Federal officials do not construct and operate transportation facilities except in rare events like the Alaska Railroad. Instead, Washington furnishes much of the public money for transportation in this country. Congress and the federal bureaucracy formulate national transportation policy, which in urban transportation may be described as the good things on which we should be spending our federal dollars. Federal officials also work very hard at ways to enforce their program goals; that is, what kinds of strings to attach to federal dollars to achieve national objectives.

The rather glacial nature and global perspective of the federal government may be contrasted with the hurry of state and local officials to do something. This is only natural. Our governors and our mayors are elected for only two to four years. It is extremely hard to do something tangible in transportation in that length of time unless it involves changing the rules governing citizens' behavior, as in a popular federal program at this time that goes under the rubric of Transportation Systems Management. As behavioral scientists know, changing the rules of the game as to who gets what portion of the same or a shrinking pie is not a task that is popular among politicians.

Unfortunately, local officials in a hurry become frustrated trying to satisfy federal paperwork requirements on program effectiveness. Some of these requirements result from recent social and environmental concerns for which many among us were the most vocal partisans. The paperwork is the federal way of insuring that national perspectives and values will be reflected in local decision making.

I would submit to you, therefore, a first problem: that local officials have great difficulty responding to federal paperwork requirements that are institutionalized as a result of the crisis atmosphere created by each great passing wave of societal concern. The resulting complexity of the process also brings with it great uncertainty as to what should happen when, and nothing ties up large organizations like uncertainty. It is the best excuse for dropping the ball or blaming the other fellow that a bureaucrat, confused by the changing demands of society and his regularly changing bosses, could desire.

In the end, however, transportation improvements must be made at the state and local level. The democratic process of doing something and getting reelected requires that the effort be made. However, in the process, distortions and conflict result from differences between national level goals and local motives reached in the context ("forged in the crucible") of local political and decision-making processes. The different behaviors resulting from these assorted values are described in the second part of this paper.

In the first part of the paper we give examples of vitally important current transportation policy issues impacted by the need to better understand individual travel choice behavior. The third and final section of the paper highlights three specific areas fruitful for study by behavioral scientists. These are (1) traveler responses to new transportation technology, (2) learning in transportation choice behavior, and (3) changing our definition of comprehensiveness in transportation planning and evaluation from a prescriptive or normative judgment on how investment decisions should be made to a more behavioral description of how these decisions are actually made. The last theme ties together many of the examples of transportation policy-related behavior raised in the paper.

## INDIVIDUAL TRAVEL CHOICE BEHAVIOR

For policy analysis purposes, individual travel choice behavior may be defined as the response of individuals to engage in travel and activity at specific locations in response to a change in their choice environment. Our interest as policy makers is generally in the aggregate of many individual travel decisions, which result in observed volumes of movement and distributions of settlement and other activities. For decision-making purposes, such information is translated into travel benefits, flow-related physical impacts, and other attributes of the travel choice environment of interest as they overlap societal objectives.

Relationships between attributes of the travel choice environment of interest to consumers and policy makers exist only by policy. For example, the fare charged—a consumer view attribute—is related to the cost of providing the service only as the result of policy. In addition, the amount of travel consumed by any particular user group is of interest only to the extent of our implicit or explicit policies in transportation.

Up to now, our understanding and data on travel choice behavior has been derived from traveler responses to transportation improvements that have enlarged the area within which masses of individuals could travel to obtain benefits at the trip end. The past few decades in urban transportation have been characterized by high-capacity, high-speed transportation improvements, such as expressways, and high-capital rail transit systems and extensions. These have made possible travel and settlement on new land, which has been incorporated into our metropolitan areas.

The American concern with new land development as a result of transportation investments dates from the early days of settlement in this country. The early toll roads, the canals, and the railroads were all built by speculators who profited more from the land opened up for development by their transportation investments than from user charges on their transportation facilities.

At present, however, our frontiers have been settled, and the current distance-conquering transportation technology (the highway) seems to have been fully exploited for its potential to open up new lands for development. In and near urban areas, the latest round of investments in interstate highways seems to have merged and fuzzed the boundaries between suburbia and settlements in rural areas outside of metropolitan areas. Obviously, the effects of these most recent investments in urban transportation are still shaking themselves out. However, it appears that major investments in land-exploiting transportation technologies are over for the time being.

The urban transportation alternatives now being considered have as their objective improving service to existing developed areas, particularly central business districts (CBD) and inner city high density areas in which large numbers of the so-called transportation disadvantaged live. These are the poor, the elderly, the handicapped, and, in general, the carless, who were not well served (or even disenfranchised) by the previous round of urban highway and suburban railroad investments. Other current objectives are energy conservation, improving the environment, improving safety, and increasing employment opportunities for the poor now generally living in central cities. Government appears to be taking seriously its traditional role of redistributing incomes and the benefits of our current wealth to those least able to fend for themselves, that is, those who are least able to buy their way out of their current problems in our nation's cities.

Therefore, we should be concerning ourselves with improving our understanding of individual travel and activity choice behavior in response to alternatives that improve service to existing developed areas and that increase the productivity of the existing transportation system. These are alternatives that involve increasing use of transit and other high-occupancy vehicles and auto and land management policies.

These changes in transportation policy open up whole new areas for behavioral science contributions. Our existing understanding of travel behavior is focused almost exclusively on the response of travelers to changes in transportation level-of-service attributes associated with the previous round of high-capital transportation improvements. These, of course, include, most importantly, reductions in line haul travel times and costs. Now we are considering alternatives that price up the use of the automobile through road pricing and auto restraint policies and that increase the cost of development to private developers through such alternatives as value capture. Even our efforts at promoting carpooling through positive incentives carry with them certain reductions in level-of-service attributes (for example, increasing travel time and often walk time) in order to group travelers in time and space for ride sharing.

By pursuing policies to reduce vehicular travel through pricing and restraint measures and to serve existing development with high-occupancy vehicles, government is, of course, colliding head on with traditional market forces associated with middle-class mobility. It is going against the dynamism of our relatively free, consumer-oriented society. It is also going against the rules of behavior of government regulatory bodies that protect the transportation franchises of public and private transit agencies against providing innovative services for people already served by existing fixed-route transit service. There may be some important conflicts between current government objectives and currently considered alternatives that are not yet well understood.

Most importantly, there is great uncertainty on whether policies intended to serve existing developed areas better may serve them worse. We do not know whether serious application of transportation management policies such as area-wide road pricing and auto restraints (as contrasted with pedestrian malls) will result in individual travel choice behavior leading to more compact cities or to center-city decline and more urban sprawl. That is, by pricing up automobile travel, either in dollar terms or by introducing additional walk time by excluding autos from substantial areas of downtown, other destinations may become more desirable than other modes in our high-density urban areas. Simply stated, people may tend to travel to areas not subject to auto restraints rather than switch to transit for destinations once frequented by car. This behavior clearly needs study by behavioral scientists. If non-CBD destinations are better substitutes than transit for auto travelers, great care should be used in the design and application of auto and land management policies in city centers.

In studies of individual travel choice behavior, behavioral scientists should look beyond the traditional concern in travel demand modeling with sensitivity to changes in transportation level-of-service attributes, such as times and costs. The emerging alternative concerns, such as high-occupancy vehicle incentives and auto restraints, confront us with important questions of how individual behavior varies not only with different transportation level-of-service variables, but with the changes in lifestyle that such alternatives as carpooling bring. As one who has carpooled for half my working life, I can tell you from personal experience that the schedule constraints of urban transit are minor compared with carpooling. The dash to get ready for the carpool in the morning introduces great stress in family situations during an already crowded and hectic breakfast period with several children preparing for school. In the afternoon, all professionals in positions of responsibility can understand the difficulty of having to leave work at the same time every day to catch the carpool. Behavioral scientists will, no doubt, consider such items as backup modes to introduce some schedule flexibility in emergency situations for carpoolers.

Even though carpooling does not have the political sex appeal that multibillion dollar expressway and rapid transit systems have for politicians (more on this follows), the potential of carpools for changing travel behavior in the aggregate is substantial. In the eastern Massachusetts region, our MASSPOOL program, an employer-based $400,000 carpool matching program, appears over two years to have reduced peak period vehicle miles of travel in the region by 3 percent and total daily vehicle miles of travel by 1 percent, by one set of estimates. Large investments in some conventional transportation system improvements would not change travel behavior by this amount in the aggregate. In addition, the impact on travel behavior of such investments would generally be to increase travel, contrary to our current energy and environmental goals.

In summary, behavioral science contributions to improving our understanding of individual travel and settlement behavior can help us plan for and respond to these centrally important recent changes in urban transportation policy: (1) the transition from new physical capacity increases in transportation to a concern for increasing the people-carrying capacity of the existing transportation system; (2) a change from treating long-run demand shifts, or development on new land, as a benefit (that is, the capitalized value of user benefits) to discouraging development on new land and stimulating revitalization of existing urban centers; and (3) the related change from concern for increasing the aggregate of user benefits for the bulk of middle-class auto travelers to concern for the incidence of benefits and costs of transportation investments.

With respect to these three major changes, behavioral scientists should bring to bear all they know about individual choice behavior as affected by personality, group dynamics, and the choice environment to provide a better behavioral basis for forecasting individual travel choices.

Behavioral scientists should also be aware that the travel forecasting techniques being used in transportation planning for the last 20 years have their own implicit rules of behavior. These are the behavior rules implied by the independent variables included (and by correlations between these and variables not included, that is, the unobserved attributes), by the changes described by the data (for example, behavior on new versus developed land, direction of change, cross-section versus time series data, that is, long-run versus short-run behavior), and by the estimated coefficients with their assumptions on distributions of tastes in the population. Included also are behavioral rules on the structure of the travel choices (for example, the sequence of choices) and choice alternatives (for example, alternative destinations) over which the models are applied.

The rules of behavior embedded in current travel forecasting techniques and our methods of estimating these models require exposure to the profession. Clearly, a better understanding of actual travel choice behavior and the choice behavior simulated by various travel models is required before we can make trade-offs in specific planning situations between the basis in behavior (and thus the logic and plausibility of travel forecasts) and the time, money, and skills required to carry out the travel forecasts. With regard to improving planning methodology, lack of knowledge on how travelers behave under different circumstances when confronted with various high- and low-capital transportation alternatives may be causing us to miss many good opportunities to save valuable turn-around time and money in the production and use of travel information in transportation policy making.


## PROBLEMS IN GOVERNMENT DECISION-MAKING BEHAVIOR

Decision making in transportation is popularly perceived as the result of group behavior, that is, how decisions are reached in groups in an allegedly democratic or participatory process involving aggregates of people interacting over time. Sociologists and political scientists are presumably more concerned than are psychologists with decision making in the context of these larger aggregates. However, I would suggest that studies of individual choice behavior by psychologists can also lead to substantially improved understanding of how transportation policy and investment decisions are reached in groups. If the same kind of regularity in behavioral responses in such situations could be uncovered as we think we have uncovered in the area of individual <u>travel</u> choice behavior, some profound predictions could be made that, no doubt, would influence government organization and decision making.

In the following subsection, several examples of individual behavior in government decision-making situations are given.

### Individual Leadership Behavior in Transportation Organizations

A first example of individual choice behavior at high levels of government in transportation is that often produced by controversy, particularly that in which the media take an interest. I refer to the good guy/bad guy posturing that takes place in order to focus the public's attention on a particular individual. For example, a politician will exploit the public's paranoia and fear of the unknown when an innovative approach to solving a particular transportation problem is undertaken. The objective of the politician is to become known, to become, perhaps, even a household word in the state or city. The impression to be left with the electorate at election time is that the politician is a fighter of government excesses and, therefore, doing something right.

An auto-restraint policy or a decision to reconstruct an urban highway that involves major traffic rerouting can be expected to provoke such behavior. One's best attempts at explaining the reasons for the particular transportation decision in a city are often only counterproductive. One soon learns to "low-profile" potentially controversial decisions that negatively affect certain segments of the populace.

This leads directly to the second mode of political behavior, that of minimizing losses and aiding constituents in ways that will be remembered (at election time). Policitians, as a breed, have a fantastic sense of what influences human behavior and, often, a superficial but extensive knowledge of all the impacts and public perceptions of our transportation alternatives. Transportation technicians, on the other hand, specialize in finding out and attempting to communicate in depth, and in jargon, the complicated reasons why an alternative makes good public policy sense, even if it disturbs some portion of the electorate.

Behavioral scientists could usefully explain why it is that people seem to perceive and remember longer the hurt inflicted

upon them than the benefits bestowed by public officials. The benefits from a transportation improvement, if they are not associated
with an obvious physical monument like an expressway or rail
transit line, are soon forgotten. Or the benefits are attributed by
citizens to their own good sense in taking advantage of the system
or the travel choice environment that confronts them. This may be
why public officials, elected, appointed, or self-appointed, expend
so much energy over so many years on a particular physical monument in transportation.

Another related problem is that the thousand small improvements that characterize today's incremental strategy in urban
transportation simply attract much less interest from powerful
leaders than major new construction projects. This is a serious
problem in transportation agencies today and leads to poor morale
on the part of large bureaucracies in these agencies. The excite-
ment of building "virile highways" and other large facilities has
passed out of their lives. Few leaders in power identify with the
thousand small products of their efforts. Behavioral scientists
should address the problem of associating benefits in the popular
mind with many small individual transportation improvements,
each of which sinks readily below the public consciousness. This
research area is important not only as it relates to morale (if not
morals) in the public sector; it is also important because popular
support will need to be rallied to the cause of increasing the productivity of the existing transportation system if today's changing
societal goals are to be realized.

The appointed heads of city, state, and federal departments
of transportation in the executive branch of government exhibit still
other styles of leadership behavior. Because most statutes vest
complete control and power in the secretary or the commissioner,
as contrasted with the department, the effectiveness of the top
person's leadership is usually decisive for the effectiveness of the
organization.

Some department of transportation (DOT) organizations are
dominated by a strong-minded boss—the one person at the top. In
some cases, that person may be highly motivated by a particular
belief in a particular solution: building new highways or, conversely, depressing existing highways in cities to alleviate neighborhood impacts. In other instances, the person may be driven by
particular objectives that are believed, however naively, to be
attainable by transportation as the tool of policy. In any event, the
strong leader at the top with pervasive influence through the structure of transportation decision making (the opposite of the Peter
Principle, as it were) is an important actor in many apparently
organizational decision-making situations. It may, of course, be

the case that such individuals surface more easily in small ponds (that is, at the state and local level) than at the federal level, where there exists more talent that inevitably becomes drawn into conflict with the strong personality.

The opposite of the strong leader is, of course, the weak leader. Behavioral scientists can supply the results of this style of leadership for themselves. However, it is generally of less interest for study since fewer tangible results (by definition?) are achieved by such organizations. Depending on one's point of view, however, such leaders may also be better because they are less dangerous in their pursuit of certain policies.

A final example of individual choice behavior in transportation decision making is horse-trading behavior. This typically, but not always, arises as part of the separation of powers in our political system. If a transportation legislative committee head or a House or Senate majority leader or other powerful legislator knows that someone in the executive branch wants something badly, high stakes horse trading often takes place. Decisions made in this way can be elusive for study since multisectoral costs and benefits are being traded off. That is, transportation may be only one area of interest to the traders, and, of course, such trading behavior is difficult to predict. You think you've got a deal, and someone comes back and wants more goodies for the same thing. Often, also, the expert horse trader doesn't really give anything, but might merely agree not to prohibit you by law from doing something you want to do, for example, reserving a lane on an existing expressway for high-occupancy vehicles (as occurred to me when I undertook such a project for the Southeast Expressway in Massachusetts). Powerful legislators can be governed by what appear to be the most parochial concerns in such situations. Motives for such behavior can also merge with the first two types of political behavior described in this section.

In other situations, legislators can be motivated by high ideals, such as redressing grievances of parties threatened, disadvantaged, or otherwise not helped by particular transportation programs. Unfortunately, such legislators often have no idea of the costs or problems introduced by the statutes they pass under these circumstances, nor are the dynamics of such choice situations conducive to considering the long-run costs. Their actions can result in severe problems and conflicts in administering statutes passed under such circumstances. Examples of these are discussed in the next section.

Problems in Administering Recent Transportation
Statutes Passed by Congress

Examples in transportation of single-objective laws passed
by Congress to protect militant minorities or redress grievances
in our society are many. For reasons worthy of study, Congress's
noble, singly considered objectives are written into law in a climate
not conducive to considering comprehensively the full set of impacts
of the laws. A fair share of the current problems in transportation
at all levels of government arise from this behavior at the federal
level. The laws are leading to high costs and serious constraints
on our ability in transportation to adapt logically and efficiently to
other societal demands (for example, tax reduction and reducing
the high cost of government).

The examples are many and well known. I need only cite a
few alpha-numeric characters to elicit immediate recognition and
groans from some if not most state and local leaders in transportation: 13(c), 504, 4f, NEPA, TCPs, and so on.

For example, 13(c) is the labor protection section in the 1964
federal Urban Mass Transportation Act (UMTA), as amended. It
requires that as a condition of federal assistance to any transit
project, the condition of any and all employees affected by the
transit project receiving assistance cannot be worsened. The
original intent of 13(c) was to ensure that, in providing federal
assistance for capital funding of new transit facilities, maintenance
workers could not be fired or receive reduced compensation. When
only capital assistance was provided by Washington, this appeared
to be a reasonable protection. Federal money should not be used
to disenfranchise labor. However, the use of federal money for
capital and operating assistance has become so pervasive over time
that almost anything that is done in urban transit involves federal
money, and the easiest thing for congressional leaders to do has
been simply to extend 13(c) protections to any transit assistance
project. One would think that federal operating (Section 5) subsidies, which, by statute, must be used "to continue or improve
transit service," could not possibly worsen the condition of labor.
However, the interpretation of labor is that the moment the transit
operator touches any federal money, transit management loses its
prerogative to introduce any efficiencies or any measures that
would in any way "worsen" the condition of labor. For example,
transit workers in Boston, who because of automatic cost-of-living
increases are paid nearly twice what other public sector employees

in the area get for comparable job categories, recently claimed that automatic cost-of-living salary increases in their contract could not be eliminated for fear of losing federal funds for the transit system. The confusion this argument caused in the minds of the Massachusetts public went a long way to providing sympathy for the transit workers as they illegally struck against "management actions which would threaten the supply of federal funds for transit in Boston."

Needless to say, 13(c) is a murky area. When state and local officials behave logically and reasonably in such circumstances, they are often told no by federal bureaucrats. These bureaucrats have in turn been told no by their legal counsels, who take the most conservative interpretations of the federal laws. The behavior of government lawyers seems to reveal less concern for challenge internally by the bureaucracy than for external challenge in court by the groups whose protections they uphold at such great cost.

At the risk of belaboring the problems imposed by congressionally passed statutes so familiar to transportation professionals, let me discuss an additional example—that of Section 504 of the Health, Education and Welfare (HEW) Act. This act is of high current interest and relates to the workshop topic of transportation for the elderly and handicapped. Section 504 guarantees equal access to federally assisted facilities for all groups in society, regardless of their physical handicaps. The law is being interpreted as applying to any federally funded transit facility (meaning all of them), regardless of the obvious intent or purpose of the transit service. For example, fixed-route buses provide transportation to those who can get to the bus line at the time the bus departs. Very few wheelchair-bound handicapped persons in urban areas fit this description. A superior transit service for these handicapped persons is door-to-door service provided by specially equipped small vehicles. Nevertheless, Section 504 is now interpreted as requiring all fixed-route buses to be expensively equipped to maintain and operate wheelchair lifts.

Millions of dollars would have to be spent in each of our major cities to retrofit existing bus systems and install elevators in rail transit stations, and so on. For this expenditure, perhaps ten or 20 wheelchair handicapped might use the system each day. It would be far cheaper to buy each of these persons a (gold plated?) Cadillac or Mercedes for these trips. Service would also not be slowed in the fixed-route facilities for all the regular passengers. Better yet, of course, is the alternative of specially equipped vans or other small vehicles to provide all the transportation service that the wheelchair handicapped would use in the context of a basic, no-frills door-to-door transportation service provided by a public transportation system.

Hearings are now taking place on Section 504 as it applies to public transportation facilities. One may hypothesize that the struggle will not end until transit systems have spent millions of dollars in the futile effort to serve what on the surface appears to be the equal protection clause of the constitution. The problem, as noted above, is the reluctance of Congress to behave in such a way as to apparently inflict a hurt on some people, in this case, to repeal a protection of a particular group that believes that protection to be a right. The situation is not helped by the fact that a non-transportation agency, namely HEW, administers the law. This agency has its own objectives and constituencies and does not bear the cost of rebuilding the urban public transportation system as mandated by the law. In fact, however, it presently pays the transportation costs of its handicapped clients. What HEW may not realize is that to the extent that its clients are really served by transportation agencies, it will save its own funds.

Problems Caused by Increasing Federal Power
Versus State and Local Power

The examples of 13(c) and Section 504 discussed above suggest a growing imbalance of power in this country between the federal government on one hand and state and local governments on the other. This sounds either highly conservative or like the lament of the local official whose role I am taking. Nevertheless, the concentration of federal power that accompanies the accumulation of monies through the federal system of taxation needs to be flagged on efficiency grounds, if for no other reason.

The system of checks and balances between branches of government that our founders had in mind seems to have worked well for behavior within a particular level of government. However, even the Federalists among our founders might be surprised at the extent of federal influence in urban transportation that has evolved over only the last 20 years. Twenty years ago, there was no federal role in urban transit. Highway building was the product of a great national consensus that peaked with the passage of the 1956 Interstate Highway Act. State and federal governments worked hand in hand to implement the great highway building partnership that started with the first Federal Aid Highway Act in 1916.

Now, with the pervasiveness of federal funds and the lack of a national consensus in transportation, the initiative seems to lie completely with the federal government. The rules governing the use of federal funds increasingly determine not only the planning efforts of states and localities but their efforts to construct and operate present-day transportation facilities as well.

I was very much impressed in state government by the speed with which state and local officials could move to obtain federal money, particularly new federal money for new local projects. The normal pace of government may be glacial, but I found the ability of local governments to hustle for federal grants worthy of the behavior of a private consulting firm. There is no question that available funds, particularly those from another level of government and thus perceived as "free," relate to and drive choice behavior in the public sector. The incentive to use monies available from the larger tax-paying unit (for example, local use of state and federal money or state use of federal money) certainly contributes to conflict and frustration when strings attached to money from the higher source appear highly unreasonable or in conflict with local objectives.

Two centrally important examples of how dollars drive state and local choice behavior in urban transportation are the Section 5 federal transit operating subsidy formula and 90 percent federal funding for Interstate Highways. In the example of Section 5 transit funding, federal operating subsidy monies are distributed to urban areas on essentially a per capita basis. This formula has little relationship to the benefits that such transit service provides to the local population. That is, in smaller urban areas, transit does not generally attract as many riders per capita of population and, therefore, does not confer as many benefits as in larger urban areas. The larger areas, though often having average population densities only slightly greater than the smaller areas, have portions of their cities characterized by more people within walking distance of any given bus route and more congestion and higher parking charges for travel by the competing mode (the automobile). Nevertheless, smaller urban areas, in the range of 50,000 to 200,000 population, will provide fixed-route and schedule transit service only to the extent that 50 percent of the cost of this service is paid for by the federal government. It is, therefore, easy to draw the conclusion that the efficiency or effectiveness of transit service in these smaller areas has little to do with political decisions to provide the service at the local level and define the distribution formula at the federal level. This is a delicate and not well studied behavior on the part of political leaders at all levels of government. However, it seems clear that 50 percent federal matching money, in many cases matched also with state money, is simply too powerful for most local decision makers to refuse.

The classic, and better studied, example of how federal monies drive choice behavior at the state level is, of course, the 90-10 matching formula for interstate highways. In this case, the federal government provides a blank check for 90 percent of the cost of highways built on specifically designated routes, regardless of the cost of building these highways. Since the state must put up only 10 percent of the cost of these highways, the obvious tendency is to "gold plate" and build the highways as large as possible to "solve" the greatest number of local transportation problems with the 90 percent federal funds. The excesses fostered by this choice behavior led to the passage of the National Environmental Policy Act of 1969, a topic falling within environmental and social impact analysis.

The above examples illustrate the financial mechanism by which the imbalance of power between the federal government and local governments is furthered. The examples illustrate the contradiction between legislated behavior and the behavior that would result from less constrained applications of efficiency criteria at the state and local level.

There are other, less distribution formula-related examples of problems caused by increasing federal power relative to that of state and local governments. I hope that by citing a few examples, I will not cause my federal friends to become defensive. Unfortunately, the difficulty of changing federal laws and regulations when they are so out of line with what is logical and reasonable at the level of one state or locality is enough to cause local officials not to try to make the change. Such efforts are "dry holes" which lead to several behaviors, possibly including a selection process which operates to divert those with more energy into more fruitful areas of endeavor. Often the irrationality of the federal law as applied to a particular local situation may affect other areas in the same way. However, the local official may not know this and may think a particular case is unique. Federal officials vary in their willingness or ability to identify a pattern of inefficiencies around the country that would help local leaders unite to alleviate the problem through political action.

Two examples come immediately to mind in this connection. Both are personal, but any local official will have a basketful, no doubt. The first example is in the area of short-range transit operations. In this case, in Lowell, Massachusetts, we ran afoul of the maintenance-of-effort requirement under the federal operating assistance Section 5 of the UMTA Act. The maintenance-of-effort provision does not allow federal transit operating money to be substituted for public monies from other levels of government to subsidize an urban transit system. In 1976, our publicly owned and inefficiently operated Lowell transit system incurred an operating deficit of approximately $1.2 million, half of which was paid by federal Section 5 money. In 1977, we contracted with a private operator to provide the same or better service and incurred a deficit of approximately $600,000. Unfortunately, because of the maintenance-of-effort requirement, the commonwealth of Massachusetts and the city of Lowell, which previously shared equally in the $600,000 per year local public subsidy (half of $1.2 million), were left with no reward for much initiative and effort to be efficient at the state and local level. Worse yet, there was every incentive to drive up the costs beyond the $600,000 deficit because the federal monies would subsidize 100 percent of the costs above the previous state and local effort of $600,000 up to the previous $1.2 million deficit. When I vigorously protested this foolishness to UMTA, I got some sympathy but nothing more.

Another and new example of the increasing concentration of federal power is in the energy area. This is the problem local officials in crowded and congested northeastern cities are having with the so-called, generally permissive, right-turn-on-red rule. This rule is one of only five mandatory measures in each newly required state energy plan for that state to receive any federal energy money. The right-turn-on-red rule was inserted into the Federal Energy Act by legislators familiar with multilane approaches at uncongested intersections with separate right-turn slots. In northeastern cities (for instance, Boston) with narrow, congested streets and omnipresent queues, the right-turn-on-red rule appears to provide very little in the way of energy savings. However, the safety problems for pedestrians trying to cross with walk signals or, conversely, the putting up and maintaining at most intersections of right-turn-prohibited signs where logic dictates indicates once again the problems in a federal system with increasingly concentrated power.

The checks to such federal power must, of course, occur through the political process. However, the few examples where controversial federal laws have been overturned in transportation have been characterized by enormous struggle. An example of this struggle was the sequence of events leading to passage of the National Environmental Policy Act of 1969 (NEPA). This act required environmental impact statements for blank check federally funded highways that were causing massive dislocations in urban areas, as noted above. In the case of NEPA, the distance between the federal program and its neighborhood impact led to a prolonged struggle and another example of the psychic energy and dollar costs of doing business in transportation at the local level (Altschuler 1969). However, this example is behind us.

As I have been charged to do in this paper, I have presented many examples of individual and organizational behavior in transportation and the way these affect transportation policy formation in various branches at various levels of government. I hope examples drawn from state level service, where constructing and operating transportation facilities take place, have not offended my federal friends. It is clear that conflicts and problems arise in transportation infrastructure decision making between different personalities in the context of group dynamics and the structure of the choice environment. The examples and perspectives cited appear well worth study by behavioral scientists. As noted before, if the same kind of regularity in behavioral response in such situations could be uncovered as we think we have uncovered in individual travel choice behavior, the new understandings no doubt would influence government organization and decision making.

## FURTHER PROBLEMS AND PERSPECTIVES ON BEHAVIORAL SCIENCE APPLICATIONS IN TRANSPORTATION

The final section of this paper on transportation policies and problems for study in the behavioral sciences highlights three specific areas fruitful for study by behavioral scientists. These are (1) traveler responses to new transportation technology, (2) learning in transportation choice behavior, and (3) changing our definition of comprehensiveness in transportation planning and evaluation from a normative view arising from the technician's art to a more behavioral description of how investment decisions are actually made.

### Traveler Response to New Transportation Technology

Transportation alternatives of high current interest include the application of new technologies, specifically those involving automated control for all or part of the trip. Demonstrations of automated ground transportation systems called downtown people movers are planned in several major U.S. cities. It is hypothesized that the downtown people movers will help revitalize central cities and will substitute for walk trips, particularly those by persons employed in the CBD. These hypothesized impacts are well worth study by behavioral scientists.

Other useful research questions raised by consideration of automated control in transportation include how human and mechanical operations can best be combined in the design of these systems. One may recall the story of how elevator buttons on high-technology preprogrammed elevators were provided for users only when they insisted on a feeling of control over their environment. It was never revealed whether the buttons were linked to the elevator controls.

With regard to short-headway automated ground transportation systems, which some feel are an important component in the next generation of (dual mode) urban transportation facilities (Brand 1976), the question arises of how people will react. How should we trade off people's comfort at viewing their surroundings against closing them off from the outside world for their own comfort and security, as is presently done in high-speed elevators? This is an example of another impact worth study by behavioral scientists.

Learning in Transportation Choice Behavior

The importance of learning in transportation decision making hardly needs restatement. How does learning occur, and how is information used by individuals? Planners propose physical, operational, and economic changes to the existing transportation system. We need to know people's reactions to these changes, both as individual travelers and as decision makers in the body politic. How does the individual, characterized by intellect, personality, and group situation (for example, family or political), learn about the choice set over which a decision can be exercised and the variables describing the choice set (physical, economic, ethnic, organizational, and so on)?

For example, much is made in current transportation planning of the participatory process in transportation. However, one of the problems in citizen participation is that different groups move in and out of the planning process as their interests are affected. Individuals do not stay with the planning process for the length of time needed to deal with decisions which trade off impacts at the various levels of detail in rational planning. At the initial regional systems planning stages, highly educated, professional participator public interest types can be expected to vocally advocate transportation alternatives (for example, rail transit) for relatively abstract environmental quality and energy conservation reasons. However, at later stages in the planning process, when details on the location and long-range impacts of the transportation alternatives become known, neighborhood residents surface as effective objectors. This is a major problem in attempting to implement a democratic or participatory process of decision making in urban transportation planning.

Behavioral scientists could usefully study learning in transportation and its relationships to basic human needs. Regarding the influence of both on behavior, behavioral scientists could explore why changes occur in popular causes and issues in transportation. Are there underlying needs in individuals and in the body politic that are constant and that provoke the strange metabolism in our society of picking up issue after issue as a popular cause and then dropping each just as quickly? A major problem in transportation

planning is that it takes us as long to institutionalize paperwork requirements to deal with some of these issues as it does for society
to drop the issue and move on to the next. We are investing great
amounts of dollars and energy, psychic and otherwise, in various
transportation alternatives to reap future benefits. The question
arises: Will anyone out there value these benefits when they finally
occur?

## Prescriptive Versus Descriptive Definitions of Comprehensiveness in Transportation Planning

The final point to be made in this paper builds on some of the
themes presented before. The point is that the current comprehensive or rational planning process in transportation may be a
transportation technocrat's normative view of real world decision
making. It is based on the kinds of information conveniently available to the technical planner at any one time. As with most normative models of human behavior, it turns out to be a poor predictor
of what actually happens in the real world. A more behavioral model
of transportation investment decision making is needed. A possible
approach on which behavioral scientists may build is supplied here.

Technicians in transportation are well versed in all the subtle
background nuances, costs, benefits, and trade-offs which must be
made to intelligently evaluate transportation alternatives. Since we
technicians know so much about these alternatives, we think the
world should join in this knowledge. We think in terms of complicated decision tables—arraying options against impacts and balancing
costs and benefits in the most complex way to reach a preference
ordering over alternatives. Unfortunately, this comprehensive
planning model is incomprehensible to most decision makers in the
real world. As noted often previously in this paper, politicians and
individuals do not think comprehensively.

I would propose an alternative evaluation model or strategy
that reflects more faithfully the typical problem orientation of decision makers and the "what-have-I-done-for-you-lately" behavior of
politicians. The overall objective of comprehensive transportation
planning, which is to achieve the optimal package of implemented
transportation actions, would, of course, be adhered to with this
alternative decision-making strategy.

The alternative evaluation model or strategy specifically ac-
commodates the rapidly changing values or concerns in today's
society. For example, given the current concern for job creation,
one may hypothesize a series of highly visible guberantorial announcements involving millions of dollars in popular rural highway projects

that prompt private investment in local manufacturing and other large-scale local redevelopment. These announcements demonstrate the achievement of these objectives so that we may be in a position to announce other transportation projects that address other objectives. The strategy takes advantage of the points gained by responding to the current most pressing societal objective—in this case, hypothesized to be job creation—(single-objective planning, if you will) and uses the points earned with the public to move to other projects that respond to other, possibly less politically popular, needs in our changing society, for example, revitalizing our major city centers.

Such sequential decision making does not involve sophisticated trade-off analysis of the costs and benefits of each project. Each project that is implemented is not the best compromise itself. However, the package that is implemented may be as close to optimal as we have any reason to hope for in our politicized and constrained environment. In addition, the package may please the public much more than a series of projects, each of which moves us ahead only marginally relative to our objectives.

Planners, in any event, are becoming very pragmatic in attempting to develop and evaluate transportation plans that are as responsive as possible to current societal goals. It is not stretching the pragmatism of the planner too far to consider, not just one project with all its costs and benefits at one point in time, but groups of transportation projects considered sequentially over a period of time. Such packages of projects, described with time as well as space dimensions, can be subjected to the same kind of trade-off analysis involving balancing costs and benefits as in the single-project example. The analysis will be more complicated and will stretch the technician's art. However, the analysis could be more behavioral and reflect how decision making proceeds in the real world. Whether this new comprehensive planning more faithfully reflects behavioral principles is certainly an area for behavioral scientists to explore.


CONCLUSION

The material in this paper illustrates many situations in transportation where knowledge of personal and political behavior is more important than knowledge of the engineering of these facilities. If highly engineered facilities backfire in terms of what we seek to achieve with them, we need not have bothered to engineer them.

REFERENCES

Altschuler, A. 1969. "The Values of Urban Transportation Policy."
In Transportation and Community Values. Special Report 105,
Transportation Research Board. Washington, D.C.

Brand, D. 1976. Dual Mode Transportation. Special Report 170,
Transportation Research Board. Washington, D.C.

# 3
## BEHAVIORAL SCIENCE AND TRANSPORTATION: AN OVERVIEW

### H. McIlvaine Parsons

My mission is to suggest how behavioral science can serve
transportation planning, policy, and management, which I interpret
to include design. Many things have to be considered, not excluding what constitutes behavioral science. Certainly we should specify
psychology and sociology, the first concerned with individual and
small group behavior, the second with larger aggregates. What
about economics and econometrics? Since buying and selling, earn-
ing and spending, acquiring and hoarding and disbursing are all
varieties of human behavior, one can think of economics as a behavioral science. Certainly, economists have based much of their
analyses and projections on presumptions about human behavior,
and they have been in the forefront of transportation planning. However, it would require someone better versed in economics to cover
the contributions from that discipline. The same goes for sociology.
Consequently, this paper will forego giving much time to aggregate
behavior in transportation or to aggregate data.

Behavioral science confined largely to psychology is still a
huge domain. First, it consists of a diversity of techniques, some
in research, some in application. A simplified listing of these can
be found in Table 3.1. This table comes first because perhaps the
way in which behavioral science can serve transportation planning
and management best is through technology transfer—the transfer
of scientific methodology to transportation from other behavioral
science experience, both basic and applied.

Second, human behavior covers a lot of ground. To structure
it, let us put the ways in which transportation affects people into
nine categories. Transportation is part of our physical, constructed
environment. The primary elements in the classification in Table 3.2

TABLE 3.1

Basic Techniques of Behavioral Sciences and Technology

---

Research
  a.  Survey (observational, self-report; questionnaire, interview)
  b.  Experiment (small scale, large scale; real world, simulation)
  c.  Modeling (computer)
  d.  Trace data, archival data
  e.  Description and analysis (system, ecological)

Application
  a.  Forecasting
  b.  Design (system/equipment/service)
  c.  Training, familiarization, education
  d.  Selection (including personnel testing)
  e.  Test and evaluation (system/equipment/service)
  f.  Allocation (modal distribution, functions and tasks)

---


TABLE 3.2

Transportation-Determined Behavior

---

a.  Locomotion (passengers, pedestrians)
b.  Activities (e.g., vehicle control, maintenance, community life)
c.  Feelings (e.g., comfort, convenience, enjoyment, stress, likes, dislikes)
d.  Manipulation (e.g., modal choice, route selection, vehicle purchase)
e.  Health and safety (e.g., accidents, disabilities, fatigue)
f.  Social interaction (e.g., privacy, territoriality, conflict, imitation)
g.  Motivation (positive or aversive consequences, potentiation)
h.  Learning (e.g., operator training, driver education, merchandising)
i.  Perception (e.g., images, mapping, sensory thresholds)

---

have helped extract order out of chaos for two other physical environments (Parsons 1976b, 1978a).

Third, what aspects of transportation must be considered? It is helpful to subdivide this into eight aspects, as shown in Table 3.3. Such a classification provides an overview of transportation as it relates to people. Each of the categories in Table 3.3 has an impact on one or more of the aspects of human behavior in Table 3.2, as shown in Table 3.4. In short, we now have a systematic way of looking at how transportation affects individuals.

TABLE 3.3

Areas of Transportation's Impact on Behavior

---

a. Entire mode or multimode situation
b. Resources (provision or design of submodes or components)
c. Arrangement: spatial (routing, distribution); temporal (scheduling)
d. Communication (e.g., trip information, signs, CB radio)
e. Protection (e.g., path enforcement, anticollision procedures)
f. Ambient conditions (e.g., weather, pollution, noise, temperature)
g. Reinforcement potentiation (e.g., cost, risks, fares, congestion)
h. Appearance (e.g., beautification, vehicle design)

---

But transportation can be subdivided for purposes of analysis in another fashion, by modes—or, if one prefers other terminology, by settings or systems—including multimode considerations and submodes. These are listed in Table 3.5. For completeness, the list includes some modes or settings that will not figure prominently in this paper.

There exist also collateral variables that moderate the effects of various transportation modes on people's behavior. Some of them are indicated in Table 3.6.

Finally, let us not forget that the people associated with any transportation system vary in a number of particulars, which will be considered in this discussion. Table 3.7 shows six characteristics that significantly distinguish people in transportation from each other and nine people categories functionally related to any transportation mode.

TABLE 3.4

Relationships between Aspects of Transportation and Their Effects on People

| Aspects of Transportation | Transportation Effects on People | | | | | | | | |
|---|---|---|---|---|---|---|---|---|---|
| | Activities | Locomotion | Social Interaction | Feelings | Perception | Motivation | Health and Safety | Learning | Manipulation |
| Resources | X | | | X | | | X | X | X |
| Spatial arrangement | | X | X | | | | | X | |
| Communication | X | X | X | | | | | X | |
| Appearance | | | | X | X | | | | X |
| Reinforcement | | X | | | | X | | X | X |
| Protection | | | | | | | X | | |
| Ambient conditions | X | | | X | | X | X | | X |
| Entire setting | | | | | | | | | |

33

TABLE 3.5

Taxonomy of Transport Systems

---

Modes (Systems, Settings)
  a. Highway (auto, truck, bus, bicycle, pedestrian)
  b. Rail
  c. Urban (bus, transit, PRT, demand-responsive, elevators, etc.)
  d. Air (commercial, private, military; airplane, helicopter)
  e. Water (ocean, waterways; conventional, air cushion, surface effects)
  f. Pipeline
  g. Space
  h. Underwater

Multimode Considerations
  a. Transfer
  b. Choice
  c. Competition
  d. Interference
  e. Commonalities (e.g., communications, safety, seating, fare collection, human capabilities and limitations)

Submodes (Subsystems, Subsettings)
  a. Vehicles
  b. Paths (constructed, allocated)
  c. Terminals and sub-terminals
  d. Traffic control
  e. Services
  f. Maintenance facilities

---

TABLE 3.6

Collateral Circumstances and Conditions

---

a. Population change, demographics
b. Land usage, zoning
c. Public policies, politics
d. Economic factors (e.g., capital)
e. Technology (change, automation)
f. Environmental impact
g. Energy (shortages, conservation)

---

TABLE 3.7

Social and Individual Descriptors

---

Difference Dimensions
  a.  Economic status
  b.  Age extremes
  c.  Health, handicaps
  d.  Substance abuse
  e.  Cultural differences
  f.  Skills

Functional Categories
  a.  Vehicle operators
  b.  Passengers (actual, potential)
  c.  Maintainers
  d.  Controllers
  e.  Managements (system operators)
  f.  Shippers
  g.  Producers (construction, manufacture)
  h.  Investors (government, private)
  i.  Communities (public, citizens)

---

These seven tables illustrate one of the contributions some behavioral scientists can make to this field—to set forth a systems approach and analysis, at least in a rudimentary form. A complete analysis would relate the variables in any table to those in all the others. It would indicate all or most of the ways in which behavioral science might be involved in transportation. This paper simply selects some of these for purposes of illustration.

At the start, behavioral scientists who are psychologists come in a number of varieties. For example, some are cognitively oriented experimentalists who are interested in human information processing and decision making. Some are social psychologists intrigued with interindividual behavior, attitudes, and small groups. Others, with an operant or behavior modification approach, investigate motivation—incentives and disincentives in behavioral contingencies. Industrial psychologists think about organizational arrangements and procedures. The psychologists within the multidisciplinary field called human factors are concerned with human performance capabilities as these are related to system and equipment design, training, and personnel selection. For other types, personality and clinical psychologists, for example, it does not seem likely that their work could be brought to bear on transportation to the same extent.

## TRANSFER OF TECHNIQUES

Let us look first at techniques that might be transferred (Table 3.1). One does not have to be a psychologist to conduct a self-report survey based on questionnaires or interviews. Some surveys have been attitudinal or preferential, some have consisted of self-reports about transportation habits. Frankly, I do not know how sophisticated these have been with regard to variable, item, and subject selection; presumably many have conformed to established technical requirements. What seems less certain is whether self-report surveys have been validated by systematic observations of what people actually do, other than simply counting people using a certain mode of travel or route. Many behavioral scientists prefer observational techniques and know how to apply them, although such techniques are more expensive than self-report surveys. Often they examine or uncover behaviors or behavioral contingencies that people might fail to verbalize, for one reason or another.

In highway accident prevention research, for example, the drivers may be more likely to reveal unsafe driving actions to observers recording these, with or without cameras, than to report them in a questionnaire survey. Although alcoholism research by psychologists has been able to make substantial use of self-reports of drinking behavior, automobile drivers who might lose their licenses might not be truthful in responding to a mail or telephone survey about the extent of their alcohol consumption, especially shortly before taking the wheel. Risk or threat of some aversive consequence is well known as an obstacle to candor, as every judge and juror could attest.

Psychologists have developed effective observational techniques with human observers, based on time sampling and event sampling and tests of interobserver reliability. Although some observational studies simply determine where people are to be found (mapping), others record what they are doing, either concentrating on some particular activity or placing behavior in a number of categories, such as the activities of passengers in an aircraft or bus. Other investigators observe and record characteristics of activities, such as speed of walking (as in a recent investigation by two Princeton sociologists of different pedestrian speeds in cities of different sizes) or the extent of crowding on subway platforms. Observational studies may employ unobstrusive techniques. Those observed do not know they are being examined and measured. Thereby the process of observation does not itself alter their behavior. Increasingly, however, questions are being raised in funding agencies about violations of privacy in situations where individuals are observed by scientific investigators without their knowledge or consent, even though they remain anonymous.

Let me quote myself (Parsons 1976a) with reference to getting data about human performance and activities in transportation:

> For this aspect of behavior, survey research can sometimes supply valuable insights that lead to further research on a more objective and experimental basis. Through questionnaires or interviews, operators of vehicles may supply self-reports about what they do or reports about what other operators do, concerning critical incidents, for example, or problems they encounter. But they are not reliable sources of information about how well they can perform their tasks, how accurately, how quickly, how safely, in the variety of circumstances they face or might face in daily operations. For example, in a survey I once conducted of aircraft pilots, respondents varied considerably in stating what they did, could do, or should do. Other studies have shown that expert opinion about performance often differs from objective data.
>
> As a result, engineering psychologists have preferred to investigate pilots' performance in representative tasks or cockpit simulators in human factors laboratories, or in actual flying. In the laboratories, both observational measurement and experimental operations have been obtrusive, without necessarily limiting the validity of the research. When different altimeter designs are being compared, or different ways of displaying aircraft-horizon relationships of the earth's geography, relative differences need not be distorted by the overtness of measurement or manipulation of input. In flight, human recording of crew activity patterns or eye-camera recording of instrument fixations need not contaminate relative frequencies. In this kind of research it is relative rather than absolute measures that are being sought. Reactivity from measurement is not as important as reliability of measurement, which is generally augmented through suitable apparatus. It all depends on what one is investigating.

In aviation research, extensive investigations have been conducted into the operations of air traffic and air defense control centers (Parsons 1972). Generally this has been obtrusive since the individual controllers have known they were being observed and their performance measured. But it has usually, if not always, been possible to keep this research from becoming reactive, as it would if the controllers believed they were being individually evaluated for proficiency. The method's advantage lies in an ability to present the radar picture to the controller through simulation, so input loads and a range of problems can be systematically varied and infrequent situations presented often enough to obtain reliable data.

Activities of aircraft passengers have been studied much less than those of pilots and controllers. The Douglas Aircraft Company years ago ran some obtrusive tests of emergency chute evacuation, with employees as subjects. Reactivity among the female subjects wearing skirts became apparent in their latencies of entering the chute. However, another Douglas passenger study was wholly unobtrusive because it relied entirely on physical trace data. To help determine the required size of receptacles of waste matter for lavatories in a projected commercial aircraft, a human factors technician travelled extensively on current aircraft—equipped with a dipstick.

It should be noted that "behavioral science" figures in the title of this paper, not "mental science." What this means is that, despite some misunderstanding in other disciplines and in the general public, most psychologists who are also scientists base their concepts neither on introspection nor on the existence of a mind, but rather on observables, that is, behavior. Behavior, however, is construed as consisting of more than actions we can see. Self-report is behavior. So are data from instrument recordings of physiological phenomena such as heart rate, blood pressure, electrical skin resistance, brain waves, and glandular secretions. From self-reports (such as rating scales) or physiological data or both, psychologists often infer the occurrence of inner, invisible reactions similar to what they may introspect as feelings, emotions, or stress. There may also be observable activity associated with the self-report and physiological data, such as laughing, crying, smiling, scowling, exclamations, postural changes, immobility, and withdrawal.

To the extent that understanding and dealing with feelings, emotions, and stress are important in matters of transportation, behavioral science can serve transportation by applying its techniques for measuring such reactions. Something like this is done already, of course, in surveys of attitudes, which often are mixtures of what people say they do and what they say they feel and thus are generally insufficiently revealing of either. Already in transportation research there have been some studies of self-reported feelings among operators and passengers of vehicles and some investigations of physiological changes in air traffic controllers, aircraft pilots, and motor vehicle drivers. For example, Michaels (1960) found that the galvanic skin (or electrodermal) response, a well-recognized stress measure, had its greatest amplitude in drivers when speed differences were highest between the test vehicle and another vehicle. In 1962 he discovered the maximum occurred when another vehicle merged in front of the test vehicle on a freeway. Helander (1978) has found associations between the electrodermal response and braking during traffic incidents. Stokols et al. (1978) investigated increases in blood pressure in commuter motorists following traffic congestion.

Much more could be done. For example, three years ago I testified as an expert witness in a suit brought by the U.S. Department of Transportation against the General Motors Corporation concerning stress reactions in a driver when steering fails in a 1959 or 1960 Cadillac due to fracture of the Pitman arm. The research literature in the transportation field failed to provide any direct guidance about the effects of this kind of sudden, unexpected stressor, although it was possible to extrapolate to this situation psychological knowledge acquired in other contexts. In analogous situations some individuals are known to freeze (do nothing) or perseverate (repeat the ineffectual response) for some seconds, thereby extending the reaction time to the emergency.


Experimentation

The scientific technique in which psychologists are most proficient, and in which most engineers and planners are less so, is experimentation. Scientific psychologists are trained in how to conduct experiments. These may involve few or many subjects. They may be laboratory or field experiments. They may incorporate more than two states (experimental and control) of a single variable. Indeed, they may include a large number of variables, each with more than two states. Most scientific psychologists know how to prevent confounding from extraneous variables and how to promote external validity as well. They are adept in the selection, sampling, randomizing, and matching of human (and infrahuman) subjects. They also know about the requirements for protecting subjects from risk. Some are experienced in simulation, both computers and mock-ups. The experiments they conduct can be large or small in scale. Experimental designs to reduce an experiment's size and complexity and, at the same time, give reasonable assurance of internal validity are known to many behavioral scientists.

Why conduct experiments? Simple observation can be useful, as I have suggested. Correlational techniques, with which psychologists are also familiar, can help relate variables to each other. But for the purpose of determining cause and effect, as in studies of motivation, for example, or of systematically assessing how well individuals perform under different levels or kinds of information load, as in investigations of vehicle operators, an experiment is the desirable technique.

Psychologists can provide several kinds of expertise in transportation experiments that involve people. They can generate good experimental designs. They can select appropriate kinds of dependent variables and associated measures. They know how to test experimental results for the statistical significance of differences among results, although, of course, statisticians can do the same, and better. They can determine how subjects should be chosen, allocated among states of variables, and controlled so confounding does not result from the subject variable. This last requirement, in particular, is not likely to be satisfied by experimental investigators from other disciplines.

A considerable amount of experimentation has been conducted by behavioral scientists in transportation, but it has been largely limited to the performance of vehicle operators, notably pilots of aircraft and drivers of automobiles (Forbes 1972). A substantial amount of simulation has been involved in much of this research. Very little behavioral science experimentation has occurred in other transportation modes or in relation to other transportation users, such as passengers. Demonstration projects by the U.S. Department of Transportation have lacked a scientific base for producing reliable data, especially in the case of bus design for handicapped passengers. Experimental tests of proposed fare collection systems for buses or rapid transit have been proposed but not carried out. The result has been unnecessary delays in improving such systems, major frustrations among passengers, and loss of fare revenue.

Subway and airport terminals have been constructed with communication systems, guidance signs, for example, that have never been systematically designed or evaluated before their installation.

They have had to be retrofitted at much additional cost and after causing many difficulties for passengers. Procedures and equipment for handling emergencies or unusual demands at control centers for urban transportation systems apparently have seldom, if ever, been suitably investigated with experimental methods, although this oversight could result in either disaster or untold inconvenience and delay. Equipment, procedures, and training methods for safe ship handling of large tankers need scientific examination in this country, resembling the research undertaken for a number of years in the Netherlands; the simulation capability is now available. The list could go on. In transportation there exist many people-pertinent aspects of planning and design where behavioral science experimentation would be both feasible and helpful.

What has prevented it? (1) Planners and designers may have presumed that testing of hardware (untouched by human hands) is sufficient. (2) It may not be well understood that, in many cases, there should be advance operational tests of new equipment or subsystems, that such tests should include systematic variations in input and users (thus becoming experimental), and that experimental tests of procedures could be profitably conducted both before and after a new subsystem or equipment is installed. (3) Responsible managements are unaware of what behavioral science might contribute. (4) Proper experimental testing might uncover serious deficiencies in planning or design, thereby embarrassing the planner or designers. (5) Experimentation costs money. (6) A more fashionable presumed alternative, computer modeling, is preferred.

Behavioral science can contribute to computer modeling in transportation and improve it by specifying the parameters of human behavior in the model. However, it may be necessary to conduct some simulation experiments first to adduce these, since in many instances they cannot be generalized from handbook data or other research. Computer modeling has been used to great advantage by behavioral scientists, although it could hardly be termed their contribution to transportation problems. It is particularly useful in dealing with aggregate data.

Use of trace data and archival data by psychologists is illustrated in transportation accident research. Trace data in the form of damaged vehicles and highway features may be examined after an accident. Accident records of individual drivers can be surveyed. Other kinds of trace data include graffiti on subway cars, and archival data include arrest records. None of these sources represent a distinctly psychological contribution to technique, although it is possible that behavioral scientists might improve the quality and reliability of both trace and archival data.

System psychologists are accustomed to describing and analyzing all the components and subsystems of a system and the manifold interactions among them. They do this because people are to
be found throughout the system, and all the people in a system must
be considered in connection with system performance, system design, and system-wide training. Although a systems approach may
be taken by persons in other disciplines, system psychologists can
provide it, in some circumstances, better than most. At least a
rudimentary systems approach has been taken by a few psychologists
in looking at demand-responsible and urban bus systems, and it
could be applied by psychologists in transportation more widely, as
in analyses of model choice. However, it is not owned exclusively
by behavioral scientists. Ecological psychologists do something
rather similar. They record where people are and what they are
doing at various times of day in a setting, such as a small community or a school. Thereby they amass a great deal of information about behavior in various situations. I do not believe they have
tried to do this in transportation settings, although there seems to
be no reason why this could not be done.

Environmental psychology is somewhat related. Its research
has been directed toward (1) social behavior in constructed environments, as expressed in privacy, crowding, personal space, and
territoriality; (2) perceptions of built and natural environments; and
(3) environmental design, that is, the effects that various constructed environments have on people (and vice versa) and ways to
improve their design for the benefit of their users. Clearly, all
three aspects of environmental psychology can be involved in ground
transportation's paths, vehicles, and terminals. Requirements of
privacy or personal space (proxemics) should be considered in designing buses or transit cars. Seating, vehicular noise, control
centers, and terminal communications are among the many user-
oriented design considerations.

Application

Now we turn from techniques for research to those for application. Psychologists can contribute to forecasting by making certain that all essential variables are included in predictions. For
example, the National Highway Traffic Safety Administration apparently omitted a significant variable when it presumed that the American public would accept an unpleasant sound as a seat belt signal
that would terminate only when the belt was fastened. If that pre-
sumption was based on data from escape conditioning, it neglected
avoidance conditioning. Drivers, it could have been predicted,

would take action to keep the sound from occurring in the first place—as they did, partly by complaining to their representatives in the Congress, who then abrogated the requirement. Drivers' resistance resulted also from the inconvenience of having to fasten a seat belt. Inconvenience as a variable in human affairs has been insufficiently appreciated in transportation, as in other fields (Parsons 1975). For example, inconvenience may well account for the modal choices made by some individuals.

Psychologists can provide consultation to those who design transportation systems, equipment, or services by drawing on what is known about human behavior from research or from experience in other contexts. This has been done widely in the field of human factors in military system planning and procurement and already to a limited extent in transportation, although it is difficult to estimate that extent. The Federal Highway Administration has a contingent of human factors specialists, as does the Federal Aviation Administration. Some are also found in automobile manufacturing. On the other hand, behavioral science appears to be poorly represented in the Urban Mass Transportation Administration, the Federal Railroad Administration, the Maritime Commission, and the manufacturers of vehicles and builders of facilities in these subdivisions of transportation.

Both operators and passengers in the various transportation modes can often benefit from learning about their tasks and roles through what is variously entitled training, familiarization, and education. Aircraft controllers are systematically trained. Can the same be said of the individuals in the control centers of the New York City subway system? Are attempts to persuade commuters to carpool being skillfully handled? How effectively are bus maintenance personnel being trained? Some years ago, the New York subway controllers were furnished badly needed simulation-based training by some psychologists. I have no information about the other matters mentioned. Since many behavioral scientists do specialize in developing training methods and applications, they may be able to make a contribution to transportation.

Personnel selection, through the definition of skill requirements and testing to find out who satisfies those requirements, seems more fitting for vehicle operators (and maintainers) than for passengers. The latter self-select. The weak and the handicapped abstain from some forms of travel, as do the poor (and the rich), the blind, the ill, and the retarded. Perhaps the task of personnel psychologists as regards passengers is to find out more about how various people lack travel capabilities and how transportation facilities can be made, through design or training, to accommodate them. As for operators, as new transportation systems are developed,

psychologists can help determine what kinds of people should operate and maintain these vehicles and how these people can be selected.
Psychologists, in the past, have been involved in the selection testing of streetcar motormen and Army taxi drivers (Lauer 1960, p.
181; Snow 1926; Uhlaner 1956; Wechsler 1926).

Psychologists have participated in the testing and evaluation
of systems and their components through inspections, use of check-
lists, and the operational tests that were mentioned in connection
with research. Tests and evaluation constitute applied research.

What should be automated? Fare collection? Vehicular guidance? Traffic flow? The question really may be, within any system function, how mechanical and human operations can be best
combined, not whether the entire function should be automatic or
manual. Engineering psychologists have been concerned with such
allocation problems (McCormick 1976), and transportation might
benefit from their participation. In person-machine systems (including computer-based management information systems), allocation decisions have often been made either unthinkingly or mistaken-
ly, simply because no one was representing the needs or capabilities
of the potential human components. Even when psychologists cannot
provide precise quantitative rationales, they can at least represent
the human elements in competitions for system roles. Although in
the past they have been perhaps more concerned with operational and
maintenance elements, they could become technical representatives
of passengers and citizens who might be affected by new transportation facilities. They could take part in decisions about modal distributions, another kind of allocation problem, by indicating how
these could be organized to the benefit of transportation users.


KNOWLEDGE ABOUT BEHAVIOR

Proceeding to Table 3.2, let us discuss briefly the transfer
not of behavioral science techniques but of substantive knowledge to
transportation from other fields. With <u>locomotion</u> there is little
transfer because it is essentially part of transportation. However,
there can be transfer of knowledge between transportation modes
and situations. Passengers move not only in and out of new Personal
Rapid Transit (PRT) vehicles but also in and out of elevators in
high-rise office and apartment buildings. Much has been learned
from the latter about how long a door should be kept open to provide
passenger access (Strakosch 1967). Such knowledge can be transferred to the former. What is known about accommodation of wheelchairs traveling in and out of buildings (American Society of Landscape Architects 1976; Kamenetz 1969; Steinfeld 1975) can be applied

to such accommodation at the entrances and exits of buses. The
requirements of the U.S. Department of Housing and Urban Development can be made known to the Urban Mass Transportation Administration of the U.S. Department of Transportation. Behavioral
scientists can effect such transfers because their interests cut
across modal and bureaucratic boundaries.

A great deal of human factors attention has been given to activities consisting of vehicle control (McCormick 1976; Van Cott and
Kinkade 1972); presumably much can be extrapolated to the control
of new transportation vehicles. The same is true about maintenance
(Van Cott and Kinkade 1972), especially electronic maintenance.
Activities, however, include more than work performance within
transportation. They include work in other areas and nonwork activities in the home, out-of-doors, and in the community. How
does transportation affect these? Although some answers are self-
evident, psychologists should be encouraged to find out and apply
more systematic information about how transportation can facilitate
such activities or how it makes them more difficult. More research
is also needed in work performance in transportation.

Earlier, the discussion of observational techniques mentioned
the effects of transportation on feelings. Behavioral science should
and could generalize to transportation modes knowledge that has
been gained elsewhere. For example, information about chair comfort acquired in studying seats in buildings (Grandjean 1973) could
be used in designing seats in buses. Knowledge about stress in com-
bat might have a bearing on stress in aircraft pilots. But as in the
case of all the main items in Table 3.2, behavioral science's role
is not only to transfer knowledge but also to develop it and to help
apply it. The knowledge needed is how transportation affects individuals, in this and the other eight listed categories. We cannot
change transportation's effects on people unless we know what these
effects are or could be. For example, we cannot go about inducing
people to like some mode (or other aspect) of transportation (if that
seems important to do) unless we know more about such feelings
concerning transportation elements as "liking" them. For instance,
can dislike be conditioned through association, as in dislike of buses
from exposure to diesel fumes when stuck in traffic behind one?
Does its convenience make the private automobile more "enjoyable"?

Manipulation covers a variety of individual reactions to transportation that, in turn, have some effect on transportation. We
choose going by light rail transit instead of by auto, and the result
is a change in the amounts of light rail transit and cars. Building
a highway is manipulation. So is resisting one. People buy and
sell vehicles for themselves or for organizations. Another manipulation, route selection, like modal choice, is a major system con-

sideration that has received much attention from planners. Like all
kinds of manipulation, ultimately it consists of the behavior of individuals. What is route selection but behavior? Psychologists can
bring a large body of basic and applied decision-making and habit-
following research to bear on why a person selects one route rather
than another or one mode above others. They can also study decision making and habit following within the transportation context.

In connection with health and safety, we all know that accidents
constitute a major set of transportation impacts on individuals. It
hardly needs saying that behavioral science will continue to be directed at accident causation and accident prevention in all transportation modes. It would be difficult to specify a worthier undertaking.
Efforts could range from identifying accident-causation contributors
such as drinking and performance errors to methods of reducing operator errors and keeping drunken drivers off the highway. Some
beginnings have been made in relating performance that leads to
accidents or prevents them to behavior in general, through cognitive
or motivational concepts (for example, Parsons 1976c). Behavioral
scientists have been less interested in the "second accident," the
damage to driver or passengers resulting from a collision; this is
more a concern of physiological than of behavioral science. Illness,
rather than accidents, has not been a major interest of psychologists,
except for some who have investigated motion sickness and effects
of reduced atmospheric pressure and anoxia in high-altitude flight
(Poulton 1970). Space flight is a form of transportation; one should
take note of behavioral science studies of both subgravity and high g
(acceleration) forces (Burns, Chambers, and Hendler 1963; Poulton
1970).

Now we come to social interaction. Social interactions include fighting, loving, imitating, talking, hiding, teaching, and so
on. What have social psychologists found out about interactions
and relationships between individuals or their actions in small
groups that might be applicable to transportation? In a paper mentioned earlier (Parsons 1976a) the author commented:

> Social psychologists appear to have neglected transpor-
> tation. Yet pilots and air traffic controllers communi-
> cate verbally with each other by radio; drivers of
> vehicles communicate with each other by stop and turn
> signals, rear lights, horns, the maneuvers of their
> vehicles, and, increasingly, citizens band radio; bus
> and subway passengers exhibit or fail to exhibit pri-
> vacy and territorial behavior and communicate with
> each other both verbally and gesturally or posturally;
> pedestrians generally avoid collisions with each other;

New York taxicab drivers talk to passengers; Amtrak
conductors give passengers misinformation or respond
negatively to cries of discomfort; owners of speeding
stinkpots rock sailboats with their wakes. Many opportunities exist for both unobtrusive and obtrusive research in social interactions in the field of transportation. Studies that readily come to mind are investigations of optimal rear lighting in automobiles.

It would be interesting to know to what extent social imitation
affects modal choice and automobile purchase; one suspects it is a
major factor. As citizen band radios have grown immensely popular, highway communication has begun to make driving less asocial.
Although the social aspects of transportation vary in extent according to mode, more knowledge applied to social behavior might be
helpful to transportation planners and designers, especially if social
psychologists tried harder to translate their research results into
explicit guidelines. In other areas of generalizable environmental
design, as mentioned earlier, social-psychological data have been
gathered concerning privacy, territoriality, personal space, and
conflict, and research along these lines would be desirable within
transportation itself.

Psychologists have developed considerable knowledge about
human motivation that can be exploited in changing or maintaining
behavior in transportation. Although the term has been variously
interpreted, by motivation in this paper is meant positive or aversive consequences and "potentiation." In travel behavior, potentiation usually means goal-setting. People plan a trip to go some-
place. Then they are positively reinforced if they get there, so
they become more likely to take more trips. If they are aversively
reinforced during the trip, as by an accident, the behavior that led
to the accident becomes less likely. Motivation consists of incentives and disincentives (penalties) and the circumstances that make
these important.

Behavioral psychologists have recently begun to apply these
principles of operant conditioning (behavior modification) to various
features of transportation (for example, Everett, Hayward, and
Meyers 1974; Hake and Foxx 1978; Runnion, Watson, and McWhorter
1978). This brand of psychology has, in my view, the most con-
vincing and useful approach to motivation, and I predict it will bring
about a substantial increase in understanding why passengers, in
particular, do what they do. However, it can be inferred that there
are also cognitive components in decision making—people verbalize
alternative courses of action—although ultimately most, if not all,
human choices depend on incentives and penalties. Humans are not

purely rational, as some economists (and others) presume, especially when people are developing, maintaining, or losing some habitual behavior, of which most behavior in transportation consists. It is important to distinguish habits from decisions; as indicated earlier, psychologists investigate both of these categories of behavior. To some extent, decision making, as well as habits and habit change, affects route selection and modal choice. Decision making is verbally mediated behavior in a novel situation. To overemphasize it, however, may risk neglecting the reinforcement (incentive and disincentive) variables underlying it and also habit structures. But with a dash of decision making, operant psychologists can discover the reasons for human actions in transportation, in modal choice, in accident behavior, in energy conservation, or simply in going from here to there (Parsons 1977). Then they can show how transportation behavior can be changed by influencing motivational variables.

Much <u>learning</u> goes on in transportation. People learn how to drive a car or fly a plane. They learn how to get from here to there, whether by auto, bus, subway, rail, plane, or boat. They learn how to build or maintain vehicles, terminals, or paths (highways, railways). They learn both by being told and by doing. Since a great deal of behavioral science consists of the investigation of learning, applied psychology should be able to contribute to training (educating) aircraft pilots and tanker helmsmen, high school and other driver-learners, railroad maintenance personnel, air traffic and bus fleet controllers, bicyclists and motor cyclists, pedestrians (for example, children and handicapped), and so on. In some of these instances, the contribution has already been substantial, as in driver education (Schlesinger 1972). Although most of this technology transfer would not involve passengers, who have less to learn than operators, maintainers, and controllers, training can be considered as persuading passengers to change their transportation mode or to carpool. It is also important in getting automobile owners and drivers to conserve energy and to change driving habits so there will be fewer accidents. If behavioral science had more influence, safety campaigns might shift their emphasis from exhortation to more effective approaches to accident reduction.

Finally, by <u>perception</u> in Table 3.2 is meant that process where reactions to sensory stimuli consist of oral, written, or graphic description (or brain-evoked potentials) rather than activities and feelings, although it may be viewed also as an intermediate stage preceding those reactions. In the circumscribed sense in which the term is used here, it might also be considered part of human information processing. Substantial behavioral science research has been conducted in perception, such as investigations of

sensory thresholds, imagery, retention, filtering, overload, under-
load (stimulus deprivation), scaling, arousal, and cultural, experiential, and social modifications. Aesthetic reactions can be regarded
as mixtures of perception and feeling. Perception (including aes-
thetics) as an effect of transportation on people has special interest
for environmental designers, including many in transportation (for
example, those who design vehicles and terminals). Although other
categories of transportation-related individuals are likely to be
more concerned with other matters, behavioral science has much
knowledge to offer about perception.

## ASPECTS OF TRANSPORTATION

Continuing this system of overview of behavioral science and
transportation, we come to the aspects of transportation that affect
people as listed in Table 3.3. They characterize every transportation mode. I will discuss them briefly, as each is related to the
aspects of behavior in Table 3.2. (A matrix of these relationships
is shown in Table 3.4.)

That one should first consider the totality of a transportation
mode or system (including a multimode situation) seems self-evident.
The entirety embraces all the interrelationships between the subdivisions and affects all of the behavioral outcomes.

Resources, the second item in Table 3.3, are the major physical components of a transportation mode or system—the paths, terminals, and vehicles and their manifold elements. These are designed and, except for some paths, constructed rather than natural;
natural paths include airways and ocean routes. Linking these to
items in Table 3.2, whether various resources are provided, how
they are designed, and how they are maintained significantly affect
users' activities, such as work performance. Continuing to link resources of a transportation mode with effects on people, consider
vertical transportation, that is, elevators. If a building lacks a
sufficient number of these or if one breaks down, people are delayed
in going to or leaving their offices or apartments. If a floor button
is too high, the traveler cannot push it. If doors close too quickly,
locomotion through them becomes difficult. This example is inten-
tionally oversimplified. Most transportation systems are far more
complex, but the same kinds of considerations apply. Human factors
engineering is the subdivision of behavioral science that should be
primarily concerned with the design (and provision) of transportation
elements and complexes for optimal human performance.

Resources also affect feelings, pro or con. A properly designed, wide enough seat in a commercial aircraft makes the occupant

feel comfortable. A requirement to fasten a seat belt, in aircraft or automobile, may produce irritation based on inconvenience. A well-designed freeway reduces stress, or increases it if it is packed with fast-moving vehicles. Resources, such as vehicles, can also contribute either to health and safety or to illness and accidents; Ralph Nader could tell you why. Resources, such as the engine room of a ship, call for learning in order to be operated. A ship's passengers must learn how to find their way to the dining room or the life boats. Resources are subject to manipulation: highways are designed, bridges built, streets barricaded, potholes left unfilled.

Picking a third aspect from Table 3.3, there are two kinds of arrangement in transportation. The location and distribution of routes (paths) is the spatial variety; the scheduling of vehicles on those paths are temporal. Each is related to locomotion (for example, walking to or from terminals), social interaction (for example, joining a friend for lunch), and learning (for example, memorizing Metro stops and timetables).

Although the communication item might be viewed as part of resources, separate consideration is desirable, partly because it has a particular effect on social interaction (for example, pilot-tower radio conversation, CB radio chatter, warning cues from the rotating indicator of a police car). Communication devices (signs) say where to go (affecting locomotion) if those in an airport, for example, are properly placed and designed (but not in Dallas–Fort Worth) or they tell you which bus goes where (but not in Manhattan). Communication may necessitate learning (if airport signs are in a language you do not understand or subway signs are lettered vertically so you have to learn to read at a 90–degree angle). Route guidance signs for motor vehicle drivers are communication devices that have been investigated for intelligibility and legibility by behavioral scientists. It seems a pity that airport and subway terminal designers have failed to make use of this kind of experience and know-how.

Protection consists of those aspects of a transportation mode that are supposed to enhance health and safety, particularly the latter. Air traffic control teams and equipment guide aircraft through bad weather to runways and prevent en route and close–approach collisions. Painted strips and curb reflectors on highways help the motorist stay in the proper lane or on the road. Buoys mark reefs and shoals and stop signs or traffic lights prevent right–angle collisions (while increasing the chances of rear-end collisions). Highway warning signs are primarily protection devices, not communication devices. It is important that the vehicle driver easily discriminate their contents, as in route guidance signs, but, though visible and legible, warning signs may do a poor job of warning.

Here is an excellent opportunity for behavioral science research, which has never been exploited to find out how well various kinds of warning signs actually affect the behavior they are supposed to influence.

This example also illustrates the differences between operant (or behavior modification) and cognitive (or human factors) approaches. These can be combined, as they were in a National Bureau of Standards study of another protection device for transportation, the lighthouse foghorn (Molino, Zerdy, and Frome 1974). In some situations, human factors investigation can, in itself, contribute to protection aspects of transportation by making them more effective. An example is the improvement of equipment, procedures, team play, personnel selection, and training in air traffic control centers. There are many protection problems in transportation, including air bags and railroad separation techniques, and behavioral science intervention should be invoked for all of them. Both human factors and behavior modification techniques can be appropriate.

With regard to ambient conditions, which affect activities, feelings, motivation, health and safety, and manipulation in transportation as well as in other constructed environments, behavioral scientists can advise, in particular on control of noise and temperature. Transportation noise can also mask auditory communication and interfere with auditory perception. Especially in nontransportation fields, behavioral scientists have been working for some time with engineering specialists to minimize ill effects from noise, heat, and cold, and there is no reason why this collaboration could not be extended to transportation. The effects of noise on activities and of heat and cold on feelings have been carefully explored but there has been little investigation of the ways in which these ambient conditions influence motivation (Parsons 1978c).

By reinforcement/potentiation in Table 3.3 is meant the events, conditions, or circumstances that induce a transportation passenger or operator to do the same thing as before or to do something different—obviously, the transportation aspects that influence motivation. These include some familiar items, such as financial cost (for example, fares), financial gain (for example, payment or savings), chance of an accident (risk), an actual accident, enjoyment in the ride (for example, scenery), discomfort in the ride (for example, heat), inconvenience or effort during the trip, getting away from something unpleasant (for example, cold), avoiding (perhaps postponing) a disagreeable event or situation, anticipating a desirable event or circumstance at the destination (for example, shopping, picking up the kids from school, or having dinner or a drink), or simply reaching the destination as planned. Reinforcement/potentiation has an impact on locomotion (we usually do not set out for places we cannot reach), learning (consequences—incentives and penalties—influence the acquisition of skills and knowledge), and manipulation (the consequence, money received, controls the behavior of selling the boat). Recent behavior modification research has emphasized financial gain through special payments to passengers for mode change or ride sharing. Money savings in tolls and parking are favorable consequences for carpooling. In the laboratory, travel behavior has been experimentally altered by favorable consequences in the form of money payments and unfavorable consequences in the form of simulated accidents (Parsons 1977, 1978b). To a limited extent, the token economies that have proved so effective in altering behavior in institutions have been introduced to transportation, and greater potentials exist. A related type of behavioral investigation of reinforcement/potentiation, based on expectancy (or instrumentality) theory, has been developed in business and industry and could be applied to transportation. It emphasizes behavioral control by anticipated consequences rather than past consequences, using reinforcement theory.

Finally, in going through the contents of Table 3.3, we come to appearance, which has effects on feelings, perception, and manipulation. Perception is clearly related to appearance and since, as noted earlier, a large segment of behavioral science is concerned with perception, psychologists may be able to offer help to planners and designers concerning this transportation aspect. Appearance also affects how much people like or dislike something, such as automobiles, Bay Area Rapid Transit (BART) subway cars, or Metro stations. It is not clear to me, however, how much direct help behavioral scientists can really provide concerning appearance or how much help designers (who are engaged in the manipulation of these environments) would want. Tastes vary: some prefer the graffiti on New York subway cars to the grime and dinginess they otherwise display; others react adversely.

I now call attention to Table 3.5, which lists eight modes or transportation systems (or settings), multimode considerations between modes, the fact that one mode may interfere with another, and some of the matters modes have in common. For any particular mode there are submodes such as vehicles, paths, terminals, traffic control, services, and maintenance facilities. Why go through such an enumeration? For one reason, to make sure everything relevant is set forth. For example, although transportation planners and managers are well aware of the problems of maintenance in any mode, these are rarely addressed in the people-related literature. Yet maintenance facilities are operated by people.

The moderating variables in Table 3.6 include most or all of the major factors external to transportation that transportation planners must consider. They are not included in the behavioral and transportation categories in Tables 3.2 and 3.3, but they do involve people and must be factored into any behavioral science inquiry that deals with policy and planning. These variables either influence planning and design, which then, in turn, affect people in transportation, or they directly affect people in transportation, whose consequent needs or demands then influence planning and design, or they do both. It is not within the purview of this paper to discuss each of them individually. In any case, they can be viewed in terms of aggregates of people and data rather than within the framework of behavioral science in this paper.

In conclusion, let us look at Table 3.7. The importance of the various categories should be obvious. Modal choice often differs according to whether a person is rich or poor. Small children or infants (with or without mothers and fathers) and pregnant women must be considered along with the aged who are poor or handicapped, hence the category age extremes. But age, as such, should not be the concern. Rather, many older people are likely to be poor (and thereby isolated) or ill (physically or mentally) or handicapped (including weak or frail). We have other categories than "aged" for these problems because they exist throughout the age spectrum in our population. Older persons who are poor or ill or handicapped fit into these other categories. Those who are not do not require mention. As an aside, inappropriate phraseology can maintain or strengthen the social prejudice against age. An unfortunate instance is the phrase "the elderly and handicapped," an example of guilt by association rather fashionable in transportation and other studies.

The category substance abusers means both alcohol addicts and drug addicts (as well as smokers). Cultural differences primarily mean language differences, although other cultural variations can be important in transportation, despite its transcultural character. Developing nations may have some problems with modern technology. In this case cultural differences overlap with skills, but differences in levels of skill can be found throughout transportation, within any culture or nation. Passengers as well as operators vary in the skills they need in their various activities.

It seems fitting to end this paper with a quick look at the people in transportation in the nine functional categories in Table 3.7: vehicle operators, passengers, maintainers, controllers, managements, shippers, producers, investors, and communities. Attention must be given to all of these in applying behavioral science to this field. The categories are interrelated. They all are affected by transportation in the ways listed in Table 3.2 and as brought about by the transportation aspects in Table 3.3. The different categories are affected differently, however. Behavioral science must consider these differences. As in most of modern technology, the people involved in transportation are as various as transportation itself.

Transportation planning, policy, and management need the assistance of behavioral science, which, in turn, needs opportunities to widen its scope and deepen its participation in transportation.


REFERENCES

The following references do not pretend to illustrate adequately what behavioral science has already done in transportation or what might be transferred to transportation from other fields. Other chapters present more extensive sets of references.

American Society of Landscape Architects Foundation. 1976. Barrier-free Site Design. U.S. Department of Housing and Urban Development. Washington, D.C.: U.S. Government Printing Office.

Burns, N. M., R. M. Chambers, and E. Hendler. 1963. Unusual Environments and Human Behavior. New York: Free Press.

Everett, P. B., S. C. Hayward, and A. W. Meyers. 1974. "The Effects of a Token Reinforcement Procedure on Bus Ridership." Journal of Applied Behavior Analysis 7: 1-9.

Forbes, T. W., ed. 1972. Human Factors in Highway Traffic Safety Research. New York: Wiley.

Grandjean, E. 1973. Ergonomics of the Home. London: Taylor and Francis.

Hake, D. V., and R. M. Foxx. 1978. "Promoting Gasoline Conservation: The Effects of Reinforcement Schedule, a Leader, and Self-recording." Behavior Modification 2: 339-70.

Helander, M. 1978. "Applicability of Drivers' Electrodermal Response to the Design of the Traffic Environment." Journal of Applied Psychology 63: 481-88.

Kamenetz, H. L. 1969. The Wheelchair Book. Springfield, Ill.: Charles C. Thomas.

Lauer, A. R. 1960. The Psychology of Driving. Springfield, Ill.:
Charles C. Thomas.

McCormick, E. J. 1976. Human Factors in Engineering and Design. New York: McGraw-Hill.

Michaels, R. M. 1960. "Tension Responses of Drivers Generated
on Urban Streets." Highway Research Board Bulletin 271: 29-43.

_____. 1962. "Effects of Expressway Design on Driver Tension
Responses." Highway Research Board Bulletin 330: 16-26.

Molino, J. A., G. A. Zerdy, and F. S. Frome. 1974. "Toward
a More Musical Foghorn." Human Factors 16: 567-75.

Parsons, H. M. 1972. Man-machine System Experiments.
Baltimore: Johns Hopkins Press.

_____. 1975. "Comfort and Convenience: How Much?" Paper
presented at the meeting of the American Association for the
Advancement of Science, 1975.

_____. 1976a. "Alternatives to Survey Research in Applied Psy-
chology: Transportation." Paper presented at the meeting of
the American Psychological Association, 1976.

_____. 1976b. "Work Environments." In Human Behavior and
Environment, edited by I. Altman and J. F. Wohlwill. New
York: Plenum Press.

_____. 1976c. "Caution Behavior and Its Conditioning in Driving."
Human Factors 18: 397-408.

_____. 1977. "Conditioning of Human Locomotion Rate on a Run-
way." Paper presented at the meeting of the Midwestern Association of Behavior Analysis, 1977.

_____. 1978a. "Residential Design for the Aging (For Example,
the Bedroom)." Human Factors.

_____. 1978b. "Highway Accident Simulation." Paper prepared
for the meeting of the Human Factors Society, 1978.

_____. 1978c. "Temperature and Motivation." Paper prepared
for the meeting of the American Society of Heating, Refrigerating
and Air Conditioning Engineers, 1978.

Poulton, E. C. 1970. Environment and Human Efficiency. Springfield, Ill.: Charles C. Thomas.

Runnion, A., J. O. Watson, and J. McWhorter. 1978. "Energy Savings in Interstate Transportation through Feedback and Reinforcement." Journal of Organizational Behavior Management 1: 180-91.

Schlesinger, L. E. 1972. "Human Factors in Driver Training and Education." In Human Factors in Highway Traffic Safety Research, edited by T. W. Forbes. New York: Wiley.

Snow, A. J. 1926. "Tests for Chauffeurs." Industrial Psychology 1: 30-45.

Steinfeld, E. 1975. Barrier-free Design. Syracuse, N.Y.: Syracuse University.

Stokols, D., R. W. Novaco, J. Stokols, and J. Campbell. 1978. "Traffic Congestion, Type A Behavior, and Stress." Journal of Applied Psychology 63: 467-80.

Strakosch, G. R. 1967. Vertical Transportation: Elevators and Escalators. New York: Wiley.

Uhlaner, J. E. 1956. "Tests for Selecting Drivers." Paper presented at the annual meeting of the Eastern Psychological Association, 1956.

Van Cott, H. P., and R. G. Kinkade. 1972. Human Engineering Guide to Equipment Design. Washington, D.C.: U.S. Government Printing Office.

Wechsler, D. 1926. "Tests for Taxicab Drivers." Personnel Journal 5: 24-30.

# 4
# APPLICATIONS OF BEHAVIORAL SCIENCE TO TRANSPORTATION: A STATE OF THE ART REVIEW

## Richard M. Michaels

## INTRODUCTION

The past 20 years have seen increasing applications of the behavioral sciences to transportation issues. Until the past decade, most of the effort was focused on two areas, engineering psychology and the psychology of personality, and then largely in traffic safety. Since that time, because of major changes in transportation planning and policy requirements, there has been a major growth in applications of cognitive and consumer psychology. The reasons for the emergence of a focus on the behavioral sciences are obvious. First, transportation as a technology is a classic person-machine system. How well it operates, in terms of safety and economy, depends upon the performance characteristics of the operator and how adaptively the system is engineered to user characteristics.

Second, how transportation is used is a product of a set of consumer decisions, both short- and long-term. The bases of these decisions, in terms of when, where, and how people choose to travel, are complex social, cognitive, and attitudinal processes. These behavioral variables are fundamental to the short- and long-range public investments in existing transport technology and its operation and management. They are equally critical to decision making for new forms of transport technology.

Third, as it has become necessary to modify transportation usage to conserve resources and improve environmental quality, critical policy decisions hinge on the ability to predict traveler responses. Policy acceptability has become a basic consideration in the larger policy process. This, of course, involves significant sociological as well as psychological considerations.

Finally, it is becoming clear that much of transportation planning and policy has been reactive, following social, economic, and political pressures. The dynamism of a relatively free consumer society has never been understood well enough to allow selective, sensitive, and efficient transportation planning. The result has been transportation investments that neglect special groups such as the elderly, the handicapped, and the poor. One consequence has been the exacerbation of social conflict and the growth of nonrational responses to transportation proposals. Again, how conflict is handled and what participatory processes are used will determine the course of the implementation of transport decisions. These are clearly social and behavioral problems of major proportions.

In sum, a variety of events in the past decade have altered the nature and orientation of transportation policy and planning. It has expanded from a largely engineering and economic frame of reference to include basic behavioral considerations ranging from social and group requirements to individual choice.

If the behavioral sciences are to add useful input to the planning process, it is essential to understand both the structure of these fields and how they can be productively applied. The purpose of this review is to examine some of the ways in which the behavioral sciences have been used in transportation. However, it is essential to view these applications in the context of both the theory and methodology of the behavioral sciences from which they derive their utility. The studies to be discussed in this paper derive from a long history of theoretical development. From a transportation standpoint we can develop a matrix of theoretical areas and areas of application, shown in Table 4.1. The columns divide behavioral science into six broad theoretical areas. The rows identify seven major areas of transportation engineering, planning, and policy that are currently of major importance. The checks in the cells of this matrix indicate the importance of the behavioral science areas to each of the transportation issues.

It should be noted that this matrix is a convenience only. The fact is that the theoretical areas are not mutually exclusive. On the contrary, they are highly interdependent. However, there is no unified general relativity theory in the behavioral sciences. Rather, there is specialized theory that draws from several subelements of behavior. It is probably best to view the matrix, not in a conventional mathematical sense, but rather as a process in which each area represents a series of transforms from input (stimuli) to output (observed behavior).

The other aspect that needs to be mentioned concerns measurement methodology. For all practical purposes, all of the human processes are stochastic ones normally requiring fairly sophisticated, multivariate analytic methods. In addition, the measures of human processes require more concern from a mathematical theory

TABLE 4.1

Importance of Behavioral Science Areas to Transportation Issues

| Transportation Areas | Behavioral Science Theoretical Areas | | | | | |
|---|---|---|---|---|---|---|
| | Perceptual Motor Processing | Cognition | Information Processing | Learning | Choice and Decision Making | Organization Theory |
| Engineering design | XXX | XXX | XXX | XX | XX | X |
| Traffic flows | XXX | XXX | XXX | XXX | XX | X |
| Travel demand | X | XX | XX | XX | XXX | XXX |
| Transportation choice | XX | XXX | XXX | XX | XXX | X |
| Investment decision | X | XX | XX | XX | XXX | XXX |
| Social impact | X | XX | XX | XXX | XXX | XXX |
| System management | X | XX | X | XXX | XXX | XXX |

Note: XXX = greatest importance; X = least importance.

standpoint than most of the conventional physical processes. This is so because humans operate in qualitative as well as quantitative domains and the relation of their metrics to objective, physical stimuli is often nonlinear, discrete, multidimensional, and variable. Hence, how to measure the subjective process and the mathematical form of these metrics is of central concern in the behavioral sciences.

Finally, the application of behavioral science to sociotechnical phenomena normally requires careful experimental design. The measurement of change and the impact of interventions rarely are simple or direct. There are, to use the behavioral scientist's term, too many intervening variables between an environmental change and resulting behavior. Consequently, the behavioral sciences, whether operating in the laboratory or in vivo, naturally develop experimental designs to discriminate among explanatory or prescriptive behavioral processes. In evaluating programs, in particular, some form of careful design is an integral part of the methodology of the behavioral sciences.

With this as background, the remainder of this paper will review a variety of studies of human behavior. Most of those selected are drawn from transportation. This review is intended to be exemplary of applied behavioral science practice. It may be assumed that the work cited is methodologically sound and the results valid. However, the reader may go to the source shown in the bibliography.

This review is organized according to the matrix shown in Table 4.1. Each of the behavioral science areas will be discussed and specific studies drawn from the transportation areas. Where research or applications are nonexistent in transportation, they will be taken from other sectors.

## PERCEPTUAL MOTOR BEHAVIOR

In transportation in general and highway transportation in particular, the operation of the system depends upon a person for its control. In essence, how efficiently and safely any transport mode performs depends on how well the person can guide and control the vehicle in the individual and collective sense. This process involves a fundamental perceptual and motor task. That is, the operator must acquire information from the driving environment, process that information, and carry out control changes on the vehicle that modify its position in time, space, and velocity. This must be done not only in the absolute sense, but also relative to other vehicles.

The process by which a person carries out this function has been the object of intensive research and development over the past 30 years in human factors and engineering psychology. This effort has not only been helpful in understanding human performance, it has also been instrumental in the design and engineering of more efficient person-machine systems.

Although this human guidance and control process involves more than simple perceptual and motor behaviors, these turn out to be both fundamental and limiting characteristics of people's behavior and, as a consequence, are basic to understanding how transportation systems can and will be used.

For the purposes of this discussion, perception may be defined as the process by which people transform physical information into human behavior. In essence, perception is the processing and conversion of basic sensory information into useful terms, in a behavioral sense. At its simplest, this involves questions of a qualitative and quantitative nature about the environment: How does a driver know that a roadway curves to the right or left; how does the operator of a transit train know when to begin deceleration in order to stop at the right place in a station; how does a pilot know the right glide path; how does a pedestrian know whether there is enough time to cross an intersection? The answers to these questions require first that the individual obtain perceptual information. The information from the environment in its human transform becomes the basis for performance behavior.

Perceptual analysis in all modes of transportation has an extensive history. It ranges from static detection of signals in terms of physical characteristics, such as intensity, frequency, and duration, to complexes of information, such as signs and symbols. It includes also dynamic detection—dynamic in time or space and in noise.

One example of this class is work done in highway transportation. A fundamental question is: How does a driver know whether or not an object is or is not in the path of travel? The question has obvious implications for safety as well as traffic design and operations. Some research (Gordon [1966] and Gordon and Michaels [1963]) suggests that the basic information is the angular velocity of the object a driver is approaching. That is, the rate of change of the angle, subtended by the object and the driver's eye relative to the path of travel, is a basic perceptual variable in determining object location while moving through an environment. In general, it has been found that if an object or element in the visual field has no detectable component of angular velocity, that fact is basic to a driver's detecting a collision course that will require some change in speed or position. The important aspect of this perceptual process is that the objects can be physically located outside the driver's path and still generate the impression of a collision course. This perceptual process has profound effects on traffic flow and operations, for it determines such considerations as lane width, bridge abutment location, shoulder width, and so on. Even geometric design standards for highways are dependent upon this class of perception. In essence, the behavioral science analysis provides a fundamental means of establishing these design criteria, for by understanding the perceptual processes it is possible to identify the form and magnitude of the information that must be provided to drivers to insure efficient system guidance.

The motor functions are concerned with the mechanics of human response to perceptual as well as cognitive information in control systems. If an auto or bus driver must bring a vehicle to a stop at a particular point, what is the nature of the operations to be performed in time and space? When should brake application begin? How accurately can braking control be exerted? What is the relation between the characteristics of the mechanical system and human action on the controls? Clearly, answers to such questions crucially determine system safety, operational capacity, passenger comfort, and feelings of security. At a second-order level, the control dynamics are critical determinants of system costs, both direct and indirect. For example, highway capacity has a maximum value because of the guidance and control characteristics of the human operator given the properties of the automobile and traffic system to be controlled. Changing the guidance or control dynamics can cause an increase or decrease in lane capacity. Clearly, application of behavioral science in the guidance and control domain offers one direction for directly increasing the performance of transportation systems.

Human control processes have been analyzed extensively, especially in military and space contexts. To a lesser degree, work has been done in the surface transportation area. In general, in a person-machine system, the human operator is required to exercise control by modifying some property of the system in response to a change in its performance. At its simplest, the controller imposes a change through one or more control devices, a stick, a wheel, a pedal, or the like. The system design and the location of the operator within it determines the nature of control response. In this context, the human may act as a differential operator. If controlling only position, one is acting as a type 0 system; if controlling rate or velocity, as a type 1 system. If the system is a closed loop, that is, if there is feedback of output response to the input, there will be a transfer function that will determine the order of the system. Thus, the control function may be described in terms of type and order.

How well the given system is controlled is determined by the dynamic properties of the human as well as the characteristics of

the system itself. One of the more important developments in
person-machine system design has been the estimation of the human
transfer function. This modeling includes not only response characteristics but also the basic physiological properties of the human
system (McRuer et al. 1965; McRuer and Jex 1966). Its importance
lies in the fact that such a model permits the design of person-
machine systems with predictable dynamic properties. It also obviously allows the evaluation of complex control systems.

Control system design is one of the more complex human engineering areas, and it is beyond the scope of this paper to review
it in any detail. Interested readers should review Frost's chapter
in Human Engineering Guide to Equipment Design (Van Cott and
Kinkade 1972). Suffice it to say that the behavioral sciences have
developed a body of theory and technique for the design of person-
machine systems that permits both highly sophisticated analysis
and evaluation of complex systems for human use. It is probably
reasonable to say that little of this body of theory has been used in
the design of surface transportation, at least in any comprehensive
way. However, many of the problems in surface transport operations and safety, as well as in planning and policy, are directly
traceable to the lack of sophistication in control system design in
particular and guidance and control in general.

The relation between the perceptual-motor processes and attitudes and subjective evaluation of systems is worthy of note. How
well a system is adapted or designed for human use determines not
only its operational efficiency and safety but also user satisfaction.
A system that is difficult to control or that demands high levels of
attention or specialized operator skills generates qualitative feelings that are one basis of user judgments of system acceptability.
Quantitative evaluations, in terms of attitudinal or rating measures,
have been used for over 20 years as part of the design process in
aerospace systems (Cooper 1957; Harper and Cooper 1966;
McDonnell 1968). Similarly, relations have been developed between
subjective acceptability and acceleration and deceleration and shock
and vibration (Chaney 1965).

In sum, the perceptual-motor properties of transport systems
are one major behavioral basis for defining the attributes of transportation systems. These properties form one domain for determining users' attitudes toward transportation. Conversely, modification of any of their perceptual or motor properties will affect
users' attitudes toward those systems and hence their choices
among alternative modes.

INFORMATION PROCESSING

Human beings are constantly receiving information or data from their physical environment. The information may be discrete, for example, a traffic control signal, or continuous, for example, speed or position. There are basic limits on both the quantity and rate at which such information may be processed. It may be noted that this processing applies to cognitive or symbolic information as well as "real" or sensory information.

Human information processing behavior can be analyzed in terms of classical information theory. At one level, the interest has been in the absolute amount of information that people can process. This depends, in general, on sensory pathways and the dimensions of the sense mode, for example, color, brightness, frequency, and so on. A variety of studies over the past 25 years have defined absolute processing capabilities, shown in Table 4.2. These led to the conclusion that human information processing was limited to the order of seven levels, or 2.8 bits of information (Miller 1956).

The rate of information processing is defined as channel capacity, the amount of information that the human can process per time unit through any sensory modality. At the most elementary level, humans can process at maximum rate of no more than 40-50 bits per second (Pierce and Karlin 1957). In general, multiple channel inputs tend to reduce channel capacity, while coding information, as in language, tends to increase channel capacity (Broadbent 1958).

The importance of information processing in transportation is simply that it defines the limits within which the human can control a system. It also suggests that there are upper limits on human capacity to organize and operate in time and space. Because the human is a limited information processor, behavior must be modified to remain within these limits if stable control is to be maintained over a system. One obvious example of this in transportation is the observed maximum in highway capacity. As traffic volume increases, the amount of information the driver must process increases. Given the dynamics of car following and its "noisiness," the information load increases rapidly. Once it approaches the information processing capacity of drivers, they must limit the information load by reducing speed or by increasing headways or both. Obviously, as speed is reduced, throughput vehicles per hour must decrease. Thus the behavioral process interacting with system design determines the upper limit of highway efficiency. If the system design could be modified so that the information rate were reduced, then drivers could operate at higher speeds at the same headways and thus increase lane capacity. Research and development in highway transportation using these behavioral science constructs have

# TABLE 4.2

## Amount of Information in Absolute Judgments of Various Stimulus Dimensions

| Sensory modality and stimulus dimension | No. of levels which can be discriminated on absolute basis | No. of bits of information transmitted, H* |
|---|---|---|
| Vision, single dimensions: | | |
| Pointer position on linear scale | 9 | 3.1 |
| Pointer position on linear scale: | | |
| Short exposure | 10 | 3.2 |
| Long exposure | 15 | 3.9 |
| Visual size | 5–7 | 2.3–2.8 |
| Hue | 9 | 3.1 |
| Brightness | 3–5 | 1.7–2.3 |
| Vision, combinations of dimensions: | | |
| Size, brightness, and hue[†] | 17 | 4.1 |
| Hue and saturation | 11–15 | 3.5–3.9 |
| Audition, single dimensions: | | |
| Pure tones | 5 | 2.3 |
| Loudness | 4–5 | 1.7–2.3 |
| Audition, combination of dimensions: | | |
| Combination of six variables[‡] | 150 | 7.2 |
| Odor, single dimension | 4 | 2.0 |
| Odor, combination of dimensions: | | |
| Kind, intensity, and number | 16 | 4.0 |
| Taste: | | |
| Saltiness | 4 | 1.9 |
| Sweetness | 3 | 1.7 |

*Since the number of levels is rounded to the nearest whole number, the number of bits does not necessarily correspond exactly.

†Size, brightness, and hue were varied concomitantly, rather than combined in the various possible combinations.

‡The combination of six auditory variables was frequency, intensity, rate of interruption, on-time fraction, total duration, and spatial location.

Source: E. J. McCormick, Human Factors Engineering (New York: McGraw-Hill, 1970), p. 92.

been done over the past decade (Rockwell and Snider 1969, p. 96), but little of it has found its way into engineering practice.

## COGNITIVE PROCESSES

The review in the two previous sections has been concerned with short-term dynamics of human behavior. As noted, this class of behavioral science focuses on real time, immediate performance capabilities and limitations. Both because of these basic limitations and because of higher order behavior, for example, goal seeking, people develop longer term processes by which to connect their pasts and futures to the present. In addition, they must have or develop long-term mechanisms for sorting or coding information, storing and retrieving it, and evaluating it. Clearly, such processes must be increasingly subjective and internal and the connections to external and observable events increasingly mediated and indirect. In essence, past and future are symbolically mediated, as must be those processes that compensate for real time limitations. There are, then, increasingly complex transforms that people make, from the elementary and observational to the interpretative and predictive. Modeling these transformations has become a central focus of modern behavioral science. The most significant aspect of this course of development is its subjective focus on internal events rather than on objective, external behavior. It is a subjective world view, one that is concerned with the quantification of qualitative properties.

One of the primary concepts in the transformation of objective to subjective information is cognitive processes. Although definition of the term has evolved over time, it will be used in this section to mean the symbolization of information in human terms. It is the process by which stable subjective meaning is attached to objective experience. The most obvious example of cognitive process is language, which represents an association of abstract symbols with concrete objects or experience.

The cognitive process is ordered in complexity. At the lowest levels, it is closely related to information processing. At the highest levels of abstract meaning, it is related to decision and choice behavior. One obvious application of cognitive processes is in recognition and interpretation of symbols; much behavioral science research has been done in this area in transportation. All of the work in traffic signing and traffic control devices is essentially an attempt to provide cognitive structure for guidance and control information. Shape, color, language, and abstract symbols are devices used for this purpose, and the effectiveness of alternative forms of information has been studied (Forbes, Snyder, and Pain 1964).

Work by Dewar and Swanson (1972) is typical of the laboratory and field research. Basically their study was concerned with recognizability of symbolic messages. They used short-term presentation of different classes of messages in the laboratory, followed by a controlled field study. They were able to measure recognition accuracy and the effect of message content and form of presentation on recognition. This laboratory technique is extremely powerful in detecting small differences in recognition, for it allows systematic control over variables of interest. Dewar and Swanson were able to show clearly in the laboratory case, although less clearly in the field study, that positive symbolic messages are cognitively stronger, that is, produce higher recognition accuracy, than negative information. This is a relatively simple finding, but the approach to optimizing message recognition and the variables essential to that apply as well to transit information systems, for example, routing and scheduling.

A higher level of cognitive process concerns the transformation of objective information into meaningful subjective data as a precedent for decision making and choice. In this vein, people process a variety of data that must be ordered and metricized to be functionally useful. How that transformation is made and by what rules ultimately determines the true, subjective basis of the decision and choice process.

A variety of behavioral science approaches have been applied to this class of problem. One is that of information integration theory developed by Anderson (1974), which has been applied to transportation (Levin 1976; Levin 1977; Levin et al. 1977; Norman and Louviere 1974). These studies suggest that people evaluate an object or experience using a multiplicative model. That is, attributes are weighted by their importance and the overall evaluation is the product. These models have been applied to subjective estimates of travel expense (Levin 1976) and mode choice (Norman and Louviere 1974). The results indicate a nonlinear relation between travelers' analyses and observable variables such as fare, travel time, cost, and so on. That is, not only is the human metric different from the objective metric, but there is also a combination rule that allows the people to integrate qualitative as well as quantitative variables in a regular and predictable manner. These results suggest that the cognitive process used to reach decisions is only indirectly related to conventional measures of transport performance or the models used in transport planning or policy. Furthermore, these results suggest that cognitive processes are far better means of market segmentation and population stratification than conventional variables such as age, income, sex, and so on (Thomas 1976).

At a higher level of cognitive abstraction, people must develop some subjective representation of their larger spatial environment. That is, in order to function in a spatial context, people must develop some internal maps which permit them to locate themselves relative to places and to define the paths to reach these places. The concept of cognitive maps is an old one in psychology. However, attempts to develop such maps of space are relatively recent (Downs 1970; Milgrim 1970; Stea 1974).

A study done in our laboratory (Stenson 1978) is exemplary of this research. Stenson's work was concerned with transportation use. He hypothesized that how people used modes of transport depends, in part, on their ability to locate sites in urban space and on their perception of distances between those sites. Using unidimensional and multidimensional scaling techniques, it was possible to develop both subjective, locational, and distance maps. The results showed that subjective perception of location and distance were major distortions of objective reality. For locations of increasing objective distance, estimates of distance were significantly distorted, and reliability of those estimates also decreased with distance from the origin reference. Other research has also shown a serious distortion in subjective spatial structure relative to objective geography (Garling 1976; Kameron 1973; Lowenthal and Riel 1972).

These studies have important implications for transportation planning. On the one hand, the trip distribution models of the gravity type predict the number of trip ends as some inverse power function of distance from an origin zone. Since travelers' subjective distance function follows the power law, then gravity models are analogs of the behavioral process. On the other hand, traffic assignment models, using minimum time path algorithms based on linear distance assumptions, are inconsistent with the behavioral process.

In mode usage, cognitive structure models suggest that whether a trip will be made and by what mode will depend on subjective location reliability and perceived travel time. If an individual does not know where a destination site is exactly located, using a fixed-route mode becomes extremely difficult and the risk of failing to achieve a destination will rise. Beyond a certain point, the likelihood of using such a mode at all or using it for anything other than limited kinds of trips will be low. This work suggests that, given the uncertainty in people's ability to locate destinations in space, people would consistently prefer point to point systems. This also may be one reason why transfers within mass transit networks are rather limited.

Studies in cognitive structure also suggest that marketing of fixed-route systems must include locational information. In fact, it can be argued that a major transit marketing requirement may be to help people develop spatial cognitive structure as a prerequisite to expanded usage of fixed-route transit systems.

It is clear from much of the work in subjective spatial organization research that there are basic inconsistencies between transportation planning as well as engineering spatial logic and the consumer perception of macrospace. If it is cognitive structure that defines the metrics of space and how travel in space is conceived by trip makers, then the development of such structure must be a fundamental basis of trip distribution, trip frequency, route choice, and mode choice. Unless the metrics of the planning process are consistent with those of behavior, the predictability and reliability of the planning process must be in question. This issue is not unique to transportation planning. It is equally an issue in policy and systems engineering, where consumer choice exists. If one objective of travelers is to reduce cognitive complexity and uncertainty, then they are likely to seek systems that perform more consistently with their subjective metrics. An understanding of those metrics and their integration becomes essential in the planning and design of transportation.

## BEHAVIOR MODIFICATION

The behavioral processes discussed involve learning. That is, by direct experience and interaction, individuals will acquire, integrate, store, and retrieve information. This process allows them to use effectively past experience in both concrete and abstract ways to manage their environments. Much of the learning implicit in perceptual, motor, and cognitive processes is naturalistic: it develops over time out of the direct and indirect consequences of behavioral action on the physical and social environment.

Learning also occurs by direction: people can be taught to behave in specific ways. This class of learning is directed by agents using both formal and informal means. Much of social organization is dependent on this learning process and involves procedures for modifying behavior to conform to social and functional norms.

Whether the learning process is naturalistic or directed, the basic theory underlying learning is well developed in the behavioral sciences. In terms of practical applications, the models most consistently used are those of operant conditioning. These models assume, in one form or another and with varying degrees of complexity, that a desired behavior will develop and endure if the occurrence of the behavior is consistently rewarded according to some schedule. The reward is a means of reinforcing the desired behavior. The rate and permanence of the learning depend on a variety of factors. Among these is the frequency with which the reinforcement is provided. The schedule may be varied, and in many cases, if not most, learning may occur faster and may be more stable when the reinforcement is not given on every trial. Once the learning is complete, the frequency of reinforcement may be reduced and, in some cases, eliminated completely.

Operant conditioning techniques have been applied for many years in education and have been expanded to industrial areas as well. Most recently, they have been applied to transportation. Some of the clearest examples of behavior modification theory used in transportation are described in work by Everett, Hayward, and Meyers (1974) and by Deslauriers and Everett (in press). In the earlier study, people who chose to ride a special bus were rewarded with tokens, redeemable for goods at local merchants according to a schedule of value. With proper advertising, the special bus was instituted along with a control group in which no rewards were offered. The study found that behavior modification was indeed effective, generating significant new ridership.

In the second study, the same procedure was followed, except that in addition to the 100 percent token reinforcement schedule, a 33 percent contingency was also used. It was found that the one-third schedule produced the same increment of ridership as did the continuous schedule.

Both these studies demonstrate the use and potential of behavior modification techniques in transportation. These are seminal studies and much work needs to be done to make effective use of operant techniques. For example, what reinforcers are most effective for transportation users? Are there optimal schedules of reinforcement? What population segments are most sensitive to what reinforcers and at what schedules?

It is well to point out that a major objective of behavior modification is to use rewards up to the point where the desired behavior becomes internalized. In theory, at that point, further extrinsic rewards become unnecessary. As learning proceeds, the inherent reward of the behavior itself becomes sufficient for the person to continue. Conversely, if it is desired to change behavior, for example, to use a bus rather than an automobile, the behavior modification process involves unlearning one response and learning an alternative. Thus, behavior modification may be concerned with learning of a new behavior or replacing one response with another. Obviously, this kind of substitution can be accomplished using behavior modification only if the properties of the substitute are equivalent to the original in terms of their rewards. This equivalence can be obtained from a combination of extrinsic as well as intrinsic rewards.

Much of transportation policy, for energy conservation, transportation usage, housing location decisions, driver behavior, and so on, involves attempts to modify behavior. Unfortunately, these attempts are based on assumptions about behavior that are limited at best, that is, to the economic nature of man. In addition, they do not involve any structured mechanisms for behavior modification. This is most obvious in relation to car- and vanpooling. These are policy options which probably can be implemented without a formal program of behavior modification (Deslauriers 1975).

## DECISION AND CHOICE

As is obvious in this review, the behavioral process involves a progression away from objective data and direct observation toward subjective analysis and indirect inference. Decision and choice behavior involves largely internal processes. In general, it is assumed that choice exists and that stable decision rules are used by individuals in selecting among alternatives. However, it is well to point out that a choice exists only if the observed individual subjectively perceives that alternatives are indeed available. Even if transit service exists, if the individual does not perceive it as a link to a desired destination, then effectively there is no choice to be made. This is very different from the case where a person evaluates the operating properties of the given modes as the basis of a mode choice decision. This distinction has been noted by Thomas (1976) and Johnson (1975), but it is often overlooked in mode choice modeling where only data on mode availability are used.

When the contextual variables preclude alternatives and no choice exists, relatively simple models of manifest behavior will suffice, involving relatively simple and obvious variables. Most disaggregate demand and mode choice models fall in this category. As Watson (1973) has pointed out, these models do well in predicting mandatory trips (for example, work trips) but are far less successful in predicting discretionary travel. It is important, therefore, to recognize that most behavioral approaches to decision and choice require that the alternatives involved be subjectively real and relevant to behavior.

When, in fact, the choice set is appropriately defined, current behavioral science theory allows a fairly sophisticated approach to developing transportation decision and choice modeling. The basic logic involves four major domains: the identification of subjective variables salient to the decision maker, the affective value or importance attached to those variables, the attitudinal scaling process used to measure the affective process, and the group of combinatorial rules, usually probabilistic, by which those scalers are employed to arrive at decisions.

The subjective variable of identification has been dealt with in a variety of ways in transportation studies. The direct approach is to identify an exhaustive set of attributes of modes and use univariate or multidimensional scaling techniques to identify those of highest subjective importance or affect. Varied studies of this type have been done in transportation over the past decade. One used paired comparisons to evaluate a set of variables considered of importance to the design of a demand responsive system (Golob et al. 1972). The preference scaling was internally consistent and produced interval measures of the set of 32 attributes. As a first-order approximation, these provided an ordering of design characteristics for a new system that would most nearly match potential user preferences.

Another study of a similar type (Michaels and Weiler 1975) used the categorical ratings of system attributes to segment mobility needs of the handicapped. Most scales measuring extent of mobility limitation are ordinal and arbitrary at best. Using scaling of attributes, it was possible to differentiate the handicapped into three groups. The most mobility limited placed more importance on access and ride attributes; values shifted with decreasing mobility limitations to service variables, as in nonhandicapped populations (Paine et al. 1967). In this case, subjective measurement of attribute or system variables provided a direct means of classification of mobility limitation.

Another study of attributes (Dobson and Tischer 1977) was directly aimed at determining the importance of affect in mode choice. Here the study was concerned with choice among three alternative modes for central business district (CBD) trips. Using semantic differential scaling, they were able to segment the population by mode use and showed that the subjective measures were better predictors of choice among the alternatives than the functional objective variables. This study demonstrates that sophisticated application of behavioral science methods can produce better estimates of demand and mode usage than conventional, aggregate or disaggregate models.

Unidimensional scaling has a basic limitation in that it assumes independence among the subjective variables under study. Depending on the objectives of an application, this may not be a serious problem, but in many cases there is a significant interaction among the variables. In these cases, the subjects are involved in a trade-off analysis. Thus the willingness to pay for transportation depends upon the attributes bought and, in theory, in some consistent relation. Multidimensional scaling (MDS) is a particularly useful tool in these situations. It permits the analysis of the attributes of importance in relation to each other. The techniques have been applied in a variety of contexts (Romney, Shepard, and Nerlove 1972). Conjoint measurement has been applied in marketing and more recently to transportation (Ross 1975). Here the technique has been used with a transformation technique to produce ratio scale measures of attributes (Johnson 1973). Hence, it is possible to determine the proportional value of the attributes and to compare across attributes. These measures provide a direct measure of utility that can be combined multiplicatively. This permits the planner to estimate how much better or worse than another one mode is perceived to be or how modifications in a mode will change its perceived value.

Another use of MDS is in differentiating subgroups in a population. From a behavioral standpoint, it is commonality of values, preferences, and attitudes that define homogeneous groups. This is over and opposed to conventional classifications on the basis of such things as age, sex, or socioeconomics. A series of studies using MDS for this purpose has been done in transportation using importance of attributes and environment (Nicolaidis and Dobson 1975; Nicolaidis and Sheth 1976). Similarly, a study of destination characteristics as a basis of destination choice used MDS to segment attractiveness (Koppelman, Prashker, and Begamery 1977).

A third approach to subjective scaling of the variables used in choice and decision is direct behavioral correlates of affective quality. Attitudes may and usually do measure affect, but there are other direct measures. One is the galvanic skin response (GSR), a physiological measure of startle or stress. In a study of route choice (Michaels 1966), summated ratings were obtained from people entering or leaving a controlled access highway and a parallel highway. In addition, GSR was measured on test drivers on both routes. It was shown that the stress differences between the two routes were greater than travel time or cost differences. Further, the attitudinal data correlated very highly with the GSR, and the attitudinal items that were most discriminating were those relating to the negative properties of the routes. Driving stress was the direct measure of the affective response of drivers to alternative routes between which a choice was made, and past experience led to the development of affective perception, which became the basis of route choice. Further, using the stress measure, it was possible to develop a diversion model that predicted route choice better than existing travel time diversion models.

Identification of the subjective variables, the affective value, and the metrics for their scaling is a continuous subjective process. However, where one starts in the process is crucial. If attitude measurement is the starting point, it is purely chance if there is any strong correlation with behavior, since the variables used are not necessarily the directly relevant ones. The fact is, attitudinal measures tap the affective domain, which, depending upon the attributes used for the scaling, may bear little relation to the real world in which individuals learn to behave. A good example is a study that used attitudinal measures, among others, to segment the transport market (Nicolaidis, Wachs, and Golob 1977). Attitudinal measures were found to be poor predictors; instead, choice constraint was most predictive. This does not negate attitudinal measures but rather demonstrates that behavioral models of choice require subjectively real alternatives for the process to be discriminating.

In a real choice situation, the final step in the process is the decision rule that forms the basis for the overt behavior. Various models exist within the behavioral sciences dealing with this decision process. One is a linear model that uses a regression approach based on the Brunswick "Lens" theory (Hammond, Hursch, and Todd 1964). A second is the information integration model of Anderson (1974) applied to transportation by Levin (1976, 1977) and Norman and Louviere (1974. A third is the trade-off analysis approach (Ross 1975; Johnson 1974), which has been used in several studies of Short Take-off and Landing Aircraft (STOL), commercial aviation, and transit marketing. A fourth is psychological utility theory (Luce 1959). This last has become one theoretical basis for disaggregate models of mode choice (Stopher and Meyburg 1975). All represent basic approaches for predicting mode choice and decision making and hence represent direct behavioral approaches to demand analysis, trip distribution, and route as well as mode choice. Although most of the theory exists to develop a rather general planning methodology, no such comprehensive behaviorally based techniques have been developed or tested.

It is worth concluding this discussion of decision and choice with the observation that the basic approach to understanding traveler choice behavior is equally applicable to planners' and policy makers' behavior. Transportation planning and policy making is a hierarchy of choices and decisions among a set of alternative courses of action. How policy makers carry out this process, especially as they become increasingly removed from the technical planning activity and increasingly closer to the sociopolitical activity, is not the least bit clear. However, it must involve the same process that has been discussed. That this is a real problem in transportation planning is evident in the current literature (Barker and Roark 1978).

ORGANIZATIONAL DEVELOPMENT

A final area of behavioral science is concerned with applied
social or group psychology. Current organizational theory is the
evolution of a movement that can be traced back to Kurt Lewin. In
general, the area has focused on group behavior, largely in industrial and organizational settings and in management practices. The
basic thrust in the application of these techniques is (1) to develop
more effective objective and affective communication among group
members, (2) to develop consensual goals for the group, (3) to improve management effectiveness, and (4) to increase productivity
within the organization. Normally, the process involves interaction
among members of the organization at different levels. The objective is to modify the organization to facilitate communication and to
afford recognition of group members' needs, as well as to provide
the opportunity to satisfy those needs within the context of the organizational goals.

At the present time, organizational development (OD) is being
used within the regional transit authorities of Seattle, Cleveland,
and Atlanta. Work done in Atlanta at upper management levels is
an example of one class of OD technique (Golembiewski and Kiepper
1976). The organizational process began at Metropolitan Atlanta
Regional Transit Authority (MARTA) with a primary task of building a management team. The process involved techniques of direct
confrontation among the top staff to develop agreement on both individual and group expectations. The purpose was to allow the participants to see both themselves and each other more clearly and
realistically. The process was evaluated using a rating system and
demonstrated significant increases in group effectiveness, coopera-
tiveness, and mutual trust.

Another OD technique is the process of developing consensual
goals for performance. Generally, the concept is to obtain from all
levels in an organization agreement on goals to be achieved at each
level. Participatory methods are used to develop the goals for both
units in the organization and individual members. A recent study
exemplifies the approach (Raia 1965). Each division manager was
required to establish the goals for the division's operation and the
means of determining the performance of the division. These goals,
in turn, were discussed with first line supervisors, who defined each
of their groups' performance goals, that is, how each would achieve
the division goals. With the performance controls in operation, each
group had feedback on its own activity. The results of the process,
analyzed by the trend of productivity over time, showed a reversal
from before to after. Productivity in the 15 plants involved had
been decreasing at a rate of 0.4 per month before the initiation of

the program. After initiation, productivity increased at a rate of 0.3 per month.

The spectrum of behavioral science theory being applied to organizations and groups is now quite extensive. It uses many of the same techniques discussed in earlier parts of this review, including work system design and behavior modification as well as social interaction methods. These all are aimed at increasing productivity, improving worker motivation and morale, and developing management structures that are more effective and efficient.

Another area where OD techniques are directly applicable to transportation is in citizen participation. The adversary nature of current public hearings is hardly conducive to either communication or decision making. One of the objectives of organizational development techniques is to reduce role conflicts and to assist people in understanding and sharing goals. Given that consensus, it becomes possible to explore alternative means of achieving those goals that can be mutually agreed upon. Although the process is complex, it has, in fact, been applied in a variety of social contexts. The techniques allow a sorting out of the real and imaginary concerns felt by the participants, planner and citizen alike. The process can bring all the participants into a common reality, and, within it, allow them to deal constructively with the transportation issues. Although various approaches to citizen participation in transportation decision making have been employed, there is no indication that comprehensive OD techniques have been applied to the problem.

CONCLUSION

The purpose of this review has been to examine the applications of behavioral science theory and technology to transportation. There has, in fact, been a long history of application of behavioral science. Its use is now increasing for two reasons. One is that the power and sophistication of the body of theory has grown. The other is that it is obvious that some of the most fundamental problems in transportation are behavioral in nature. If resource constraints are a given, then the need to change transport user behavior must be a fundamental consideration in design, planning, and policy making. Conventional economic and legal reinforcers alone cannot be used to achieve these changes. From work done in the cognitive, behavior modification, decision and choice, and organizational areas in the behavioral sciences, there are clearly more powerful and cost-effective means available to augment conventional policy tools. Recent work in the energy conservation area suggests some promising approaches.

In transport planning, behavioral science research is demonstrating the limits of conventional demand and trip distribution models, which appear to be narrow descriptions of highly constrained
manifest behavior. Certainly the sequential and independent models
currently in use do not reflect the integrated and learned process
that travelers develop in making travel decisions. Further, the
linear concept of time and space used in current design, planning,
and operating procedures is inconsistent with the proven behavioral
frame of reference. Human perception of space is not linear and
time perception is elastic. Yet it is the spatial orientation of travelers that underlies their choice of destination, mode, and route.
The principles of cognitive organization and information processing
offer an alternative means to develop travel demand models, models
having greater predictive power and generality than those we now
apply.

Existing planning methodology is empirically based on manifest travel behavior. The process, as now employed, uses past behavior to predict future transport needs. Since it is needs, attitudes,
and cognitive structure that determine behavior within technological
and social constraints, observed past or present actions are poor
predictors of future behavior. Unless the planning process utilizes
basic behavioral processes, it can only perpetuate the transportation
technology currently in use and poorly predict future social or behavioral responses as requirements. This is one of the reasons why
the emergence of social resistance to highways was largely missed
by planners, engineers, and policy makers. The same may be said
about elderly and handicapped transportation demands. Approaching
transportation policy and planning without understanding the underlying behavioral forces must at least reduce the cost effectiveness of
transport decision making and at worst generate social responses
that prevent rational planning and policy. It is clear that the current
state of the art in the behavioral sciences is sufficient to provide
these essential inputs to transportation planning and policy.

## REFERENCES

Anderson, N. H. 1974. "Information Integration Theory: A Brief
Survey." In Contemporary Developments in Mathematical Psychology, edited by D. H. Krantz, R. C. Atkinson, R. D. Luce,
and P. Suppes, vol. 2. San Francisco: Freeman.

Barker, W. G., and J. J. Roark. 1978. "The Role of the Urban
Transportation Planner in Public Policy." Presented at the
Southwest Division of the Association of American Geographers
Spring Meeting, April 15, 1978, at Houston, Texas.

Broadbent, D. E. 1958. Perception and Communication. New York: Pergamon Press.

Chaney, R. 1965. Whole Body Vibration of Standing Subjects. Boeing Co., BOE-D3-6779.

Cooper, G. E. 1957. "Understanding and Interpreting Pilot Opinions." Aeronautical Engineering Review 16: 47-52.

Deslauriers, B. C. 1975. "A Behavioral Analysis of Transportation: Some Suggestions for Mass Transit." High Speed Ground Transportation Journal 9: 13-20.

Deslauriers, B. C., and P. B. Everett. (In press.) "The Effects of Intermittent and Continuous Token Reinforcement in Bus Ridership." Journal of Applied Psychology.

Dewar, R. E., and H. A. Swanson. 1972. "Recognition of Traffic-Control Signs." Sponsored by Committee on Motorist Information Systems. Highway Research Record, vol. 414.

Dobson, R., and M. L. Tischer. 1977. "Comparative Analysis of Determinants of Modal Choices by Central Business District Workers." Transportation Research Record 649: 7-13.

Downs, R. M. 1970. "The Cognitive Structure of an Urban Shopping Center." Environment and Behavior 2: 13-39.

Everett, P. B., S. C. Hayward, and A. Meyers. 1974. "The Effect of a Token Reinforcement Procedure on Bus Ridership." Journal of Applied Behavior Analysis 7: 1-9.

Forbes, T. W., R. F. Snyder, and R. F. Pain. 1964. "A Study of Traffic Sign Requirements II: An Annotated Bibliography." College of Engineering, Michigan State University. Lansing.

Garling, T. 1976. "The Structural Analysis of Environmental Perception and Cognition." Environment and Behavior 8: 385-415.

Golembiewski, R. T., and A. Kiepper. 1976. "MARTA: Toward an Effective, Open Giant." Public Administration Review 36: 46-60.

Golob, T. F., E. T. Canty, R. L. Gustafson, and J. E. Vitt. 1972. "An Analysis of Consumer Preferences for a Public Transportation System." Transportation Research 6: 81-102.

Gordon, D. A. 1966. "Experimental Isolation of the Driver's Visual Input." Highway Research Record, vol. 122.

Gordon, D. A., and R. M. Michaels. 1963. "Static and Dynamic Visual Fields in Vehicular Guidance." Highway Research Record, vol. 84.

Hammond, K. R., C. Hursch, and F. J. Todd. 1964. "Analyzing the Components of Clinical Inference." Psychological Review 71: 438-56.

Harper, R. P., Jr., and G. E. Cooper. 1966. "A Revised Pilot Training Rating Scale for the Evaluation of Handling Qualities." Report No. 153, Cornell Aeronautical Labs. Ithaca, N.Y.

Johnson, M. 1975. "Psychological Variables and Choice between Auto and Transit Travel: A Critical Research Review." Working Paper No. 7509, Institute of Transportation and Traffic Engineering, University of California. Berkeley.

Johnson, R. M. 1973. "Pairwise Non-Metric Multidimensional Scaling." Psychometrika 38: 11-18.

_____. 1974. "Trade-Off Analysis: The Measurement of Consumer Values." Journal of Marketing Research 11, no. 2.

Kameron, J. 1973. "Experimental Studies of Environmental Perception." In Environment and Cognition, edited by I. Ettelson, pp. 157-67. New York: Seminar Press.

Koppelman, F., J. Prashker, and B. Begamery. 1977. "Perceptual Maps of Destination Characteristics Based on Similarities Data." Transportation Research Record 649: 32-37.

Levin, I. P. 1976. "Comparing Different Models and Response Transformation in an Information Integration Task." Bulletin of Psychometric Science 7: 78-80.

_____. 1977. "Information Integration in Transportation Decisions." In Human Judgement and Decision Processes in Applied Settings, edited by M. F. Kaplan and S. Schwartz, pp. 57-82. New York: Academic Press.

Levin, I. P., M. K. Mosell, C. M. Lamka, B. E. Savage, and M. J. Gray. 1977. "Measurement of Psychological Factors and

Their Role in Travel Behavior." Transportation Research Record 649: 1-6.

Lowenthal, D. , and M. Riel. 1972. "The Nature of Perceived and Imagined Environments." Environment and Behavior 4: 189-208.

Luce, R. D. 1959. Individual Choice Behavior. New York: Wiley.

McCormick, E. J. 1970. Human Factors Engineering. New York: McGraw-Hill.

McDonnell, J. D. 1968. "Pilot Rating Techniques for the Estimation and Evaluation of Handling Qualities." AFFDL Technical Report No. 68-76, U.S. Air Force Flight Dynamics Lab. Wright-Patterson Air Force Base, Ohio.

McRuer, D. T. , D. Graham, E. S. Krendel, and W. Reisener. 1965. "Human Pilot Dynamics in Compensatory Systems." AFFDL Technical Report No. 65-15, U.S. Air Force Flight Dynamics Lab. Wright-Patterson Air Force Base, Ohio.

McRuer, D. T. , and H. R. Jex. 1966. "Effects of Task Variables on Pilot Models for Manually Controlled Vehicles." Paper presented at advisory groups for Aerospace Research and Development Specialists Meeting on Stability and Control, September 25, 1966, Cambridge, England.

Michaels, R. M. 1966. "Attitudes of Drivers toward Alternative Highways and Their Relation to Route Choice." Highway Research Record, vol. 122.

Michaels, R. M. , and N. S. Weiler. 1975. "Transportation Needs of the Mobility Limited." Transportation Center, Northwestern University. Evanston, Ill.

Milgrim, S. 1970. "The Experience of Living in Cities." Science 167: 1461-68.

Miller, G. A. 1956. "The Magical Number Seven, Plus or Minus Two: Some Limits on One Capacity for Processing Information." Psychological Review 63: 81-97.

Nicolaidis, G. C. , and R. Dobson. 1975. "Disaggregated Perceptions and Preferences in Transportation Planning." Transportation Research 9: 279-95.

Nicolaidis, G. C., and J. N. Sheth. 1976. "An Application of Market Segmentation in Urban Transportation Planning." Publication No. 2149, General Motors Research Laboratories. Warren, Mich.

Nicolaidis, G. C., M. Wachs, and T. F. Golob. 1977. "Evaluation of Alternative Market Segmentations for Transportation Planning." Transportation Research Record 649: 23-31.

Norman, K. L., and J. J. Louviere. 1974. "Integration of Attributes in Bus Transportation: Two Modeling Approaches." Journal of Applied Psychology 59: 753-58.

Paine, F., et al. 1967. "Consumer Conceived Attributes of Transportation: An Attitude Study." Department of Business Administration, University of Maryland, College Park.

Pierce, J. A., and J. E. Karlin. 1957. "Reading Rates and the Information Rate of a Human Channel." Bell Telephone Technical Journal 36: 497-516.

Raia, A. P. 1965. "Goal Setting and Self-Control: An Empirical Study." Journal of Management Studies 2: 32-53.

Rockwell, T. H., and J. M. Snider. 1969. "Investigation of Device Sensory Capabilities and Its Effects on the Driving Tasks." RF 2091 Final Report, Research Foundation, The Ohio State University. Columbus.

Romney, A. K., R. N. Shepard, and S. B. Nerlove, eds. 1972. Multidimensional Scaling: Theory and Applications in the Behavioral Sciences, Vol. 2. New York: Seminar Press.

Ross, R. B. 1975. "Measuring the Effects of Soft Variables on Travel Behavior." Traffic Quarterly 29: 333-46.

Stea, D. 1974. "Architecture in the Head: Cognitive Mapping." In Designing for Human Behavior, edited by J. Lang, C. Burnet, W. Maleski, and D. Vachin. Stroudberg, Pa.: Dowden, Hutchinson and Ross.

Stenson, H. 1978. "Cognitive Factors in the Use of Transit Systems." Final Report, US-DOT-IL-11-0008, Urban Systems Laboratory, University of Illinois at Chicago Circle. Chicago. Pp. 157-68.

Stopher, P. R., and A. H. Meyburg. 1975. Urban Transportation Modeling and Planning. Lexington, Mass.: Lexington Books.

Thomas, K. 1976. "A Reinterpretation of the 'Attitude' Approach to Transport-Mode Choice and an Exploratory Empirical Test." Environment and Planning A, 8: 783-810.

Van Cott, H. P., and R. G. Kinkade, eds. 1972. Human Engineering Guide to Equipment Design. American Institute for Research. Washington, D.C.

Watson, P. L. 1973. "Predictions of Intercity Modal Choice from Disaggregate, Behavioral and Stochastic Models." Highway Research Record 446: 28-35.

# 5
## APPLICATIONS OF BEHAVIORAL
## SCIENCES TO ISSUES IN
## TRANSPORTATION PLANNING

### David T. Hartgen

INTRODUCTION

Transportation Planning Evolution

In the fields of transportation, housing, health, energy, and
environment, rapid changes are now taking place. Individually,
these disciplines have evolved rapidly over the last 20 years. They
have also become more integrated and functionally aligned, as we
recognize that many problems and issues in modern society are, in
fact, closely interrelated and not amenable to easy solutions along
functional lines. As one of these disciplines, transportation planning is no exception; it has undergone vast changes in objectives,
structure, and approach in the last 15 years. During this period,
the methods used in transportation planning changed radically, from
those oriented to broad, long-range investment questions to "micro,"
short-term concerns for the distribution of benefits and costs of
transportation services to various subgroups in society. The rate
of such change seems to have increased over the last ten years
(after a period of relative stability in the middle 1960s) and is likely
to continue to accelerate. While the general subject of such change
is too broad to cover in this paper, it should perhaps be briefly
summarized, as in Table 5.1.
   There has been increasing realization on the part of the transportation planning profession that methods and procedures developed
in the early 1960s are, generally speaking, inadequate to address
the issues of today (Neels, Cheslow, and Beesley 1978; Stopher and
Meyburg 1975, 1976). While these methods fall short in a number
of ways (also summarized in Table 5.1), dissatisfaction with them

can be attributed primarily to their complexity and data intensive-
ness and their inflexibility in dealing with even the most simplistic
of behavioral questions. This has led to a back-to-basics movement within the profession, as it were, in which the basic approaches
and structures of travel are being reanalyzed with increasing fervor.

TABLE 5.1

Trends in Transportation Planning Methods

| Trends in Transportation Planning, 1965-68 | Problems or Shortcomings of Conventional Methodologies and Techniques |
|---|---|
| Decreasing scale of analysis | Complex in analytical structure |
| Shortening time horizon of studies | |
| Broadening detail of analysis | Data intensive |
| Greater public input | Inflexible to many policies |
| Broader evaluation | Lacking in behavioral content |
| Requirement for faster turnaround | Not constraint-bound |
| Greater concentration on disadvantaged | Oriented to major invest-ments |
| Greater interest in low-cost options | Lacking in group-impact detail |
| Greater use of demand shift policies | Insensitive to minor policies |
| Smaller, more specialized data sets | |
| Greater use of opinion and perceptual information | |
| Greater behavioral content of methods | |
| Greater concern for constraints | |
| Greater concern for policy analysis | |

Reanalysis of Basics

The back-to-basics movement has two streams of thought,
both of which can be roughly viewed as more behavioral in content
than previous approaches. On the one hand are a variety of analytical and primarily mathematical extensions that make use of data
collected and utilized at the individual level, that is, disaggregated
data (Stopher and Meyburg 1975, 1976; Charles River Associates

1976; McFadden 1978; Bouthelier and Daganzo 1978; Atherton and Ben-Akiva 1976; TRB 1973). These methods are evolving to a high degree of analytical complexity, borrowing liberally from both mathematical psychology and the general subjects of mathematics and statistics. Research has recently been completed at the federal level summarizing recent developments in this area and their applications to transportation planning (Charles River Associates 1976). Yet already that major study is viewed by some as out of date.

A second, and perhaps more basic, train of thought has taken the view that the mere disaggregation of observations to their elemental level does not, in itself, constitute an increase in behavioral understanding. In fact, the methods and procedures used in the first approach still treat individuals and contexts alike within empirically determined market segments. The second approach has emphasized instead the social and psychological aspects of travel behavior and has also resulted in numerous recent research efforts (Golob, Horowitz, and Wachs 1977; Jones 1977; Fried and Havens 1977; Brog, Herrwinkel, and Neumann 1977; Margolin and Misch 1977; Louviere et al. 1977; Dobson et al. 1978; Hartgen 1977). Research continues on these topics, as exemplified in the following:

1.  the ongoing National Cooperative Highway Research Program (NCHRP) studies of new approaches to travel behavior (Fried and Havens 1977);
2.  Federal Highway Administration's (FHWA) May 1978 Conference on Applications of Behavioral Concepts to Transportation Planning;
3.  recent activities in Europe (particularly England) on travel behavior and household decision making (for example, Jones 1977);
4.  a September 1978 conference in France on the psychology of travel behavior;
5.  current plans for the Fourth International Conference on Travel Behavior to be held in Europe in 1979; and
6.  various applications from social sciences, particularly in the area of household decisions, roles, and social structure.

Parenthetically, the author believes that the second approach is, over the long run, more viable and more likely to bring a greater understanding of travel than the first approach. It is difficult to understand how any model can be any more behavioral or causal in structure than its theory and input variables (Hartgen and Wachs 1974). The central criticism of the present disaggregate approach is that it emphasizes the analytics of model construction rather than the basics of input variables, the ways in which they describe the choices open to individuals, and the process by which individuals evaluate those choices to make decisions.

Objectives

My intent is to look with a fresh view upon the general subject of applications of the behavioral sciences to transportation planning, with particular emphasis on a number of central questions. My objectives are the following:

1. Concentrating on four topic areas (see below), covering in sum numerous elements of transportation planning, to identify issues that suggest and are amenable to the application of behavioral science principles.
2. To evaluate the potential of behavioral science principles to assist in the analysis of these issues.
3. To recommend particular areas of focus from which detailed research needs, areas of application, or a tentative conclusion of an unproductive alley can be developed.

While I hasten to add that these thoughts are my own, it perhaps should be mentioned that my view of the subject is tempered by my experience as a transportation researcher in a large applications-oriented transportation planning agency, and, at that, a researcher with some experience both in studying the behavioral sciences and in describing their value in coherent terms to sometimes skeptical policy makers.

BEHAVIORAL SCIENCES: A QUICK OVERVIEW

The general nature and content of the behavioral sciences have been described in previous chapters by H. McIlvaine Parsons and by Richard M. Michaels. However, it will be useful to briefly summarize the behavioral sciences, so that a common baseline is established.

Initially, it should be pointed out that even social and behavioral scientists themselves do not agree upon the meaning of the general phrase behavioral science (for example, Brit 1966). Some are inclined to take a broad, sweeping view and include not only psychology and sociology but also anthropology, economics, education, history and political science, marketing and business, and parts of certain other fields, such as geography. Others take a narrow view and include only certain elements of the first three fields. In the course of reviewing the general subject matter of these disciplines, it becomes apparent that a very large part of the general material in these areas is not obviously applicable to transportation planning. On the other hand, under certain circumstances it is clear that most, if not all, of the material dealt with in the subject area could be used by transportation planners for perhaps quite specific or limited purposes. For the purposes of this paper, I have taken the view that the behavioral sciences comprise those elements of psychology, sociology, business, marketing, economics, and geography that deal primarily with the individual as a behaving entity, viewed both separately and as a member of groups and society, and the ways by which individuals operate in response to changing environmental conditions. Thus, my definition would include most if not all of social psychology, a large part of sociology, only some anthropology, economics, and geography, and some business and marketing.

Similarly, one could develop an extremely detailed list of materials covered in the behavioral sciences. While it may be useful in other contexts to develop such a list, I have chosen to note only those that may have some general application to transportation planning. The subject matter of the behavioral sciences is broken into six general groups, as shown in Table 5.2.

Within each of these general subject areas, a number of subareas of particular interest or concern to social and behavioral sciences are identified.

## ISSUES: EVOLUTION AND BEHAVIORAL APPLICATIONS

The subject matter for this paper has been organized under four themes: short-range transit operations, transportation for the mobility limited, environmental and social impact analysis, and energy and transportation. Numerous other topics in transportation could have been proposed (for example, Wachs 1977; TRB 1976). The selection of these themes is based upon the following criteria: (1) Since a wide number of applications of behavioral science principles are apparent or perhaps even obvious in transportation planning, the subject matter here should be broad enough to demonstrate how the applications can be fully utilized. (2) Issues in transportation planning are evolving very rapidly, and it would seem that the relevance of this paper would be significantly increased if knowledge from it could be applied to issues of critical importance in planning as they continue to evolve.

With that background in mind, this section will review briefly the evolution of planning methods and procedures in each of the four chosen areas, with an eye toward identifying the central unresolved questions and issues in today's transportation planning environment. Further, I will show how the behavioral sciences, as a group of disciplines, contain material that may be fruitfully applied to various

## TABLE 5.2

### Behavioral Sciences: A Classification
### for Transportation Planners

| General Area | Subjects |
|---|---|
| Cognitive and psychic structure | Attitude theory and measurement<br>Attitude change<br>Perception<br>Beliefs<br>Emotions<br>Motivation<br>Personality |
| Behavior | Behavior (revealed preference<br>  and behavior intent)<br>Modification of behavior<br>Attitude-behavior linkages |
| Learning | Learning theory<br>Decision theory<br>Diffusion theory and innovations |
| Social structure | Roles and norms<br>Status and class<br>Lifestyle<br>Life cycle (family)<br>Culture<br>Society<br>Socialization |
| System design | Human factors<br>Personal space |
| Groups and organizations | Social organization<br>Group dynamics and leadership<br>Organization development |

questions relating to each of these issues and what subjects within the behavioral sciences have been successfully applied or have been shown to be not particularly relevant to these four transportation topics.

Short-Range Transit Operations

While it would seem to the external observer that short-range transit planning, operations, and analysis would always have been a central element of transportation planning, this is not the case. In fact, such activities have been a recent arrival for most transportation planning agencies, even transit operators. During the 1960s, heyday of long-range planning, virtually every city of 50,000 or over developed a multimodal long-range transportation plan, incorporating both transit and highway elements. These plans often described in general terms how systems are intended to operate at some distant point in time (usually 20-25 years), but they contained much less information on the actions necessary to reach those goals. Neither did they address critical day-to-day problems, either in the highway or transit world.

While transportation planners were engaged in this activity, transit operators increasingly were faced with inability to meet rising costs from farebox revenues. During the late 1960s, transit costs began to escalate rapidly and ridership continued to decline. As a result, most transit operations went from shaky ground to wet quicksand; many operations simply went out of business or were taken over by public entities. Federal funds available at the time for transit capital assistance were of little use in stemming the tide of transit company failures, since the issue was not one of capital fund availability but rather of operating assistance. In the early 1970s, therefore, several states and local governments, and eventually the federal government, began to assist transit operations. In the meantime, transit planning activities at all levels of government continued to expand in response to the availability of funds from the Urban Mass Transportation Administration (UMTA) and FHWA for planning purposes. It is now common to find many large transit operations with at least one resident transit planner, and in addition most metropolitan planning organization (MPO) staffs (local elected officials directing transportation planning, development, and implementation) and state agencies have individuals skilled in these areas. Whether these doctors can stanch the flow of red ink from transit operations is a matter which remains to be seen.

Lest this be taken to mean that the primary activity of such individuals is deficit analysis, it should be pointed out that transit

planners today are also heavily involved in the analysis and planning of new or revised services for the riding public through a
variety of fare, service, and marketing actions. Route scheduling
and location, frequency of service, fare levels, various promotion
fares, and the like are typical subjects. Modern transit studies
also work to provide mobility for special groups, to save energy
and improve air quality through increased loadings, and to provide
better service to employment sites, high density locations, and
special activity centers. Transit planners also study complex
labor/management/equipment systems and all the activities connected with such business.

   In spite of this, the overshadowing gloom of a deficit environment exists and acts to constrain the services provided by most
transit operations. Inevitably, then, improvements in service and
fares will be traded off against the availability of public financing.
Few new transit services break even, and the operator must therefore continually pick and choose among available opportunities,
knowing that in the end it is local, state, and federal tax support
that enables the system to exist. There is no escaping this reality.

   As transit becomes more dependent on society rather than on
the farebox as its source of livelihood, the central role of transit as
a public versus a private service must continually be evaluated
against increasingly scarce public dollars. The issue of local financial support for transit service—its extent, its nature, and the degree to which it should increase subsidies for a decreasing market—
is likely to remain the central question for transit planners and
analysts over the next ten years (see Table 5.3).

   A number of important subissues extend from these two issues.
Particularly important is the consolidation and efficiency of transit
service, as it expends public dollars in an ever increasing proportion. This is closely related to cost and allocation of the transit
service to various geographic and demographic groups. A considerable amount of the transit planner's time is spent dealing with
these questions, and the transit operator is primarily concerned
with the effective and efficient delivery of these services in the allocated amounts. As mentioned earlier, responsibility for transit
costs among the various publics, transit managers, and riders of
transit systems is also a central question. The ability of transit
operators to accurately estimate demand and cost in response to alternative service arrangements is critical to effective operations.

   Tables 5.3, 5.4, and 5.11 attempt to show schematically how
various concepts and techniques in behavioral science have been or
might be applicable. At present the most extensive applications of
behavioral science principles to short-range transit operations and
analysis have been in the areas of attitude theory and measurement

TABLE 5.3

Issues and Methods in Short-Range Transit Operations

| Key Issues | Subissues | Behavioral Science Methods |
|---|---|---|
| Role of transit as a public (supported) or private (business) service | Consolidation/efficiency | Organization development/behavior |
| | Cost and allocation of service | Labor relations |
| Local financial support for transit | Responsibilities for cost among rider/public | Management structure |
| | Demand potential, cost analysis | System design |
| | | Social structure |
| | | Society |
| | | Lifestyle/status |
| | | Attitude–behavior link |
| | | Modification of behavior |
| | | Attitudes and opinions |

TABLE 5.4

Applications of Behavioral Sciences in Short-Range Transit Operations

| Subject | Typical Applications |
| --- | --- |
| Present | |
| Attitude theory/measurement | Mode choice of consumers |
| Behavior and revealed preferences | Attitudes toward transit service |
| Modification of behavior | Community views and support |
| Decision theory | Changes in behavior if service improved |
| Potential | |
| Organizations development | Structure and behavior of transit properties |
| | Transit management |
| | Labor relations |
| Motivation | Factors influencing transit choice |
| | Reasons for support of transit services |
| | Ways to encourage people to use transit services |
| Behavior modification | Increased acceptance after experience with transit service |
| Learning | Inclination of various groups to try out new services |
| Diffusion | Inclination of different user groups to use such service at different |
| Status and class | rates |
| | Development of specialized marketing campaigns |
| Life cycle and family | The allocation of roles within households |
| Human factors | Transit systems design |
| Personal space | Internal vehicle layout |

and their relationship to behavioral phenomena. Numerous studies now exist concerning the structure of modal choice (for example, Charles River Associates 1976; Atherton and Ben-Akiva 1976; Golob, Horowitz, and Wachs 1977; Gilbert and Foerster 1977; Golob and Recker 1977) and perceptions and attitudes toward transit service by various groups of riders and nonriders (for example, Golob, Horowitz, and Wachs 1977; Margolin and Misch 1977; Dobson et al. 1978; Hartgen 1977; Gilbert and Foerster 1977; Donnelly et al. 1975; Golob and Dobson 1974; Hartgen 1974). The literature in this area is rapidly expanding. These ideas have been extended in mathematical form using individual decision theory from mathematical psychology (Stopher and Meyburg 1975; Restle and Greeno 1970). Extensions of the models of Luce and Raiffa (Restle and Greeno 1970) have had widespread application in transit planning, particularly in mode choice analysis. While some of this activity has been oriented to long-range transit planning, it can be equally applicable for short-range transit planning and operations.

Transit service will ultimately rise or fall on its use by the public. Such use is a behavioral phenomenon, subject to the usual rules of perception and evaluation and impinged on by a variety of personal and situational constraints. It should be apparent that many other concepts and techniques from the behavioral sciences could be useful for short-range transit operations and analysis. These are also shown in Table 5.4. Of particular interest is the whole area of labor and management, a field that is well evolved in the behavioral sciences but until recently has not seen significant application in transit operations.

Transportation for the Mobility Limited

Perhaps expectedly, the first round of urban area transportation plans were singularly devoid of detailed information on travel characteristics or requirements for any special groups, including the mobility limited. Concern for these groups began to evolve in the late 1960s as the geographic and temporal scale of transportation planning decreased and more emphasis was placed upon the requirements of special subgroups within the population. Greater general interest in transportation system accessibility and mobility for special groups accelerated this trend.

For a variety of physical and psychological reasons, mobility limited persons often were not capable of taking full advantage of transit systems. Initial analyses of transportation systems for the mobility limited were confined to modifying existing transit systems. In many ways, existing transit systems were found inadequate for special group requirements. A variety of activities at the federal level resulted in federal law and regulations to provide planning requirements and transportation services for the elderly and the handicapped and, more recently, to retrofit existing systems to provide access. Parallel with this activity, the development of fully accessible vehicles for transit operations has proceeded.

A separate and almost unrelated evolution took place in nontransportation areas. The late 1960s witnessed a significant increase in the vocalization of demands, particularly by the physically handicapped. They asserted that a variety of services provided by society should be made accessible to them in a fully integrated way. Thus, recent Department of Health, Education and Welfare (HEW) guidelines require full accessibility in all public buildings and related facilities.

It is perhaps unfortunate that the issue of transportation accessibility has not been at the forefront in the evolution of these issues. Rather, transportation has taken a back seat, and transportation planners have found themselves generally reacting to rather than influencing the direction of policy on this subject. So the key issues in transportation services for the mobility limited are likely to continue to revolve around broader national questions, particularly those concerning the nature and quality of services provided by society. It will be critical to understand and agree upon the degree to which accessibility is either a right or privilege and what amount of it constitutes fair and equal treatment for specialized user groups—in transportation as well as issues across the board.

The position of the handicapped citizen lobbies has been that separate service, while it may be superior in quality, does not constitute equal service because it is not integrated. In this view, one of the primary objectives of transportation actions should be to improve, encourage, and enable the physical and psychological integration of the handicapped into modern society. This simply cannot be done by the provision of separate systems. However, recent applications and demand projections show that specialized physical systems to alleviate transportation accessibility problems of the handicapped or the elderly do not, in fact, lead to significant additional utilization. At the same time, such actions require large costs, particularly for retrofitting (estimated at $4-10 billion). A central issue in transportation is that of cost versus effectiveness. It can be demonstrated that the dollars thus spent could be utilized to provide a far higher level of service to these groups in other ways, either through chauffeured systems or specialized services, rather than through the removal of physical barriers on existing systems. This issue, and its implications for taxpayer dollars, is at the heart of the question.

As Table 5.5 shows, transportation planners will likely be concerned with a number of subissues surrounding the question of cost effectiveness. These include the nature of demand for transportation systems, the implied particular physical and service requirements for serving different groups, the projection of future travel behavior and of future lifestyles, and the utilization of existing client-agency transportation.

All of these questions have obvious behavioral content and can be analyzed to some extent with behavioral science methods and concepts. Referring to Tables 5.6 and 5.11, the most extensive use of these principles has been in the human factors area, to design fully accessible transportation systems (for example, NCHRP 1976). Considerable use has also been made of attitude and opinion measurement and theory (Miller 1976; Hartgen, Pasko, and Howe 1977; Paaswell and Recker 1976), travel behavior (Hartgen, Pasko, and Howe 1977; Falcocchio et al. 1977; NCHRP 1976), and, more recently, lifestyle (Wachs and Blanchard 1977; Gillan and Wachs 1976). Numerous other typical areas would be of potential use to planners, particularly roles and norms and socialization.

Environmental and Social Impact Analysis

While it is true that transportation plans developed in the 1960s proposed a number of major facilities for metropolitan areas, these plans generally did not affect facilities then in the planning or development stage, nor did they appear to have major impact on the decline of highway construction in the 1960s. Highway construction was already being slowed significantly, due in part to a variety of broad social and national factors outside the highway construction area. Preeminent among these were:

1. increasing concern on the part of the public for environmental conservation and improvement of air quality,
2. increasing (in the 1970s) realization of the scarcity of energy resources,
3. concern for significant detrimental impact on neighborhoods within urban areas (often accruing to precisely those individuals and communities that did not benefit significantly from the highway project itself),
4. significant increases in the involvement of citizens in the general activities of government, and
5. realization that escalating construction costs combined with scarce public dollars meant increasing inability of local governments to meet even the local share of federal construction projects.

TABLE 5.5

Issues and Methods in Elderly and Handicapped Transportation Services

| Key Issues | Subissues | Behavior Science Methods |
|---|---|---|
| Nature of transportation service equality | Demand: response to service | Attitudes |
| | | Behavior |
| Separate vs. integrated systems | Implied requirements for service | Human factors |
| Nature of reasonable and fair service | Projection of elderly and handicapped travel behavior and lifestyles | Life cycle/lifestyle |
| Service cost vs. effectiveness | Service coordination with ex-services | Role/family |

Behind all of this activity, of course, was the belief that the government, generally, was not attuned to the needs of its citizens, particularly those living in the dense urban portions of metropolitan areas. The sum total of these trends was effectively to bring urban highway construction and investment to a crawl by the early 1970s.

TABLE 5.6

Applications of Behavioral Sciences in Transportation
for the Mobility Limited

| Subject | Typical Applications |
| --- | --- |
| Present | |
| Human factors | Design of vehicles and transportation system access |
| Attitudes | Perception of handicapped and/or elderly toward transit systems |
| Behavior | Mode choice and trip generation |
| Lifestyle | Evolution of travel patterns |
| Potential | |
| Perception and beliefs | Views of transportation accessibility and mobility |
| Attitude-behavior link | Relationship between behavior and attitude |
| Decision theory | Methods by which the elderly and handicapped make travel choices |
| Roles and norms | Behavior in a variety of social and structural contexts |
| Status and class | Background for describing travel patterns |
| Socialization | Process by which elderly and/or handicapped adopt specific roles and behaviors |
| Personal space | Interior vehicle design |
| Group dynamics and organization development | Structure of lobby groups and their activities |

Federal programs were undertaken at that time to shift the emphasis of urban transportation investment from one of capital construction of highway projects to transit construction and investment and also to maximize use of existing transportation systems. The decline in highway investment was further accelerated by the 1977 Clean Air Act Amendments, requiring the detailed evaluation of a variety of low-capital actions that might improve air quality. Requirements for State Energy Conservation Plans also suggest low-capital actions in the transportation sector, particularly in vanpooling, carpooling, and public transit, as well as moderately effective actions such as reduced speed limits. In sum, the heyday of major highway construction is over, at least in urban areas, and with it probably has also died the necessity to evaluate and analyze the impact of major transportation actions on the urban environment and on urban society.

The key issues (see Table 5.7) that transportation planners will have to deal with in the next several years concerning transportation investment, therefore, will revolve more around the questions of demand shifts versus transportation system expansions and improved maintenance and use of existing facilities versus new facilities. The issue of transportation access versus its social and environmental costs will continue to be important but is likely to decline in relative significance, taking a back seat to the previous issue. We should also expect to see increased concern for the equitable distribution of costs and benefits of transportation actions among the various demographic and geographic groups in society.

In support of such studies, transportation planners will continue to be called upon to analyze the nature of transportation impacts, although the scale and complexity of such impacts is likely to shift toward the low-cost noncapital action. This means that new work will be required to identify and measure impact values and their associated weights, as viewed by the public and its various lobby groups. Transportation investments must be designed to be compatible with both the environment and with society as a neighbor. A good example would be present concerns about improvement in air pollution and efficiency of automobiles, about noise around airports and along major highways, and about maximum use and operating efficiency of existing transportation facilities. As the scale and time frame of transportation planning shrinks, the magnitude of public involvement in immediate and proposed transportation actions is likely to increase. Transportation planners ought to be readying themselves now for dealing with a variety of new actors who are concerned primarily with short-term impacts of transportation investments.

TABLE 5.7

Issues and Methods in Environmental and Social Impact Analysis

| Key Issues | Subissues | Behavioral Science Methods |
| --- | --- | --- |
| Transportation access vs. social impact | Identification of impacts | Organization behavior and group dynamics |
| Demand shift vs. system expansion | Identification and measurement of impacts, values, and weights | System design |
| Distribution of costs/benefits of transportation actions | Design for compatibility | Evaluation methods |
| | | Roles/norms |
| | | Culture/society/status |
| | | Attitudes and opinions |
| | | Perception |

TABLE 5.8

Applications of Behavioral Sciences in Environmental
and Social Impact Analysis

| Subject | Typical Applications |
|---|---|
| **Present** | |
| Attitudes and opinions | Community views of transportation actions |
| Community cohesion | Studies of community impact |
| Groups | Citizen involvement processes |
| Human factors | Design of facilities to reduce pollution |
| **Potential** | |
| Perception and beliefs | View of transportation projects |
| Roles and norms | Positions of actors in citizen groups |
| Status and class | Differences in communities and neighborhoods |
| Society and socialization | Project impacts on communities |
| Group structures | Understanding lobbies and pressure groups |

In such an environment, the behavioral sciences can be easily applied by the transportation planner (see Tables 5.8 and 5.11). Environmental and social impact analysis to date has utilized only a few central areas from the behavioral sciences, primarily those concerned with attitudes, opinions, and community cohesion related to transportation impacts (for example, USDOT 1975, 1976; Institute on Man and Science 1976). Second, much work has been done on citizen participation and the way in which groups and organizations operate in both public and private sectors (Jordan et al. 1976; Yukubousky 1973; Smith et al. 1975; Veland and Junker n.d.; Manheim et al. 1971). Third, some work has incorporated human factors design into systems development, particularly in air and noise pollution. Fourth, some studies have examined the impacts of transportation facilities on a variety of demographic and social groups (for example, Crane and Partners 1976; Frisken and Emby 1975), although the analysis has not normally been conducted consistent with the kinds of studies done by social scientists. (This work has normally been conducted by transportation engineers as part of an environmental impact statement.) In addition, it would appear that a number of other subjects from the behavioral sciences would be appropriate, particularly roles and norms and socialization.

Energy and Transportation

A central shortcoming of most metropolitan area transportation plans developed in the 1960s is that they failed to consider a variety of price or supply constraints on fuels. In developing these plans, no account was taken of the possibility that petroleum and its derivatives would eventually decline in supply, driving up price and reducing demand. In fact, a review of the 230-odd long-range plans prepared fails to show more than a handful that even mention the possibility and, of those that do, none, to the author's knowledge, deal with energy constraints in a way to suggest that that concern should be real. Further, proposed transportation investments developed from these plans make no mention of energy constraints, neither are they based upon a realistic estimate of the probability of such an occurrence. Even today it is a rare agency that studies in a comprehensive way the nature of transportation energy supply and its implication for the future.

Perhaps, then, it is not surprising that the transportation planning profession as a group was caught largely off guard by the 1973/74 energy crisis. That crisis, while short in duration and magnitude, was severe enough to demonstrate the critical dependence of the United States on foreign energy supplies, particularly in terms of the continued growth and viability of our economy. Where possible, individuals reduced discretionary travel and took minor actions to cope with the crisis; there was very little shift to alternative transportation modes, nor was there any change in car purchasing or residential moving behavior (Stearns 1975; Keck et al. 1974). Evidence suggests that it was the availability of energy supply, rather than gasoline price (which increased 60 percent) that primarily influenced demand (Neveu 1977; Peskin et al. 1975; Skinner 1975). But while considerable research has recently been published on energy constraints and the effectiveness of various energy conservation options in the transportation sector (Rubin et al. 1975; Transportation Systems Center 1976; NCHRP 1977), very little of this material has found its way into transportation planning practice.

While another such crisis may not occur in the next five years, we are likely to be entering a period of increasingly stringent requirements with respect to energy conservation for transportation. Eventually, the price of present petroleum products may be driven up so much that alternative fuels will be required as substitutes, or significant shifts in travel behavior, and perhaps lifestyles, may result. Key issues (see Table 5.9) in the next several years will revolve around transportation energy conservation, conversion, and reduction in immediate use of energy resources, while continuing the present or a reasonable level of personal mobility. Actions that should be taken to address these concerns in an effective and fair manner will be of great interest to local transportation planners, if for no other reason than that they are primarily outside the range of local influence. Energy policy is being developed at the federal level and, at least in the short term, there is little a local planner can do to significantly influence transportation energy conservation in his own locale.

Such proposals will likely fall with differential impact upon various demographic and geographic groups, as during the energy crisis (Stearns 1975); the distribution of costs and benefits of transportation actions to conserve energy will thus become important. Allocation of scarce energy resources is likely to be of concern during relative shortfalls. Allocation of resources may be scheduled on an individual and family basis, as well as within, and perhaps among, states and urban areas. Over the next 15 to 30 years, planners will deal with long-term conversion from petroleum-based transportation energy resources to other products, with the impact that such conversion is likely to have on travel, the economy, and society.

Considerable research is needed now (some has begun; see NCHRP 1978) to understand the way in which travel behavior is likely to change in response to a variety of energy conservation incentives and disincentives. Critical to this understanding is knowing how individuals and decision-making units place priorities on travel and allocate scarce resources for its completion. Transportation planners will also have to identify and evaluate alternative courses of action to conserve energy at the state and local level.

A number of obvious applications of behavioral science principles to this general issue are summarized in Tables 5.10 and 5.11. It is ultimately a question of whether the behavior of individuals can be modified in such a way that energy is conserved. Essential to this process is an understanding of how individuals perceive and view the energy crisis. Attitude theory and measurement, as well as perception and beliefs, are likely to play important roles in this process. Some headway has been made in understanding attitudes on energy conservation, but the effort has only scratched the surface. Similarly, the principles of behavior, behavior modification, and the relationship between attitudes and behavior are critical and obvious linkages between the energy issue and the behavioral sciences. Decision theory (how individuals make

TABLE 5.9

Issues and Methods in Energy and Transportation

| Key Issues | Subissues | Behavioral Science Methods |
|---|---|---|
| Energy conservation/reduction in use | Changes in behavior (incentives, disincentives) | Attitude/opinion measurement |
| Implementation of effective and fair policies | Priorities on travel | Behavior and behavior modification |
| Differential impacts | Identification and evaluation of actions to conserve | Evaluation methods |
| Allocation of scarce resources | | Culture/society |
| Long-term conversion and ancillary impacts | | Lifestyle |
| | | Attitude change |

TABLE 5.10

Applications of Behavioral Sciences in Energy and Transportation

| Subject | Typical Applications |
|---|---|
| Present | |
| Attitude theory and measurement | Attitudes and opinions about energy use |
| Behavior | Present energy use patterns |
| Potential | |
| Attitude change | Views toward consumption |
| Lifestyle | Changes in U.S. energy consumption |
| Behavior modification | Changes in behavior in emergencies, etc. |
| Decision theory | Choice under constraints |
| Group structure | Pressure groups, lobbies, etc. |

TABLE 5.11

Linkage between Behavioral Science Concepts and Conference Workshops

| Behavioral Science Concepts/Techniques | Short-Range Transit Operations and Alternatives Analysis | Transportation for the Mobility Limited | Environmental and Social Impact Analysis | Energy and Transportation |
|---|---|---|---|---|
| Cognitive structure | ○ | ◐ | ○ | ○ |
| Attitude theory/measurement | o | • | • | ○ |
| Attitude change | o | o | o | o |
| Perception | • | o | o | o |
| Beliefs | • | • | • | – |
| Emotions | – | • | • | – |
| Cognition | • | • | – | – |
| Motivation | o | • | – | – |
| Personality | – | • | – | – |
| Behavior |  |  |  |  |
| Behavior and revealed preferences | ● | ◐ | ○ | ○ |
| Modification behavior | o | • | • | ◐ |
| Attitude/behavior link | ◐ | o | o | ◐ |
| Learning | o | • | • | o |
| Decision theory | ○ | o | • | o |
| Diffusion/innovations | o | | – | o |
| Social structure |  |  |  |  |
| Roles/norms | o | o | – | o |
| Status/class | o | o | o | o |
| Lifestyle | • | ◐ | o | ◐ |
| Life cycle/family | • | o | • | o |
| Culture | • | • | ◐ | o |
| Society | • | • | o | ◐ |
| Socialization |  | o |  | o |
| System design |  | o |  | – |
| Human factors | o | • | ◐ | • |
| Personal space | o | | | – |
| Group/organization |  |  |  |  |
| Social organization | – | o | • | o |
| Group dynamics/leaders | • | o | ◐ | • |
| Organization development/management | o | • | ○ | • |

Key:
| Obvious linkage | ○ |
| Probable link | o |
| Possible link | • |
| Unclear link | • |
| No apparent link | – |

Degree of Innovation
| Extensive | ● |
| Partial | ◐ |
| Research environments only | ◐ |
| Minimal | ○ |

104

choices) is another obvious area of study. Since energy usage is in many ways a product of lifestyle and culture, a considerable portion of behavioral science concepts in these areas is also applicable to the problem. It is fair to say that, while very little of such material has been studied and brought into the transportation energy area so far, the potential payoff in doing so would appear to be great.

## SUMMARY AND CONCLUSIONS

In this paper I have reviewed the evolution of central issues in four key subjects relating to transportation planning and described how the projected direction of these issues is likely to require the input of behavioral sciences as an aid to their solution.

Some comments are appropriate at this point. First, while I hasten to add that I have not conducted a thorough analysis of the behavioral science literature with a view toward application (see Appendix A), it appears to me that the most obvious present applications in transportation planning are those concerning attitude theory and structure, with lesser, but also important, applications in behavior and attitude-behavior linkages, lifestyle, and community culture. Studies of personal space and human factors also have received considerable attention, and certain management principles are being applied in transit operations.

Second, it should also be apparent from my discussion that there are a large number of subjects within the behavioral sciences that are, at least on the surface, directly applicable to the kinds of problems and issues that transportation planners will encounter in the four subject areas. Particularly applicable would be further work in the attitude/behavioral link, perception, and most particularly in the area of social structure, especially life cycle and family, culture, and society. An overlooked area of application that may have considerable potential for some studies is group structure and organizations, particularly group dynamics, and principles of management. I have attempted to summarize all of these broad trends in Table 5.11.

I have purposely not dealt in detail with the methodology of the behavioral sciences, since in many ways it is not significantly different from that used in transportation. However, certain approaches might be highlighted for exploration as potentially useful:

1.  Experimental designs in laboratory settings (for example, Louviere et al. 1977; Levin and Louviere 1978)
2.  Quasi-experimental designs for before-after studies (for example, Tischer and Phillips 1978; Howe and Hartgen 1976)

3. Content analysis (for example, Krishman and Golob 1977)
4. Structural equations and path analysis (Dobson et al. 1978)
5. Participant-observer methods
6. Social indicators and unobtrusive measures

It should also be pointed out that the diffusion of innovations (in this case the diffusion of behavioral sciences ideas into the transportation planning profession) is itself a behavioral process. It generally often requires positive action on the part of both the giver and the recipient. The conference for which this paper was written has been organized and sponsored by transportation planners in the belief that their superficial knowledge of the behavioral sciences suggested an opportunity for their profession and the behavioral sciences to develop a lasting and significant bond of interaction, to the mutual benefit of both groups. It is fair to say that the behavioral sciences have not been overly concerned with such issues as transportation theory and policy making. While we do not suggest that it ought to be otherwise, it is our belief that the application of behavioral science principles to a variety of governmental disciplines, including transportation, is an area that should be given considerable attention by behavioral scientists. It would appear to us that, for some very critical reasons—many of which are described above—transportation planning would be an obvious point of contact between the disciplines. It is our hope and belief that this paper, and the conference for which it was prepared, will strengthen this bond for the joint good of both communities.

REFERENCES

Atherton, T. J., and M. E. Ben-Akiva. 1976. "Transferability and Updating of Disaggregate Travel Demand Models." Record No. 610, Transportation Research Board (TRB), pp. 12-18.

Bouthelier, F., and C. F. Daganzo. 1978. "Aggregation with Multinomial Probit and Estimation of Disaggregate Models with Aggregate Data." Paper presented at TRB, January 1978.

Britt, S. H. 1966. Consumer Behavior and the Behavioral Sciences. New York: Wiley Press.

Brog, W., D. Herrwinkel, and K. H. Neumann. 1977. "Psychological Determinants of User Behavior." Report of the 34th Round Table on Transport Economics. Paris.

Charles River Associates. 1976. "Disaggregate Travel Demand Model." Final Report, National Cooperative Highway Research Program (NCHRP) 8-13.

David A. Crane and Partners. 1976. Impact Assessment Guidelines. Final Report, NCHRP 8-11.

Dobson, R. D., et al. 1978. "Structural Models for the Analysis of Traveler Attitude-Behavior Relationships." Transportation Research Board, 1978. In press.

Donnelly, E. P., et al. 1975. "Statewide Public Opinion Survey on Public Transportation." Preliminary Research Report No. 80, New York State Department of Transportation (NYSDOT), Planning Research Unit.

Falcocchio, J., et al. 1977. "Travel Patterns and Mobility Needs of the Physically Handicapped." Record No. 618, TRB.

Fried, M., and J. Havens. 1977. Travel Behavior: A Synthesized Theory. Final Report, NCHRP 8-14, TRB.

Frisken, F., and G. Emby. 1975. "Social Aspects of Urban Transportation: A Bibliography." Report No. 30, Joint Program in Transportation, New York University.

Gilbert, G., and J. F. Foerster. 1977. "The Importance of Attitudes in the Decision to Use Mass Transit." Transportation 6: 321-32.

Gillan, J., and M. Wachs. 1976. "Lifestyles and Transportation Needs of the Elderly in Los Angeles." Transportation 5: 45-62.

Golob, T. F., and R. Dobson. 1974. "Assessment of Preferences and Perceptions toward Attributes of Transportation Alternatives." Special Report No. 149, TRB.

Golob, T. F., A. Horowitz, and M. Wachs. 1977. "Attitude-Behavior Relationships in Travel Demand Models." Paper presented at the Third International Conference on Travel Behavior. Adelaide, Australia.

Golob, T. F., and W. W. Recker. 1977. "Mode Choice Prediction Using Attitudinal Data: A Procedure and Some Results." Transportation 6: 265-86.

Hartgen, D. T. 1974. "Attitudinal and Situational Variables Influencing Urban Mode Choice: Some Empirical Findings."
Transportation 3: 377-92.

_____. 1977. "Ridesharing Behavior: A Review of Recent Find-
ings." Preliminary Research Report No. 130, NYSDOT, Planning Research Unit.

Hartgen, D. T., M. Pasko, and S. M. Howe. 1977. "Forecasting
Non-Work Public Transit Demand by the Elderly and Handicapped." TRB.

Hartgen, D. T., and M. Wachs. 1974. "Disaggregate Travel Demand Models for Special Context Planning: A Dissenting View."
In Special Report No. 149, TRB.

Howe, S. M., and D. T. Hartgen. 1976. "Irondequoit-Wayne Expressway: Study Design." Preliminary Research Report No.
101, NYSDOT, Planning Research Unit.

Institute on Man and Science. 1976. "Social and Economic Impacts
of Highway Projects." Rennselaerville, N.Y.

Jones, P. M. 1977. "New Approaches to Understanding Travel
Behavior: The Human Activity Approach." Paper presented at
the Third International Conference on Travel Behavior.

Jordan, D., et al. 1976. Effective Citizen Participation in Transportation Planning. U.S. Department of Transportation (USDOT).

Keck, C. A., et al. 1974. "Changes in Individual Travel during
the Energy Crisis 1973-74." Preliminary Research Report No.
67, NYSDOT, Planning Research Unit.

Krishman, K. S., and T. F. Golob. 1977. "Using Focus Group
Interviews and Workshops to Develop Transportation Concepts."
Paper 2428, General Motors Research Labs.

Levin, I., and J. Louviere. 1978. "Functional Analysis of Mode
Choice." TRB.

Louviere, J., et al. 1977. "Application of Psychological Measurement and Modeling to Behavioral Travel Demand Analysis."
Center for Behavioral Studies, University of Wyoming.

Manheim, M., et al. 1971. Community Values in Highway Location and Design. MIT.

Margolin, J. B., and M. R. Misch. 1977. "Handbook of Behavioral Strategies in Transportation." Washington University.

McFadden, D. 1978. "Quantitative Methods for Analyzing Travel Behavior: Some Recent Developments." Paper presented at TRB, January 1978.

Miller, J. 1976. "Latent Travel Demand of the Handicapped and Elderly." Record No. 618, TRB.

NCHRP. 1976. "Transportation Requirements for the Handicapped, Elderly, and Economically Disadvantaged." Synthetics Report No. 39, TRB.

_____. 1977. Transportation Energy: Synthetics of Current Practice.

_____. 1978. Requests-for-Proposals Projects 8-22 and 8-23.

Neels, K., M. D. Cheslow, and M. Beesley. 1978. "Improving Demand Forecasts for Urban Area Travel." Draft paper, Urban Institute.

Neveu, A. 1977. "The 1973-74 Energy Crisis: Impact on Travel." Preliminary Research Report No. 131, NYSDOT, Planning Research Unit.

Paaswell, R. E., and W. W. Recker. 1976. Problems of the Carless. Report prepared for USDOT.

Peskin, R. L., et al. 1975. "The Immediate Impact of Gasoline Shortages on Urban Travel Behavior." Northwestern University.

Restle, F., and J. G. Greeno. 1970. Introduction to Mathematical Psychology. Addison-Wesley.

Rubin, D., et al. 1975. "A Summary of Opportunities to Conserve Transportation Energy." Transportation Systems Center (TSC).

Skinner, L. E. 1975. "The Effect of Energy Constraints on Travel Patterns: Gasoline Purchase Study." Federal Highway Administration (FHWA).

Smith, D. C., et al. 1975. "Manual for Community Involvement in Highway Planning and Design." FHWA.

Stearns, M. D. 1975. "The Behavioral Impacts of the Energy Shortage: Shifts in Trip-Making Characteristics." USDOT.

Stopher, P. R., and A. H. Meyburg. 1975. Urban Transportation Modeling and Planning. Lexington, Mass.: Lexington Books.

_____. 1976. Behavioral Travel Demand Models. Lexington, Mass.: Lexington Books.

Tischer, M. L., and R. V. Phillips. 1978. "The Relationship between Transportation Perceptions and Behaviors over Time." Transportation Research Board. In press.

Transportation Research Board. 1973. Urban Travel Demand Forecasting. Special Report No. 143.

Transportation Research Board Executive Committee. 1976. "The Ten Most Critical Issues in Transportation." Transportation Research News, No. 67, Nov./Dec. 1976.

Transportation Systems Center. 1976. Transportation Energy Conservation. Office of Technology Sharing.

U.S. Department of Transportation. 1975. Environmental Assessment Notebook. Washington, D.C.

_____. 1976. Social and Economic Effects of Highways. Washington, D.C.

Veland and Junker Assoc. N.d. "A Manual for Achieving Effective Community Participation in Transportation Planning."

Wachs, M. 1977. "Transportation Policy in the 1980's." Transportation 6: no. 2.

Wachs, M., and R. D. Blanchard. 1977. "Lifestyles and Transportation Needs of the Elderly in the Future." Record No. 618, TRB

Yukubousky, R. 1973. "Community Interaction Techniques in Transportation Systems and Project Development." Preliminary Research Report No. 50, NYSDOT, Planning Research Unit.

# 6
# THE MACROSOCIOLOGY OF TRANSPORTATION

## Samuel Z. Klausner

### THE SOCIAL ORGANIZATION PERSPECTIVE
### ON TRANSPORTATION

Social action is more likely to be effective and worthy when it
is grounded in theoretically correct sociological research.  Historically, the sociology of transportation has developed in response to
the needs of government regulators and transportation producers,
operators, and users.  Traditionally, they have appealed for solutions to problems as conceived by the various actors in a transportation system.  Planners and operators ask behavioral scientists,
for instance, to estimate the impending demand for roads, vehicles,
and transportation manpower.  Whether or not this is the strategic
question, the response has tended to fit that formulation.  Behavioral
scientists have been predicting patronage: the number of potential
paying riders or packages, their origins and destinations, and the
transportation modes they will choose.*

---

*Typically, expected patronage has been estimated from in-
formation on the numbers of residents or workers or the amount of
goods produced in an area combined with estimates of when and
where these people and goods might move.  More recently, researchers have assessed the ideas, attitudes, preferences, or plans
of the individual travelers or of those who dispatch and receive
goods.  The volume of traffic flow is, typically, estimated by aggregating these data on individuals.

===

The author wishes to thank Wilma C. Marhafer and Diane E.
Davis for the preparation of this manuscript.  The comments of the

This paper will consider transportation as a social organizational, or macrosociological, phenomenon. Traditional studies of the transportation behavior of individuals will be examined from a social organizational perspective. The predictions proffered in that research, may, it will be argued, gain in precision when the social and cultural context of the individual behavior is considered. More importantly, the judgment of transportation policy makers will be enhanced by a more comprehensive image of the societal system in which they intervene. Transportation policy is, after all, societal policy.

The prediction of demand, to stay with this example, is, generally, not an end in itself. It is among many of society's calculations regarding transportation. Planners and managers use information about demand to guide their investment decisions, to plan present operations, or to propose new transportation systems. Demand estimation considers the public as a source of travelers. The public is also a source of investors. As boosters or detractors of transportation, their votes in control of public and private funding are more telling for transportation than their contributions to the farebox. Businesses along the right-of-way become public actors dealing with the social and environmental changes accompanying the development and operation of transportation systems. Communities become political actors when the costs to them of transportation seem disproportionate to the advantages the system offers. Public actors may enter negotiations, some civil and some raucous, with legislators, policy makers, and policy-implementing executives.

Transportation is a peculiar type of social organization meeting a need for coordination among other social organizations more directly implicated in social production and the maintenance of social mores. Relations among society's political, economic, religious, familial, among other organizations, generate travelers for the transportation system. This is a topic in the microsociology of transportation and will be discussed in the first section of the paper. The economic and political organizations shape and control transportation. Reciprocally, the character of transportation influences

steering committee on an earlier draft are also gratefully appreciated. Errors of fact or omission of course remain with the author. The views expressed herein are those of the author and should not necessarily be attributed to the New York State Department of Transportation or the United States Department of Transportation.

the economic and political life of society. These are topics in the macrosociology of transportation and will be discussed in the later sections.

A transportation system emerges out of the relations among the organizations of society to meet a requirement of those organizations and, ultimately, to facilitate the contributions of those organizations to the society. Travelers are organizational delegates produced in the network of organizational relations. Their personal attributes influence the way they carry out organizational behests. The following section of this paper discusses the behavior of travelers as organizational delegates. One type of transportation analysis models their behavior in terms of the physical facilities implicated in social organization of transportation and conceives of travelers as if they were physical objects distributing themselves in space. A review of studies in this mode is followed by an exploration of some uses and some limits of this analytic style. The microsociology of transportation, in a more symbolist mode, studies individual transportation behavior as a function of its organizational context and of the individuals' personal attributes. The next part of the paper deals with the effect of these on transportation decisions.

A macrosociological analysis of transportation views it as an organization among organizations. So much of transportation today is carried on by organizations specialized for that purpose, such as railroad or trucking companies. Its infrastructure is controlled by unique agencies within government, such as federal commerce regulators and state highway departments. For most of human history, transportation was an arm of, and administratively incorporated in, organizations of production. Societal characteristics that promote the development and growth of independent organizations for transportation will be explored in the next section of this paper. The social processes that develop transportation as an independent activity include those through which community and government control transportation. The penultimate section reflects on ways in which economic and political organizations in industrial societies shape transportation to their particular needs.

Both the macrosociological and the microsociological analyses offer the planner general, abstract propositions to assist in thinking about transportation and its problems. Typically, those propositions are probabilistic expressions of transportation/society events that do not account for every case, just most of the cases. The planner is, ordinarily, concerned with a particular case. The concluding pages reflect briefly on the use of scientific generalizations in constructing policy for particular historical situations, a matter of weaving the knowledge of the scientist together with that of the artisan.

## ORGANIZATIONS PRODUCE TRAVELERS:
## A CONCEPTUAL INTRODUCTION

Societal organizations are arrangements of social activities. The persistence of a particular arrangement is determined by its success in serving a societal function.* Societal functions (the contribution of a smaller to a larger unit) and processes (mechanisms by which the units operate or change) are implemented in relationships among organizations. It is customary to classify social organizations in terms of their principal societal functions.†

Societal organization is determined by both social and physical arrangements of relationships. The social organization of society is defined by the patterns of cultural rules that specify the actual and potential relationships and that govern behavior in them. The physical organization of society is defined by the way these social activities are related in space and sequenced in time.

Transportation is a form of social activity that coordinates the social and physical organizations of society. Without this coordination, members of society could not be socially related while being physically distant. Society would not be distributed across its resource base and would not be able to evolve beyond the possibilities offered by the most parochial settlement. Propinquity would be the major factor determining social relationships. Transportation reduces (or, in some instances, increases) spatial and temporal impediments to social relationships. In the light of this

---

*The nature of that function may not be obvious to the individual actors in these organizations. Social organizations may be distinguished from social institutions. The term social institution refers to a set of rules, norms, and value standards by which organizational activities are conducted. An organization refers to an arrangement of actors toward the realization of some social value. Each organizational type, such as industrial or commercial, is represented by concrete organizations such as factories and banks organized around some palpable goal.

†Economic organizations are arrangements for obtaining human and material resources. Religious and familial organizations are charged with maintaining internal social order, and political organizations with imposing the will of the society on its members or on another society. Health, educational, and religious and familial organizations, in another respect, develop, guide, and motivate members of the society to fulfill the myriad of behaviors expected of them.

social function, it develops norms about who and what to transport
and when, where, and how. Transportation facilitates face-to-face
social relationships or material exchange between actors otherwise
spatially separated. Thus, transportation tends to negate the space
that may separate socially joined actors.

Further, the translation of distance into time permits an actor,
physically separated from the site of action at one moment, to join
in action at that site at another moment. Related social activities
may thus be synchronized. Production, for example, may involve
the synchronization of work at several sites. Deliveries of material and workers are matched to the sequence of production activities. Similarly, the production process is synchronized with the
worker's household activities. Transportation, thus, also tends to
negate time by enabling actors, initially distant from one another,
to interact sequentially.

By transiting space within a duration, transportation articu-
lates the activities at one site with those at another. The durations
vary with the technologies to determine which activities may become interdependent. Both the social and the spatio-temporal
organization of society are shaped by the transportation possibilities.

The measure of the success of transportation is the extent to
which it facilitates the ordering of these two components of society.
Transportation may be assessed in formal and in substantive terms.
The formal success of a transportation system, expressed in
cybernetic language, is positively proportionate to the amount of
social complexity that it structures, and it is negatively proportionate to the level of complexity of the transportation system.
Formal success is in introducing the greatest simplification in the
relations among social units with the minimum of complexity in
the transportation system. The substantive success of a transportation system is measured by the degree to which it facilitates the
realization of social values—economic values, welfare, education,
family cohesion, and so on. Transportation aims to achieve these
ends by the physical movement of people and goods in ways consistent with social rules.

The substantive success may be evaluated in terms of technical, social, and moral performance. The rate and direction of
flow of people or goods is a measure of the technical performance
of a transportation system. Technical performance must be justified by its contribution to social performance. The social performance of transportation is measured by the extent to which
social groups are enabled to materialize their relationships in the
light of the technology and the rules governing its use. The social
performance must be justified in moral terms, through judgments
of social purpose. The social relationships materialized should be

morally worthwhile. Technical and social performance and moral values are not always maximized together. A disjunction between them constitutes a social problem. Engineers and social managers are accustomed to the challenge of a situation in which technical capability falls short of meeting social needs. When their technical achievements yield little social or moral advantage, they experience the technical victory as hollow and look to behavioral scientists for an understanding of the nature of social performance.

The measurement of transportation performance, in these terms, has been rudimentary. The following section begins with a review of some social ideas that have grown out of concern for the technical performance of transportation.

## THE BEHAVIOR OF INDIVIDUAL TRAVELERS: THE MICROSOCIOLOGY OF TRANSPORTATION

### The Physicalist Model of Human Behavior: Some Uses and Some Limits

#### The Physical as Social Proxy: A Simplifying Strategy

The transportation system is a social system that includes physical facilities, primarily vehicles and routes.* A social analysis of transportation would focus on the relations between actors around the use of the physical facilities of transportation. Such a social analysis would employ the language of social science. In two senses, however, the social system may be treated as if it were a physical system, a space-time event, and physical language may serve as a proxy for social. First, the physical objects in the social system may be taken as proxies for the human actors. This is a simplifying strategy that produces the pseudosocial models common in engineering systems analysis or operations research. Second, the physical aspect of social actors may be abstracted for attention from all of their other characteristics. This is the approach of demography and human ecology in which members of a population are, indeed, space-time objects.

--------

*Physical resources are relevant for social action as objects of consumption, as facilities for attaining social objectives, or as carriers of symbolic meaning. The relation of society to its physical resources is three-termed: two or more actors deal with each other with reference to a physical resource. For example, the actors may bid among themselves to consume gasoline or to use vehicles and roads.

The first approach, the simplifying strategy, is illustrated by an example from traffic studies. Furutani (1976) models traffic flow in terms of the interacting behavior of individual cars. Putatively, he is modeling the interaction of the drivers. The movement of cars is a proxy for the activities of persons, but the laws derived to account for that movement are physical, not social, laws. As one car approaches, another traveling ahead of it tends to accelerate. If this "flight behavior" is suppressed, "platoons" of cars are created. Such phenomena are explicable in terms of social norms that control the drivers' orientations to speed limits, their ideas about police surveillance, and their commitment to courtesy on the road. Furutani, however, ignores these complications, using data only on car speeds and directions and on their approach and separation to generate statements about traffic flow. This exercise is valuable for its traffic flow imagery. It provides practical, rough-and-ready rules of thumb for traffic management. The planner, with longer range concerns, will combine information from such models with behavioral information to arrive at an understanding of the mind of the individual driver and the behavior and culture of the collectivity of drivers.

Transportation policies are social interventions. Nevertheless, they too may be expressed in terms of physical proxies. The transportation operator is said to provide seat-miles, to compute load factors, and to measure distances between off-ramps, when the actual concern is with the behavior of travelers as they connect activities at their origins and destinations.

When social acts bear a fixed and known relation to physical objects, the objects are perfectly good proxies. Thus, the number, density, or queueing behavior of social actors at the wheel may be estimated from data on the movement of their vehicles. However, to inquire into the decisions that generate those densities, behavioral terms such as demands, needs, or role expectations must be introduced. These behavioral terms remain as the unspecified exogenous variables when the model is limited to observed movement patterns (Encel 1975).

This simplifying strategy offers an advantage for both data gathering and theory building. The rules of traffic movement have a certain generality across social situations. Variations in movement may be examined in relation to contextual physical factors, such as road width or car lengths, under changing social conditions, such as speed limits, displays of accident-wrecked cars, or laws governing the ages for licensing drivers.

However, this physicalist frame of reference cannot support acceptably reliable or valid long-term predictions. Social actors interpret the physical and social conditions with reference to some norm and motive to arrive at a behavioral decision. Prediction, therefore, depends on knowledge of these interpretations. The predictive variables are personality and societal characteristics of the actors that predispose them to interpret situations and to behave in one or another way. Driver behavior in response, say, to speed limits would not be the same for drivers from different cultures. Social theoretical interpretations are needed to anticipate changes in traffic flow that occur with neighborhood development or in response to communal clashes, as in Beirut, or in conjunction with a police strike, as in Montreal, or when enemy planes suddenly appear overhead, as may happen any place in the contemporary world.

In the above examples, the physical objects are treated as proxies for the social events in which they participate. Some researchers, mistaking the part for the whole, may treat them as if they were the event. In a relatively popular work, Schaeffer and Sclar (1975) talk of the walking city, the tracked city, and the rubber city, arguing that these forms of locomotion shape society. They assert, for example, that the tracked vehicle, because of its speed and limited routing, is responsible for the development of suburbs, politically and physically separate from industrial areas and from slums, and that the auto contributes further to the stratification of cities. Such assertions are suspect. Early cities, which were walking cities, had ethnic, religious, and occupational sectors. Tanning, for instance, partly because of its environmental impact and partly because of its need for water, was isolated from the residential zones and often from other occupational activities.

Transportation technology may facilitate social change. It opens possibilities for change but does not cause change. The railroad makes it possible for industry to use vacant land and to locate closer to market towns. Land values do not automatically follow the trolley. Land speculators may promote a trolley line in order to facilitate population shifts to the land they hold and so increase its value.

## The Physical Aspect of the Social: A Useful Abstraction

A second way in which the physical comes to stand for the social is by abstraction of the physical from the social aspects of society itself, its population (as in demography) and its spatial distribution (as in human ecology). In the above example, vehicles were proxies for the social activities in which their riders engaged. Here the individuals themselves are considered as objects distributed in space. The behaviors of the objects (persons) are described by their enumeration, rates of entry into and exit from the system, and rates of migration through it. The behavior is also considered understandable in these terms, there being no need to introduce symbolic terms referring to personality and cultural processes to anticipate their movements. The gravity model uses this abstraction to predict patronage of transportation. The expected traffic volume between two points is calculated as directly related to the size of the residential and transient population at the two points and as inversely related to the distance between the points (Sommers 1970). Proximity of population is, however, but one factor in assessing potential travel. A consideration of decisional factors would improve the prediction.*

The gravity model may be modified by entering a measure of destination attractiveness, as indicated, for instance, by the income of the population at the destination (Sommers 1970). The gravity model may be modified to take account of such a social factor without abandoning the physicalist frame of reference. The researcher may, for instance, take the rate of movement in one or another direction as a proxy for attractiveness, whatever its motivational or cultural basis. This is the previously discussed simplifying strategy.

Demographic and ecological analyses, supplemented by social and psychological analyses, may increase the accuracy of longer range predictions. Characterizing organizations as industrial, household, education, and so on is an approach to delineating the transportation-relevant relations in which they may enter. Measures of trip purpose, as perceived by individuals, or of market segmentation, as an economic classification of organizations, are indicators of organizational characteristics relevant to transportation.

Those who use the physicalist model in transportation research tend to concentrate on attributes of individuals while neglecting the emergent effect of the organization of the individuals. Physical mechanics, sometimes fluid mechanics, has had more

---

*A political barrier such as the Berlin Wall reduces travel to near zero, in part by influencing the decisions of potential travelers. The value of assessing potential travel demand based only on spatial distribution of populations of various sizes should not, however, be underestimated. The degree and direction of association between population attributes and travel may be understood in terms of a social decision variable. The size of the population may then be entered as a weight in the equation, giving the actual amount of shift in demand by the probabilistic coefficient of association.

influence on the physicalist model applied to transportation than
have theories of electromagnetic fields. As in mechanics, the individual is the unit of observation, and systems are reconstructed
by aggregating the attributes of these individuals. Behavioral research, in this spirit, may isolate the psychological characteristics of individuals from their social context and then attempt to
account for group decisions by aggregating the attitudes or opinions
of those individuals. The microsociology of transportation is not,
simply because it gathers data from individuals, a prisoner of this
methodological individualism. It is, after all, sociology, a way of
studying the collective.


Individuals and Their Decisions: The
Microsociology of Transportation

### Levels of Aggregation and Organization

The lion's share of contemporary behavioral science studies
of transportation has been microsociological. Not all studies,
however, have used physical proxies for individual behavior. The
prediction of demand on the basis of psychological characteristics
of individuals is another aspect of the microsociology of transportation.

Here, too, as mentioned above, the individualistic bias has
been regnant. Characterizing the traveler community by aggregating characteristics of individual users masks the emergent or
organizational character of transportation.*

---------------------

*Summing the characteristics of members of a group may fail
to identify characteristics resulting from the way the group is organized. An expression of the average per capita wealth of the community does not distinguish an aristocratic society, having a few
wealthy and many poor members, from a society with a more democratic income distribution. These two political forms, as different
ways of organizing social power, lay out different highway systems.
The use of aggregate measures of individuals to characterize
collectives has an attraction because of the accessibility of summary statistics of government and of organizational data acquired
for administrative purposes. Often these data may be available in
the form of time series, such as traffic-flow reports. If these
measures are treated as indicators of collective events, with due
attention to the interpretation problem that this entails, the accessible aggregate data sets are very useful.

Sample survey research may divert attention from group effects. Sampling typically identifies isolated random units and is thus a procedure that limits one's ability to observe social interaction among the sampled units. The attributes are measured and treated as if they do not depend on the connections among the individuals in and out of the sample. Thus, Ryan, Nedwek, and Beimborn (1972) interviewed individuals in 373 households seeking citizens' views and values regarding a planned highway. The impact of the highway was not, however, randomly distributed in the community. The dislocation of 1,300 not randomly dispersed households in a ten-mile area was expected. The advantages of the highway were enjoyed by particular groups within the community while other groups endured its disadvantages. Survey sample results might have diluted this result. Surveys may compensate for such a deficiency by dealing with relational attributes or, by "snowballing," may reach out for social networks. The important thing to keep in mind is that the individual acts as part of and in the name of a larger social reality.*

Behavioral researchers have written of the need for disaggregating transportation data. Disaggregation would preserve the diverse transportation behavior characteristic of subgroups of travelers. Disaggregation is, in practice, merely partitioning already aggregated data. Typically, the so-called subgroups are simply social categories, such as males and females, the elderly and the young, blacks and whites. The issue of emergent levels of organization is less pressing in such cases since no social networks are presumed. Where, however, the units of analysis are social organizations, such as households, firms, or churches, the level of organization reflected by the data is crucial.†

———————————

*The same authors report on a public hearing attended by 2,000 persons from sponsoring agencies, government offices, citizens' groups, church organizations, motor clubs, and labor unions. The organizations represented at the hearings might well have provided their data base. Opposition to a highway might come from a few organizations; however, it does not follow that the remainder of the community will oppose those organizations. Small protest groups and judicial action have frequently delayed highway development.

†The level of organization effect is illustrated by Stopher (1977). The individual transportation decision is a function of an activity location and of a transportation opportunity possessing some utility. A transportation opportunity is defined by a variety of social

A more organizationally meaningful disaggregation is obtained by taking organizational rather than individual attributes as the classificatory dimensions. The division of labor is one such dimension. Thus, destination is meaningful because the occasions for travel increase as labor is further divided. More importantly, the social meaning of travel, whether for work, pleasure, family reunion, religious pilgrimage, or the like, may be recognized through the types of divided labor, or organizations, that are linked. A functional distinction between households, commercial organizations, educational organizations, health organizations, and so forth, distinguishes among organizations according to the role they play in the larger society. Productive organizations have not only a social division of labor, financial, administrative, and so forth, but also a technical division of labor around stages in the production process. Technically divided labor may be spatially separated, as, for example, are the automobile engine plant, the body plant, and the assembly plant.

The social process of agglomeration offers a second dimension for disaggregating transportation data. Agglomeration is a tendency to concentration. Political agglomeration is a tendency for organizational control to become increasingly centralized. Geographic agglomeration is a tendency for organizational activities to become increasingly centralized at fewer and fewer locations. Organizations may be distinguished according to their scope of control, the range of activities dominated by a single head. The large organization with concentrated control may promote its own custom transportation system, as does the military. Locational concentration often means that those bound to its catchment area travel greater distances to interact with it.

The concrete connections between organizations is a third dimension of classification relevant to transportation. Individual households may be connected to other households in the kinship group. Personnel and resources may be exchanged between

———————————

elements beyond the route and vehicle schedule. The utility for the individual is laced into but not identical with the utility for the organization. The trip is generated by a social organizational relation. An organization selects individuals as its travel delegates. A family, for instance, may delegate one of its members as a shopper. Whether this is a man or a woman or a child depends on the culture and conditions of that household. Simply enumerating the shoppers would miss the organizational participation through its delegate and the cultural rules for selecting the delegate.

households.* The classification of travelers according to trip purpose is a proxy for organizational connections. The traveler role is viewed in the context of other roles, such as family roles. The family, for instance, influences the relative location of residence and work, the decisions about where to live and which job to take.

Transportation influences nontravelers as well as travelers. Also part of the picture are the role partners of the travelers, either property owners, residents with homes near the right-of-way, or business, manufacturing, or service activities whose workers or clients use the transportation system. These forms of disaggregating—by division of labor, agglomeration, and connectivity—are not based on characteristics of individuals. They are based on characteristics of the organizations. Further discussion of this matter brings us to the macrosociology of transportation; it will be discussed further under that heading. Meanwhile, let us return to the issue of individual behavior as influenced by organizational context.

## Individuals as Social Delegates

Individuals make their transportation choices under social constraint. This section discusses how organizations select individuals for trips and some of the constraints the organization imposes on individual choices. A work trip is a delegated trip. One or more members of the household are delegated to enter the productive economy. The remaining members of the household, principally the children, the elderly, the infirm, and sometimes a spouse, are supported by transfers from the earners. The character of the household constrains the choices which the delegate makes. Income, for instance, influences the choice between automobile and mass transit. The social norms governing individual roles influence choice. Thus, an orthodox Jew will not travel on the sabbath, nor are most women likely to travel on a Philadelphia subway after midnight. Attributes of the personalities of the household members influence their entry into roles which require more or less traveling.†

---

*Foley, Lee, and Appleyard (1970) class users or potential users of the Bay Area Rapid Transit (BART) system in San Francisco according to whether they are captive or dependent users, marginal users or optional users. The distinction rests on the transportation choices, other than BART, available to them. Captive users have no access to the automobile as an alternative.

†The modal choice is a function of attributes of the individuals. Paaswell and Edelstein (1976) found the dial-a-ride program used

The relation between the household and the firm or some other social organization generates trips. Acting in their business roles, individuals actualize the relation between organizations. Sales personnel or executives are more likely than other employees to be delegated to travel. Rules of the firm govern the destination, the distance, the time, and whether they fly economy or whether an executive may exchange a first-class ticket for two economy fares to cover travel for a spouse. The travel rules of a firm are conditioned by those customary in a specific industry or by a sponsoring agency's regulations regarding reimbursement.

A worker's choice between car or public transit is a function of the worker's place in the household. The destinations of several workers in the same household as well as the pattern of authority and deference, alluded to above, condition the choice. For example, in an urban black family in which the husband is a skilled laborer and the wife is an office worker, the man is likely to drive and the woman to use mass transit. The woman is more likely to work in the central business district while the man may travel to a suburban point not well served by transit. In addition, however, black male household heads have more authority over car use than do their white counterparts and are likely to exert that authority. A family may also negotiate such a decision, considering, for instance, which member might more likely be penalized for tardiness.

The delegated character of the traveler is recognized by Popper, Notess, and Zapata (1976). They formulate it in terms of a derived demand for transportation. Travel by the elderly, for

---

disproportionately by those elderly in poor health and by those more despairing in their outlook on life. The unhealthy are hindered by social rules from obtaining or from operating a car. They also may be less able to manage bus travel. As a consequence, they are prime candidates for the dial-a-ride service, which calls for them at home and delivers them to their destination at a cost below that of a taxi. This population, excluded from the usual forms of transportation, resorts to an innovative form when it is offered.

The relation of their households to the social service agency, not the dial-a-ride service, provides the motive for the trip. The transportation facility should not be confused with what it facilitates, Michaels (1974) recognizes and applies this distinction between the facility and what it facilitates. He says that the validity and reliability of a model of, for instance, trip generation will be higher when the model is constructed of behavioral rather than physical measures. This matter was discussed above.

instance, is occasioned by visits to social service agencies. The relation between households of the elderly and community activities occasions these trips of individuals. Through transportation, individuals link the two activity loci and so enact the interorganizational relation.

A final example shows the interaction between the social norms and the individual response to those norms. Wilde (1976) examines the formal and informal rules governing driving in order to understand conflict between road users. Conflict arises when drivers deviate from the rules or when drivers conform to discrepant rules. Some rules may increase and others decrease danger on the road. Traffic regulations about passing on hills and signaling when passing are legislated rules, while rules about how close to pass a car are informal, rooted in courtesy of the road or in common sense. These rules increase safety. An informal rule that one should speed up when being overtaken in order not to be passed would increase danger. Yet, this is an unspoken behavioral guide for some drivers, who treat their position on the highway as a significant symbol of dominance. *

## Individual Choice under Social Constraint

The argument may be recapitulated briefly. Travel is occasioned by relationships between organizations. It emerges to coordinate the social and the physical networks of these organizations. The organizations as a whole, however, do not interact. Individuals delegated by them interact. Organizational interaction becomes

---

*The discussion has been moving from the sociological, the analysis of social organizations, to the social psychological, the influence of groups on individual behavior. Commitment to rules may be thought of as an attitude, a predisposition on the part of the individual to behave in a certain way under defined circumstances. Attitudes, by providing an interpretation of the situation, assist the person in adapting to it. As such, attitudes are not established outside of social behavior but are an aspect of a social act, to use George H. Mead's formulation. The attitude toward a situation expresses deeper personality tendencies, which, in turn, are outgrowths of the previous experience of the individual. Because of the repetitive character of situations, an attitude toward those situations becomes a learned response, is internalized in the personality, and, for practical purposes, may be treated as a trait of the individual, a psychological characteristic.

actuality through the travel of delegated individuals. The requirements are modified by individual travel choices, which, in turn, are influenced by individuals' attitudes.

Organizational requirements are but one element in determining the transportation mode. The relative geographic positions, community norms regarding transportation, and the occupational culture and income of the worker contribute to a decision to take the bus, take the car, drive alone, drive in a car pool, be driven by a spouse to the plant, or drive the spouse to work and then drive to the plant, and so forth. The meaning for the individual of the relative geographic locations is reflected in an attitude of willingness to travel. Community norms are adopted as internal behavioral directives and are thus exposed to the individual's more basic disposition to act in accord with or contrary to the norms. The cultural meanings of the various modal choices appear on the individual level as attitudes toward the modes.

The assessment of individual choice is often accomplished through the measurement of expressed choice. The attributes of transportation toward which attitudes are measured in behavioral research tend to be drawn from common sense rather than from a theory. They are sometimes identified from complaints about the system or from rationalizations for not using the system. These latter attributes are impediments to the use of transportation, and, it is suggested, removal of these impediments would increase patronage. Thus, Rosinger, Connell, and Stock (1967), examining both riders and nonriders of transit, assess factors such as trip time, convenience, accessibility, information available about system operation, comfort, social mixing of race and class, safety, security, prestige of riding, cost of fare, and condition of equipment and facilities. Attitudes toward these attributes are used to develop measures of user needs, factors influencing the decision to travel in a particular system.

These elements can provide rather immediate and practical guidance to a transit operator. It is certainly useful to know that riders prefer one type of seat over another. In a larger sense, however, the analyst would want to be sure that these are not simply convenient rationales by which riders, really unaware of why they like or dislike transit, make their own decisions meaningful to themselves. The operator could discover that after the preferred seats were provided, ridership remained unchanged while nonriders shifted their complaints to the feeling of security. Reliance on common sense, paradoxically, may obscure the true sense underlying the decision to ride.

Once there is some certainty that the measured choices reflect underlying, and reasonably stable, expressions of attitude, the researcher seeks to account for that attitude. Underlying personality dispositions, one source of attitude, are a focus of the psychological study of transportation. Personality influences the location of a home, the onerousness of travel time, the search for privacy in travel, the significance of independent control over the situation of travel, and willingness to pay for travel by one or another mode.

The social context is relevant developmentally in the formation of underlying personality dispositions. These dispositions are fed by internalized cultural meanings. The basic interpretation that the individual makes is that of meaning of the situation for the self.

The social context is also relevant as a contemporary source of situational events evoking personality response. Hartgen (1974) recognized that different social variables may control the mode choice of different groups of travelers. A search for the meaning of travel for the individual is a way to discover these variables. Personality characteristics, in the context of socially prescribed norms, influence individual responses to trip characteristics, such as frequency of stops by vehicles or the headway of vehicles. Hartgen investigated a number of these characteristics, including, for instance, time in transit and comfort of seats. Trip purposes differentiate categories of travelers; thus, judgments on these matters are found to vary with trip purpose.* For those traveling

---

*Trip purpose has also been used to classify potential travelers. Miller (n.d.), for instance, measures latent demand, the trips that would be taken were certain populations, such as the handicapped and the elderly, not excluded. He asked respondents about the frequency with which they shop for groceries, go to a movie, go to work, shop for clothes, go to a barber or hairdresser, or go to church. This may be an overspecification of trip purposes for the aims of transportation research. The variable of interest is the intensity of the social and space-time linkages between the household and its various activity settings. The specific trip purposes are individual reflections of organizational links. They may be scale items, or indicators, referring to the classes of social activities in which members of households engage. To obtain food, for instance, a person may eat in restaurants, eat at a parent's table, cook at home, have meals-on-wheels delivered to the home, and so forth. Each alternative for obtaining food has different implications for traveling outside the home. As elements in the scale, they may attest to a more general underlying source of transportation demand.

to work or to shop, small differences in cost may become a salient consideration. Fares for the trip to work may be computed against earnings and the cost of travel to various stores may be weighted against relative prices of items in those stores. The fares are less crucial, more inelastic, for family or recreational travelers. The model of the rational economic man maximizing benefits and minimizing costs is most nearly applicable to the business trip. It would be a mistake, however, even in this case, to ignore factors other than cost. The willingness to bear the cost of a recreational trip reflects the level of expenditures socially expected for vacations. The traveler would be sensitive to the comparative costs of several operators covering the same route. Yet cost may pale into insignificance for religious trips such as pilgrimages.

Attitudes are dispositional traits, elicited in certain circumstances. The circumstances and the repertoire of responses to the circumstances are subject to social norms. Norms of social responsibility indicate when it is legitimate to protest an inconvenience and against whom the protest should be directed. The individually expressed choices, therefore, are tied to the reigning social and political philosophy of the society. In responding to the choices, the planner must discriminate between occasions when the problem is simply one of convenience and when the issue is deeper and requires a deeper response.

Choices are made sequentially and may be thought of as following a decision tree. The choice of a job requiring commuting is an early one and is followed by decisions to use one or another mode at one or another time or with some frequency, perhaps alternating it with other modes or not alternating it at all. Different factors control the successive choices. Burnett (1974) discusses conditional or spatial choice processes and activity sequencing in relation to trip linkages. The likelihood of taking one kind of trip affects the likelihood of taking another kind of trip. This relation of conditional probabilities is true of the trips of a particular individual and is true of the trips of various individuals.

SOCIAL SYSTEMICS: THE MACROSOCIOLOGY
OF TRANSPORTATION

Division of Labor and Agglomeration:
Underlying Social Processes

A travel requirement arises from the relative geographic locations of organizations that are already socially interdependent. The amount of travel generated depends on characteristics of the organizations and of their interrelations. This section continues the description of the types of organizational behavior that influence the propensity to travel and then leads into a consideration of how societal control of transportation helps shape it in the image of its society. The section concludes with some remarks on the impact of political and economic organizations on transportation. The microsociological discussion was able to draw on current studies. The tradition in macrosociological thought about transportation informs the discussion in a more diffuse manner and so will not be cited with reference to particular points. (References to the literature in this area are given in Klausner, Masnick, and Santo, 1977.)

Two social organizational processes, introduced above, influence the level of transportation in a society: the social division of labor and organizational agglomeration. The social division of labor, as applied to social organizations, implies an increasing number of more specialized organizational units. As Durkheim argued so cogently, divided labor becomes socially interdependent labor, the basis of organic social solidarity. Socially specialized activities become locationally specialized. The differentiation of tasks means a dispersion in the locations at which those tasks are accomplished and, thus, an increasing number of activities and locations to be connected. Trips are required between these locations to integrate them socially. Smelting and mining differentiate both as organizational specialities and in location. They remain socially interdependent and so must be connected spatially. The ore is thus moved from the mine to the smelter. The more narrow the specialization, the larger the number of activity sites which emerge and the more transportation is required to effect an exchange of goods between them.

The agglomeration of specialized activities into fewer, but larger, units arises, particularly if they are economic units, to achieve economies of scale in administration and in production. It also overcomes the friction of space between socially linked activities. The reemergence of the food bazaar in the contemporary supermarket or the colocation of an electrical utility and dwelling units using its waste heat are illustrations. Activities may be assembled to enjoy a synergic effect. The clustering of independent retail stores handling the same class of merchandise, such as a series of jewelers on the same block, illustrates this. Concentration extends the radius of the catchment area from which customers are drawn. A concentration of activities generates more travel by creating occasions for longer trips rather than by increasing the number of trips. Fewer but longer trips are made to the supermarket than were made to the corner grocery store. Further, customers minimize costs at these marketing stations by providing, as it were, their own freight haulage. The automobile traffic, because of its custom character, exceeds that of the delivery truck traffic it displaces.

Agglomeration has a political or managerial aspect. Interdependent specialized activities tend to come under unified control. The possibility of concentrating them at fewer locations permits a more direct and thorough exercise of that control.

The acceptance by a person of more and more role responsibilities is an individual cognate of the social agglomeration process. Transportation permits the same person to participate in activities at dispersed sites within a relatively short space of time—the critical length of time being the point at which absence from a given role creates a problem. Social rules about the number and compatibility of specialized tasks one person may assume, what sociologists call the complexity of the role set, govern the extent of shuttling between locations. The more rapid the travel, the more locations at which an individual may perform. The greater the number of tasks and sites that fall to each individual, the greater the possible productivity of a population of a given size.

Transportation itself is subject to these two social processes. In its primitive stage, transport is part of the organization which it facilitiates. Traders are the operators of caravans and ships. On the other hand, a company organized for the purpose of providing transportation moves the goods and people of a number of organizations. Its personnel includes drivers and mechanics and executives and those who build the routes or produce the vehicles. These are specialists with a full-time commitment to transportation. Specialized transportation companies also tend to centralize their terminals and transfer facilities. To the extent that economic and political arrangements abet this trend, the result is a few large automobile manufacturers and a few dominant railroads, trucking concerns, and bus lines.

Historically, transport systems have been categorized in terms of the mode. A transport mode is defined by the physical media through which or over which vehicles move. The respective peculiar technological problems encountered in moving through air, land, or water require the development of peculiar classes of vehicles and routes. These, in turn, require occupational specialties to build and operate them. Each mode is thus associated with its own form of technical division of labor, its own conditions of work, and its own type of labor contract. The mode is not defined simply by the medium but by the way the medium is engaged by means of a technology. Railroads and motor traffic are distinct modes of overland travel. The division of labor among social organizations served by transportation, as noted above, increases the demand

for transportation. The technical division of labor within transportation results in a system more flexible and more adapted to the
various demands upon it.

Competition between the modes is competition between the
clusters of occupations developed around the respective technologies
and the social organizations supplying them and the organizations
they serve. Government regulatory systems are called into being
by the interaction of these occupations and organizations in their
business roles. Therefore, regulatory agencies are organized to
parallel the modes of transport.*

In the introductory section above, a function of transportation
was described as the ordering of the relation between the space-
time network of activities and the network constructed by social
connections of activities. The modal differentiation of the transport
system implies that there are as many types of social ordering by
means of transportation as there are modes of transport. Transportation is not a homogeneous system providing an undifferentiated
function for society. Whether industrial worksites are linked by
air, rail, or road affects the social structure of industry. A development of this point would lead to a discussion of the impact of
transportation on society, but that is the subject of another paper.
The theme of this paper is how to think about the demand that society
imposes on transportation. Transportation remains the dependent
variable. The following pages touch briefly on how society controls
the selection among modes, as well as other features of the transportation system.

How the Community Controls Transportation

Were transportation planning limited to decisions whether to
run buses on five-minute or ten-minute headways, the day-to-day
experience of the planners would be as good a guide as many sophisticated demand estimations, if not better. If a long-range decision
is pending, such as whether or not to install a rapid transit system

---

*Modal organization is, nevertheless, more significant as a
way of characterizing transportation suppliers than of characterizing clients. In fact, the preeminence of the modal-split problem in
transportation research is a projection more of the problem of competition among suppliers than of the problem of convenience for
clients. Any system for categorizing clients would be constructed
around a notion of trip purpose—business travel, recreational travel,
and the like.

involving tunneling and laying of tracks and expected to influence the tax base, property values, and the distribution of the labor pool and of worksites, more than an extrapolation of current usage is needed. Demand is, however, the primary way in which the community controls transportation in a market-oriented economy.

Transportation is shaped by the democratic force of consumer sovereignty, always operating in a constrained market. The concept of consumer demand has been offered as an explanation of how particular systems came into being. Michaels (1974), for example, notes that what people in the aggregate have chosen uniquely defines transportation history in the United States. Thus, he says, people have chosen railroads, highways, and aviation, in that order. Actually, demand helps account for the functioning and development of established transportation forms. The initial building of the railroads, however, did not necessarily depend upon traveler demand. The potential farebox must have been only a slight incentive for those interested in developing the rights-of-ways. Congress recognized that fact in allocating privileges to encourage railroad building. The government's political interest was in extending control over territory newly incorporated into the United States.*

Demand is also a form of control in a more inclusive sense of the term. When an industrialist asks that a transit route be run to his plant or when a neighborhood association presses for more frequent services than ridership would seem to justify, decisions to subsidize and to build transportation systems are influenced.

A transportation economy is politically constrained in a number of ways, including the interest group pressures indicated above. The terms of the franchise, the routes to be served, and the times and frequency of service are not simply reflexes of farebox receipts. They are determined in bargaining between a transportation operator and a government agency. The political influence of the communities along routes and of those at the terminuses influence transportation decisions. The decisions are subject to the distribution of political power in the community, its income level, its willingness

---

*The introduction or origin of the system is best traced according to the rules of technological and cultural innovation. The anticipated performance is part of the motive for introducing a system. The acceptance or rejection of the innovation depends on functional factors as well as on cultural compatibility of the transportation system with other activities of the society. In our society, these other activities have been largely economic and political.

to vote a bond issue and attitude toward taxation, trends in land values, relationships between ethnic groups in the area, and norms regarding the use of transit by each ethnic group or each income stratum, among many other things. Does a bus become the turf of one ethnic group or age group, discouraging its use by other sectors of the population? The fact and feeling of personal security on existing systems may influence the public pressure on government for transportation alternatives. Home-to-work and work-to-home travel is influenced by changing labor force requirements of industries in the area. This, in turn, is influenced by changing markets for their products. The demand for work trips is also a function of the number, distribution, and social character of the households. The ratio of workers and, therefore, of work trips is also a function of the number, distribution, and social character of the households. The ratio of workers and, therefore, of work trips to total household members is higher in nuclear family households and in single-parent households than in traditional families. Changing community attitudes toward women working and ensuing formal and informal labor rules regarding the hours and places in which women may work influence the level of travel demand in general and that exerted by women in particular. Changes in the type of industry in the area affect numbers and characteristics of travelers as well as the level of traffic at different times of the day. White-collar work will draw women out of the home, as will a national emergency. The residential distribution of families at various stages in the family life cycle and the numbers of children in school influence residential distribution and, thus, the volume and destinations of travel by women in various age categories. Authority and deference attitudes between household members influence who drives the car, who is a passenger, and who travels to work by public transit.

Community control of transportation is expressed through governmentally enacted rules such as those governing parking, direction of traffic flow, speed limits, air pollution and noise standards, and so on. Some of the rules are expressed directly in terms of behavioral requirements, while others euphemistically refer to physical conditions to be obtained, leaving the behavior necessary to obtain them implicit and unspoken.

Criminals have a dramatic effect on the use of transportation by the rest of the community. While it is not customary to consider criminals as instruments of social control, and they certainly do not reflect conscious decisions of the organized society, they are indubitably a crucial factor influencing the composition of transit ridership and public decisions regarding transit security. Criminal influence is exerted indirectly through the behavioral, administrative,

adjustments to crime by the riding public, the govern-
he police.

s also influence one another through congestion. Con-
s not exclude riders at random but turns away those who
transportation options available to them, either by virtue
or of their location along the route.

Control not only retards but may promote use of transportation. Thus, community policy may favor one mode over another,
as in the shift from light rail to bus transit in Los Angeles. Use of
a line may increase exponentially as it becomes a fad or fashion,
each additional user increasing the probability of attracting the
next user until some threshold is attained.

Policy makers are guided by the profitability of transit investments. The governmental official cannot limit the concept of
profitability to the book balance of the operating company but must
attend to it in community welfare terms. Minimum service may be
maintained to a strategic area of the city or to special populations,
such as the elderly, even when not immediately justified by the
farebox.

Governmental regulation of transportation is conducted at the
state and local levels of government. This division arises on the
basis of territorial responsibility, but they also have functionally
divided responsibilities. Local authorities have greater responsibility for highway feeder systems than for longer-range highway
systems. They monitor traffic flow, police surveillance, traffic
lights, and an array of traffic signs. They franchise public transportation, including taxis. Some transportation labor settlements
are attained on the local level. Land use control, excepting that
of public land, is local. The state constructs and maintains longer
highways and controls the rights of individuals to operate motor
vehicles through its licensing and testing procedures. The federal
government, of course, controls the largest highway system but,
perhaps more significantly, monitors transportation as a business
through such agencies as the Interstate Commerce Commission.
Railroads, trucks, and airlines engaged in interstate commerce
are particularly affected by federal regulation. Central to the
analysis of governmental regulatory action as a form of social control of transportation is the basic criterion by which a society determines this allocation of authority. For instance, societies that
place driver licensing power at the federal rather than provincial
level would have a more uniform code, as well as one less likely to
take provincial social conditions into account. Centralized licensin
would probably go further to standardize criteria in terms of physical competencies and would pay less attention to the cultural vari-
ability in notions of adulthood and responsibility.

These pages do not provide an exhaustive catalog of the agencies controlling transportation and the forms that their control might take. The basic form of control is through demand, in the narrow sense of seats and fares, as generated in interorganizational relations. The processes of division of labor and agglomeration have been noted as being among the more important influences on level of demand. Transportation is further controlled by the community through its political agencies, which, in turn, are influenced by the interests of various social organizations. Again, the issue of demand in the broader sense of institutional control revolves around interorganizational, macrosociological considerations.

Dominant Social Organizations: The
Shaping of Transportation

Not all social institutions, organizations, or activities have an equal share in determining the character of transportation. In industrial societies, organizations of instrumental control, such as the military, the government, and industry, have a predominant influence on the national transportation system.* The form of this large system in turn influences the local networks that may be linked to it. Government, in its military and police role, must be able to project a credible force at a distance. Roads and highways and the air transport network are located to facilitate the deployment of troops. These organizations, in meeting their own needs, develop vehicles which may be more widely adopted. The military contribution to the development of the airplane has not been inconsiderable.†

---

*Social institutions may be divided into those oriented to task accomplishment (instrumental) and those that function primarily through integrating social relationships (solidary or expressive). The economy and the polity illustrate the former, and religion and the family the latter.

†The automobile, probably the most significant influence on contemporary transportation, has been adopted, supported, and diffused by the family, a solidary rather than an instrumental organization. However, as will be explained below, the family in our society is dominated culturally by the economy and the polity. The family is the means by which the automobile has proliferated. The influence on family structure, activities, and residential patterns of the instrumental institutions is a more basic factor, indirectly determining the automobile culture.

Economic organizations shape the transportation network in a more diffuse way. Routes of trade follow the distribution of economic actors and result from a myriad of economic acts. Organizations of primary production are, perhaps, among the most influential of economic organizations. Coal and iron mining do not choose their geographic location. Primary production provides the largest single source of shippers of freight by rail. Mining operators have dominated railroads, and railroads have, at times, dominated coal mines.

Organizations of secondary production are more flexible in their locational decisions. These organizations may select a location on the basis of their needs for energy, labor, and materials and on the basis of their relation to markets, as all of these are conditioned by transportation. One way of optimizing this situation is to influence the type of transportation available. Industrial and agricultural location theory has conceptualized this issue from the perspective of the productive enterprises. A locational analysis is relevant, as well, from the perspective of transportation systems. Transportation policy is affected by the way economic or political activities tend to locate themselves and, as a consequence, generate transportation demand in both the narrow and the broad senses of the term.*

The service characteristics of transportation are geared to the travel needs, actual and potential, of members of economic and political organizations. The operating characteristics of travel systems are matched to their bodily capacities. Thus, we have the

---

*Households, as sources of labor, distribute themselves with respect to work sites and, in so doing, influence transportation demand. Economic requirements modify but are not the sole determinants of household locations. Were occupation the sole factor in residential location, cities would not be segregated by race and ethnicity. Resort communities, for instance, are less influenced by jobs. Religious and racial clusters in such communities are even more prominent than in urban areas. Kinship groups, acting through households, promote family visiting and recreational travel and press toward culturally homogeneous living. The resort or vacation community is one of the few locations in our society in which the solidary association offers major resistance to the force of the instrumental institutions. The service economy, including barbers, cleaners, and food purveyors, and municipal services, such as water treatment plants and incinerators, are located with respect to households and worksites. They thus add their weight to the already dominant determinants of transportation.

tradition of arraying vehicles to serve healthy individuals during their working years.

Since the transportation systems have emerged under the influence of the instrumental institutions, certain social organizations tend to be excluded or, at least, less well served. Educational institutions may fall in this category. Small schools may follow the lead of the service economy, locating in residential areas in walking distance of the household. When schools become larger they draw from a larger district and require specialized transportation systems of their own. Health and religious organizations also try to locate themselves with respect to the population distribution determined by the political and economic systems. The clients and workers of these organizations use the in-place transportation system. By using the system on a different schedule from those traveling to places of employment, they may even serve to reduce the peaking problem. To the extent that hospitals need emergency transportation, they supplement the network with their own transportation. Religious organizations may also institute supplementary specialized transportation systems. Buses which enable members of fundamentalist churches to visit sister churches are an example.

The transportation system is not uniquely suited to serve every firm or every individual, even within the economy. Some businesses do not succeed in attracting transit service to their locations, perhaps because they have less political influence than others who compete for the service. The requirements for using the system may exclude the elderly and the handicapped as well as small children. The excluded tend to respond by withdrawing from the system or by trying to change the system.

The elderly and the handicapped tend to withdraw. This reinforces the tendency to ignore them in service planning and contributes to the perpetuation of their transportation disadvantages. Paaswell and Edelstein (1976) write about the exclusion of the elderly as they are deprived of access to activity centers and stores. Banks and doctors move from a changing neighborhood in which the elderly remain and so exacerbate the exclusion. The elderly make trips as often as younger people do, maybe even more often, to the grocer, to medical and religious activities, or to engage in social life. Car use as such, these researchers find, does not decrease as people become older. The elderly, however, are less likely to be car drivers and more likely to be passengers, dependent on others for transportation. The availability of an auto is related more to income than to age and physical condition. A wealthy handicapped person may have a chauffeur. The elderly shift from the car to walking when the activity is nearby. Otherwise

they use the bus and perhaps the taxi. When these forms of transportation are inadequate, they are disadvantaged.*

An attempt to change the system is a second response to exclusion. Change may be sought either within or without the rules.
The former conjures up the image of political influence and of
public hearings on transit. The latter includes transportation
crime. For example, firms may bribe city officials to adjust a
route or pay a premium directly to a bus driver to encourage him
to make an unscheduled stop.


## SCIENCE AND ART IN TRANSPORTATION PLANNING

The thrust of this paper has been to outline the kind of behavioral science information transportation planners and policy
makers need for effective planning. In closing, it is appropriate to
indicate the limited usefulness of scientific knowledge when taken
alone.

Transportation research results in general statements regarding the probability of certain events. The assertion that transit
usage will peak more on Friday than on Wednesday evening is a
general descriptive statement. The assertion that the higher the
income, the greater the likelihood of access to a car is an analytic
general statement. These likelihoods of occurrences refer to a
universe of occasions. Transportation operators and planners are
concerned with a concrete transportation system at a specific time
and location. The abstract statement does not predict any particular situation because, as a single generalization, it reflects but one
aspect of the full relationship of people to transportation.

The historical method offering a detailed description of a
sequence of events, rather than the scientific generalizing method,
offers information nearer to that used by planners. History describes particular events and the concrete connections between

---

*Wachs and Blanchard (n.d.) describe how transportation
operators have adapted to the elderly by, for instance, offering a
reduced fare for off-peak travel. Taylor and Sen (1976) describe
the travel disadvantage of impoverished female heads of household
receiving AFDC. They travel most in the midday, using a bus or
walking. If they travel at night or in the evening, they do so as
passengers attaching themselves to other people who travel. Most
of their trips are for shopping or social and recreational activities
rather than for work.

particular events. General scientific statements provide a broad understanding of the particular event of interest by placing it in an array of many similar events. Such insights give a planner a sense of what to look for. This is recognized, for example, by Bouchard, Lehr, Redding, and Thomas (1972), who find that statements of community values are unidentifiable in any usable form except within the framework of project development, that is, in a concrete social situation, in a particular neighborhood, or in a religious enclave. The data-gathering method of choice is that of participant observation. Field methods have, in common with the historical method, a sense for the concrete case. As traditionally applied, though, field methods underestimate the force of history. This calls for an art of social study. An observer or a practitioner who has a political sense and is substantively familiar with people and their activities, motives, interests, and influences is usually a successful political artisan.

This approach, applied alone, has its limitations. The artisan of social research may not have a broad view, may be bound to local experience, and may not control his own values. Thus, general statements are useful as correctives.* An interweaving of the scientific study of transportation, as described in this paper, and the art, which others may describe, can provide knowledge of the case at hand needed for transportation planning.

REFERENCES

Bouchard, R. J., E. L. Lehr, M. J. Redding, and G. R. Thomas. 1972. "Techniques for Considering Social, Economic, and Environmental Factors in Planning Transportation Systems." Highway Research Board, Highway Research Record, no. 410, pp. 1-7. Washington, D.C.

Burnett, P. 1974. "Disaggregate Behavioral Models of Travel Decisions Other than Mode Choice: A Review and Contribution

---

*The planner may extend his or her historical understanding by involving citizens in the process. Citizens would include a variety of people drawn from many sectors of the society. Schimbler, Chastain, and Corradino (1973) describe how to put together a citizens' advisory committee with representatives from government bodies, agencies, semi-public agencies, private industry, and community influentials. Learning from such a group is part of the art of transportation planning.

to Spatial Choice Theory." In Transportation Research Board Report 149, Behavioral Demand Modeling and Valuation of Travel Time. Washington, D. C.

Encel, S. 1975. "Social Aspects of Communication." IEEE Transactions and Communications, vol. com-23: 1012-18.

Foley, D. L., D. B. Lee, and D. Appleyard. 1970. "Social and Environmental Impacts of the BART System: Needed Research." Highway Research Board, Special Report 111, Impact of the Bay Area Rapid Transit System on the San Francisco Metropolitan Region.

Furutani, N. 1976. "A New Approach to Traffic Behavior, II: Individual Car and Traffic Flow." International Journal of Man-Machine Studies, no. 6, pp. 731-42.

Hartgen, D. T. 1974. "Attitudinal and Situational Variables Influencing our Urban Mode Choice: Some Empirical Findings." Transportation 3: 377-92.

Highway Research Board. 1973. "Citizen Participation and Social Indicators." Highway Research Record, no. 470. Washington, D. C.

Klausner, S. Z., G. Masnick, and Y. Santo. 1977. "Thinking Sociologically about Transportation." Philadelphia: Center for Research on the Acts of Man.

Kriken, A. G., W. H. Bottiny, and F. I. Thiel. 1972. "Estimating Community Effects of Highways." Transportation Research Board, Transportation Serving Community Needs, Transportation Research Record, no. 528, pp. 9-14.

Lee, J. W., D. L. M. Covault, and G. E. Willeke. 1972. "Framework for Using Social Indicators to Monitor, Evaluate and Improve a Public Transportation System." In Use of Economic and Social Environmental Indicators on Transportation Planning, Highway Research Board, Highway Research Record, no. 410, pp. 24-26. Washington, D. C.

Louviere, J. J., and K. L. Norman. 1977. "Applications of Information-Processing Theory to the Analysis of Urban Travel Demand." Environment and Behavior 9: 91-106.

Michaels, R. M. 1974. "Behavioral Measurement: An Approach to Predicting Transport Demand." In Transportation Research Board Report 149, Behavioral Demand Modeling and Valuation of Travel Time, pp. 51-57. Washington, D.C.

Miller, J. A. N.d. "Latent Travel Demands of the Handicapped and Elderly." Report to the Urban Mass Transportation Administration, pp. 7-12. Washington, D.C.

Murawski, C. A., and F. L. Ventura. 1976. "Social and Environmental Impacts of Dual-mode Transit Systems." In Transportation Research Board Report 170, Dual-mode Transportation. Washington, D.C.

Paaswell, R. E., and P. Edelstein. 1976. "A Study of Travel Behavior of the Elderly." Transportation Planning and Technology 3: 143-54.

Paaswell, R. E., W. W. Recker, and V. Milione. 1976. "Profile of a Carless Population." Transportation Research Board, Transportation Research Record, pp. 16-28. Washington, D.C.

Popper, R. J., C. B. Notess, and R. N. Zapata. 1976. "Demand for Special Transit Systems to Serve the Rural Elderly." Transportation Research Board, Transportation Research Record, pp. 1-6. Washington, D.C.

Rosinger, G., K. F. Connell, and J. R. Stock. 1967. "Design of Urban Transportation for the User." Battelle Memorial Institute, Columbus Laboratories.

Ryan, C. R., B. P. Nedwek, and E. A. Beimborn. 1972. "An Evaluation of the Feasibility of Social Diagnostic Techniques in the Transportation Planning Process." Highway Research Record, no. 410, pp. 8-23.

Sacco, J. F., and H. M. Hajj. 1967. "Impact of the Energy Shortage on Travel Patterns and Attitudes." Transportation Research Board, Transportation Research Record, pp. 1-11. Washington, D.C.

Schaeffer, K. H., and E. Sclar. 1975. Access for All: Transportation Growth. Baltimore: Penguin Books.

Schimbler, C., T. H. Chastain, and J. C. Corradino. 1973. "Formulation of Effective Citizen Involvement in the Development of a Major Aviation Facility." Highway Research Record, no. 470, pp. 1-11. Washington, D.C.

Sommers, A. N. 1970. "Towards a Theory of Traveler Mode Choice." High-speed Ground Transportation Journal 4: 1-8.

Stopher, P. R. 1977. "On the Application of Psychological Measurement Techniques to Travel Demand Estimation." Environment and Behavior 9: 67-80.

Taylor, L., and L. Sen. 1976. "Travel Behavior and Mobility Patterns of Low-Income Residents of Syracuse, New York." Transportation Research Board, Transportation Research Record. Washington, D.C.

Wachs, M., and R. D. Blanchard. N.d. "Life-styles and Transportation Needs of the Elderly in the Future." Report to Urban Mass Transportation Administration of U.S. Department of Transportation, pp. 19-24.

Wilde, G. J. S. 1976. "Social Interaction Patterns in Driver Behavior: An Introductory Review." Human Factors 18: 477-92.

# 7
# TRANSPORTATION ISSUES ANALYSIS

## INTRODUCTION

As was discussed in this book's Introduction, there are four immediate and substantive issues facing transportation planning and policy: energy conservation, transportation for the mobility limited, social and environmental impact analysis, and transit management and short-range planning. Each of these areas involves significant behavioral questions, many of which require answers before rational planning and policy decisions can be made. Consequently, each issue was the subject of direct study at the conference by groups of both transportation specialists and behavioral scientists. The purpose of these dialogues was to analyze the direct and indirect implications of the issues, using the behavioral scientists to aid in identifying some of the major behavioral issues that are important for improving decision making, planning, and operations in these areas.

The products of these discussions are summarized in this chapter by the discussion leaders. Their purpose is to define the field of concern and to identify priority behavioral science issues that need resolution. Each of the four sections reflects an interpretation as well as a summary of the dialogue and reflects the frame of reference of the transportation specialist in the context of communication with behavioral scientists.

Finally, the chapter contains an overall interpretation of the dialogue. The purpose here is to review the discussions from a behavioral science perspective and to identify some implications from both the behavioral sciences and transportation planning and policy.

# Transit Management and Short-Range Planning

## Peter B. Everett, G. J. (Pete) Fielding, and David Goss

At the first meeting of the workshop on transit management and short-range planning it was decided that the group should focus on three general topics to which behavior science research and theory could contribute. The first topic is the internal management of a transit organization. The second topic deals with a transit system's relationship to consumers and potential consumers (that is, marketing). The third topic addresses the political variables and support constituencies to which transit management must be responsive.

## INTERNAL MANAGEMENT OF A TRANSIT ORGANIZATION

### Issues

Several issues relevant to the internal management of a transit organization were discussed. These issues can be broken into two categories, those that focus on vehicle operators and those that focus on management.

It was noted that operators fall into two very different character types. One is typified by the older, usually white male who has been a loyal employee for many years. This person performs well on the job but, beyond the specific job tasks, gives little creative input (for example, suggestions) to transit operations. The person is often alienated from the system, yet follows orders quite well. The second class of operators is typified by the young male (commonly black) who is more aggressive in assuring his rights as an employee and asserting his influence on operations. Yet the person tends not to be as reliable as the one in the first group. Absenteeism and lateness for work, primarily from this second type of employee, constitute a significant labor problem.

Three characterizations of the environment in which an operator functions are fairly common. First, there is little contact between management and operators, other than during pay periods or infrequent meetings. The operator's major contact is with the public. Such a situation makes ordinary management techniques more difficult. Second, the majority of management controls over operators tend to be punitive (for example, reprimands, letters of warning). There is little use of incentives (reinforcement) for appropriate behaviors. Finally, operator contracts, indeed most transit labor contracts, commonly are based on criteria other than job performance. The impact of this situation on productivity is potentially significant.

Several issues that focus on transit management were also brought up. Among these was a concern for the source of new managers. As the older managers retire, what sorts of academic programs might be training new people for these positions, and what are the personal attributes and skills required for transit management? Contemporary transit managers must be responsive to diverse constituencies (for example, federal, state, and local governments; consumers; politically responsive boards; commercial enterprises). Additionally they must be versed in a wide range of contemporary management skills ranging from theory to modern analytical techniques, including computer applications. Finally, it was noted that middle management is often not fully integrated into the transit organization, as manifested by lack of knowledge or lack of understanding of organizational objectives.

## Discussion

Much discussion of the above issues centered on institutional characteristics or barriers that seem to promote some of the internal management problems. For example, it was noted that operators are often caught between management and consumer desires. Management may insist upon loading and discharging passengers at designated stops only, while a friendly (consumer-oriented) operator may violate this dictum. The group also noted that some operator selection tests seem to discriminate against individuals with initiative.

Comments relevant to management were many. One of the most salient was that realistic goals and objectives for the transit organization often are lacking, and accordingly, management does not know when it is "winning" (doing the right thing). Strong group consensus was noted when the observation was made that transit management meets primarily with other transit management personnel (for example, via professional meetings) when discussing techniques, advances, strategies, and so forth. This could lead to inbreeding and the dissemination of bad management practice. Management from other types of organizations may be able to stimulate new thinking and introduce new techniques and should be invited to transit management conferences. Transit managers also should be encouraged to attend management development courses provided primarily for the private sector.

Two major institutional barriers to innovation in regard to operators and management were discussed. One is that public work, with its attendant job classifications and rigid pay schedules, often stifles innovation. The private sector, on the other hand, can easily redesign an organization and roles within it, while simultaneously being encouraged with tax write-offs for these endeavors. Second, federal funding has emphasized start-up or first costs for transit systems. A funding program that cannot support continuing costs mitigates against management innovation.

## Future Research Needs

There are several concerns under the topic of internal management that could be addressed from the perspective of behavior science theory and research. For example, the area of employee and management motivation could be looked at from the viewpoint of behavior modification to analyze the reinforcers (incentives) that might increase productivity. This could be done either by analyzing successful operations or by short-term experimentation. Much could be said for a better analysis of the environmental factors that currently operate as reinforcers or punishment for operators and management. Attitudinal research could also help determine variables that impact motivation. The use of organizational development techniques (for example, team building, career planning, internal communications, human relations training) could be applied to humanizing the transit organization and in turn impacting motivation.

Another area of behavior science contribution involves training and testing programs for transit employees. For example, what type of college course work might best train individuals for transit management? How could innovation or better management skills be introduced into the thinking and actions of current management? It would be useful to develop testing procedures for transit operators that would simultaneously select the many desired attributes for this position. It is well to point out that research is needed to determine what these desired attributes are!

Finally, research needs to address the important issue of a transit system organizational structure. Transit systems operate in complex environments, often under conflicting mandates and political realities. Research that correlates different organizational structures with success would be of significance. Documented experimentation with innovative organizational models should also be encouraged.

## CONSUMER RELATIONS

At the introduction of the consumer relations topic, the workshop moved immediately into a group discussion. The discussion centered around transit marketing in general, that is, the best comprehensive strategies to satisfy existing patrons while simultaneously attracting new riders. Five marketing subemphases evolved: transit marketing per se, market segmentation, transit information and education, transit incentives and disincentives, and research and implementation strategies and techniques.

There were many comments in regard to transit marketing and the place marketing occupies in the organizational structure of a transit system. This position ought to be on at least an equal basis with planning and operations so that an integrated systematic marketing approach (dealing simultaneously with product-service, price, and promotion) could be implemented.

The discussants then observed that marketing was a "hot" transit topic a few years ago but has since lost some of its luster for the following reasons: First, transit marketing commonly was viewed simply as advertising and promotion and was not implemented in a systematic fashion. Next, transit marketing resources were quite constrained. Further, there were few standardized indexes, or rules of thumb, with which managers could evaluate marketing efforts. Finally, the potential payoff for expensive market research was not understood, and most marketing efforts were simply turned into advertising campaigns.

The discussion of market segmentation ranged from comments on how to do market segmentation to its application. Generally, much segmentation has been carried out, but examples of implementing what the segmentation studies suggest are less evident. For example, there are not many good cases of truly different types of transit services for various market segments. When different services exist, there is less than ideal integration between them. There is the danger of building a transit system around one market segment, such as the transportation deprived or the poor, and then expecting it to attract other segments, for example, middle-class car drivers. Indeed, middle-class car drivers may be even less prone to use transit once it is used predominantly by the transit deprived. The goal of making energy conservation and use of mass transit attractive to car drivers may be in conflict with the goal of transportation for the transportation deprived from a marketing point of view. Wide-scale social acceptance of change does not typically originate from the deprived, or have-nots. Appropriate segmentation studies with implementation could conceivably circumvent this problem.

The discussion then turned to transit information aids and education. Little empirical evidence for effective information aids exists; this is an important area for research and application. The relationship of the geographic transit route structure to consumer comprehension of the system is also important. If human perceptual variables were incorporated into route design, consumers might understand a transit system much better.

Transit education, as part of a comprehensive transportation education program, should be offered as an integral component of public education. Transportation education should be incorporated into programs for people of all ages. In particular, it would address topics as varied as how to read a transit map to knowledge about transit's relative level of energy consumption.

The small amount of systematic, controlled research on transit incentives and disincentives has not led to specific conclusions about their effect on transit ridership. Very little is known about incentives other than economic ones. The incentive/disincentive value of travel time, comfort, security, safety, and stress was discussed. Research is needed to factor out people's cues for comfort, security, and safety. From his experience, one participant noted that perceived and actual security and safety were probably more salient incentives/disincentives than price manipulations. There were several comments on the problems inherent in focusing on incentives or disincentives alone, not considering their joint implementation. Behavior modification could offer a systematic framework from which to view and research appropriate incentives (reinforcers) and disincentives (punishers) for transit use.

The final item discussed, in terms of consumer relations, was research and implementation strategies and techniques. There are severe problems with using data collected and reported by one transit system. For example, the data could have been collected in a fashion unique to a particular system and not transferable to another situation. Further, a selective bias of appropriate/inappropriate data could emerge. Comment was made on the need for short-range demand models that are easy to implement.

There is a need to carry out more transit experiments to assess salient variables that alter ridership and to view research in an incremental fashion. First, an attitude survey might be carried out. A concept could then be developed and implemented, on a limited scale, in experimental fashion. If the experiment is judged a success (according to prestated objectives), full-scale implementation of the program could occur. This incremental method is contrasted to full system implementation based on only preliminary data such as market segmentation carried out via a survey instrument.

Regarding future research needs, it is fairly evident that the behavior sciences could contribute much to the consumer relations topic. Cognitive and perceptual psychology and communication theory could contribute to the design of transit information aids. Behavior modification and marketing theory have the potential to pinpoint the salient incentives and disincentives for transit usage. Attitudinal and psychophysical measurement techniques, psychophysiological indicators, and theories of small group dynamics could help segment transit markets and measure their reactions to service variables. Theories of learning could contribute to the design of transportation education programs. Finally, and of great importance, the experimental and field research techniques developed by the behavioral sciences would be of significant value in determining the transit variables that impact the consumer and potential consumer.


POLITICAL VARIABLES AND
SUPPORT CONSTITUENCIES

Issues and Discussion

The first focus was on defining the constituent groups for public mass transit. These groups are many and include riders, unions, transit organizations (for example, individual transit systems, American Public Transit Association), merchants served by transit, planners, media, the transportation disadvantaged, the elderly, and the handicapped. These groups are quite diverse and often do not agree on transit goals and objectives. Furthermore, each individual group vacillates from dynamic to static phases, depending on current circumstances.

The observation was made that highways, for example, have strong advocates in the construction industry and in politics. Political advocates have been backed by citizen majorities because highways mean economic development. In contrast, transit, broadly defined to include paratransit, does not automatically engender such strong advocate groups, making the task of garnering and maintaining support more difficult. In sum, the varied and complex constituencies for public transit pose a substantial challenge to transit management in carrying out the planning, implementation, and maintenance of transit services.

Two conditions seem to be necessary in order to initiate new transit programs. First, there must be a general societal approval of the need for such a program. Second, a strong nucleus of individuals must carry the plans through to completion. In developing the transit program, these leaders must first develop broad support for the plan. Second, they must obtain legislative support and, finally, administrative support. Attention to these subtle sociopolitical factors can truly enhance and ease the planning and implementation of new transit programs.

The discussion moved from planning to the maintenance of constituent support for an existing transit operation. The central theme was that very clear goals and objectives for a transit system must be set and then met if public support is to continue. It was noted that it is quite dangerous (politically) to adopt unreasonable goals or, in other words, to promise too much.

Public involvement in goal and objective setting is important. Goals and objectives developed in this way tend to be viewed favorably by the public, and the process mitigates against feelings of alienation. Further, it promotes public understanding of the constraints and realities of transit operations (for example, budgets). This creates a public educated about transit so that an organization does not have to hard sell the attributes of service.

Once realistic goals are set, preferably via public participation, the most important tasks are evaluating the transit system and giving feedback about it to constituents. "Our ridership goals were met or exceeded this year" is a statement that will surely contribute to continued support. It was noted that often the media are primary evaluators of transit service. Attention and care should be continually paid to media relations so that accurate and timely pictures of what they find are developed.

The discussants also noted the contexts of general goals and objectives of transit. In the early 1960s a dominant theme was the reduction of urban congestion. This evolved in the mid-1960s to providing service for the transit dependent; this was a time of much social unrest over the conditions of deprived groups in general. In the early 1970s the central goal became environmental considerations; energy concerns have dominated from 1974 to the present. However, an equally dominant goal evolved in 1978 and will be very strong over the foreseeable future. This goal is monetary. Transit must operate under the constraints of taxpayer revolts while simultaneously providing energy-efficient and cost-effective transportation alternatives to the private automobile. Transit must be sold on its economic efficiency both to society and to the individual. For this reason, transit economic audits and energy audits might be evaluation data that should be made public.

## Future Research Needs

Two major efforts for the future were recommended. First, it was suggested that work be carried out to help transit organizations cope with changing political environments. Research on community power structure and techniques for identifying interest groups could be applied to this task. Specific attention should be paid to group identification techniques that are not biased and that promote a better representation of the community. A case study analysis of successful group identification techniques would be useful. Once theory, research, and the case studies have defined maximally effective identification techniques, they should be tried out under controlled conditions to gather additional data for further refinement.

The second endeavor that deserves attention is to develop techniques by which transit operators might identify a community consensus on goals. Approaches such as attitude surveys, communication-innovation dissemination techniques, persuasion techniques, and social movement theory might be of help. Developing better techniques for generating citizen participation in both planning and implementation stages also would help. Parallel to the effort to develop community goal assessment techniques is a need for methods and strategies of transit system self-evaluation to know whether the community-derived goals are being met.

# Environmental and Social Impact Analysis

## Robert E. Skinner, Jr. and Mary Lynn Tischer

## INTRODUCTION

The charge to our workshop was to examine environmental and social impact analysis related to transportation projects with respect to the three conference objectives: identify issues, evaluate potential application of behavioral science methods, and recommend focus areas and opportunities for further research.

For the purpose of the discussions, social impact assessment represents an attempt to focus on and systematically analyze the effects of transportation actions on individuals and social and cultural systems. It involves forecasting the probable social consequences of events, those secondary effects of transportation actions that alter, either positively or negatively, the structure or functioning of the social order. Implicit in this idea is that transportation serves a linkage function by interrelating and structuring the larger systems. Social impact assessment recognizes the dynamics of the interrelationships and seeks to understand how the systems will alter in the presence of a change in transportation inputs to the systems.

Environmental impact assessment involves judgment of the social as well as physical effects of transportation activities but is often used to indicate the physical impact on the ecosystem, air quality, and noise levels. In such a case, the tertiary impacts on the social and economic systems are implied.

Impact research is generally project-oriented. The impacts are thus bounded by geographic area or community limits. They are also focused on relatively short-range repercussions of the transportation actions. One analytic assumption generally made is that all other elements of the system of interest are unchanging and the research questions revolve around the singular impacts of the transportation action.

Because one goal of the social impact analysis process is to involve publics in decision making about projects that affect them, the scope of our workshop also included opportunities for applying behavioral science techniques to citizen participation programs and activities.

152

During the workshop, we found it difficult to focus exclusively on environmental and social impact analysis without first discussing and seeking consensus on some broader issues. Specifically, we discussed issues related to the general utilization of behavioral information in transportation planning. As a consequence, a number of the conclusions and recommendations that were developed by the workshop are not strictly limited to environmental and social impact analysis.

The remainder of this report will first describe the frameworks used to guide our discussion and then summarize workshop findings and recommendations.

## TOPIC 1: DISCUSSION FRAMEWORKS

Identification of impacts presumes an understanding of the interrelationship between the environment and the transportation system. It appeared necessary to begin a discussion of impact assessment with a general discussion of the role of behavioral sciences in specifying the system interactions.

During our deliberations two different but related discussion frameworks emerged that were used to guide and focus our discussions. It can be noted at this point that we found it very difficult to maintain a constant focus, and these frameworks proved helpful in this regard. In addition, the frameworks provide a needed perspective for interpreting some of the workshop conclusions summarized in subsequent sections.

The first discussion framework is based upon the nature and role of behavioral information in transportation planning. It can be stated in three questions of increasing breadth and policy significance:

1. Why do people respond as they do to transport systems, services, choices, and the like?
2. If we wish people to change their response to these various transportations, how do we accomplish it?
3. Ought we attempt such changes?

For the sake of expediency, we attempted to focus on the first two of these questions; however, the third kept reoccurring in our discussions. This was expressed most frequently by one of the behavioral scientists present; he noted that rather than attempting to modify behavior to utilize sometimes ill-conceived transport systems, we should seek behavioral assistance in designing systems to better meet user needs.

This latter viewpoint is represented to some extent in the second discussion framework which identifies three possible steps in the use of behavioral science techniques in transportation planning: (1) diagnostic research, (2) collection and use of attitudinal information, and (3) prediction.

Diagnostic Research

Diagnostic research linking behavior and transportation is concerned with developing a fundamental understanding of how travel decisions are made and the primary and secondary level social interactions and effects that result from these decisions. Diagnostic research should provide the foundation needed for the subsequent collection and direct use of attitudinal information in system design and in the predictions of the behavioral consequences of transport actions.

The general view of the workshop was that much needs to be done in the area of diagnostic research, particularly as transportation planning shifts its emphasis from major capital investments to the management and operation of existing facilities and services. There are many transportation systems management (TSM) actions, especially those involving demand modifications/restraint, for which the behavioral response is highly uncertain and the potential indirect social impacts could be adverse, affecting the overall effectiveness of the entire action.

One example that was cited as an illustration of this phenomenon involves staggered work hours. Staggering work hours directly affects work-trip timing and can reduce peak-period demands. However, less directly, staggered work hours may lead to lifestyle changes for not only the worker but other household members as well. These lifestyle changes may include modifications to the total household tripmaking for work and nonwork purposes. In addition, the degree and type of lifestyle changes will affect, in turn, the citizen acceptance of a staggered work hour program. Generally, transportation planners are unprepared to deal with anything more than the direct transportation consequences of staggered work hours or many other TSM actions.

Collection and Use of Attitudinal Information

This step involves the direct use of behavioral and attitudinal information in project planning. Most importantly, this information should be used to assist in dimensioning the problems to be solved or goals to be attained by transportation improvements and in the development of alternatives.

It is at this point that planners should be concerned with using behavioral information to design more responsive transport systems rather than with attempting to modify behavior to utilize specific transportation facilities. During the workshop discussions, Pat Burnett described some relevant research she had conducted which involved the use of attitudinal information in identifying and refining specific transportation alternatives for analysis.

Though not everyone always agreed, there were a number of behavioral research techniques mentioned that could be used for both diagnostic research and the collection of attitudinal information for use in problem definition and alternatives development. These included focus groups, attitude surveys, construct elicitation, key person interviews, opinion leader interviews, and game simulations.

### Prediction

The prediction of the consequences of various transport actions using behavioral methods would seem to be a logical extension of the first two analysis steps discussed above. There was general agreement in the workshop, however, that at least in terms of many social impacts we do not yet understand the interrelationship enough to attempt prediction. Furthermore, the view was expressed by some that the primary benefit of behavioral knowledge related to social impacts will be obtained through a better understanding of present needs and attitudes. To some extent, a general mistrust of predictive techniques was noted, considering our present level of understanding.

### TOPIC 2: QUALITATIVE VERSUS QUANTITATIVE INFORMATION

The workshop participants agreed that transportation planners have not sufficiently and effectively incorporated the use of qualitative information into the planning process. We felt this was particularly critical to the assessment of social and environmental impacts.

Qualitative information is important in its own right for problem definition, alternatives development, and impact evaluation. Moreover, it is often more directly usable by decision makers than quantitative information. Qualitative information is also important as a precursor to the collection of quantitative information. Qualitative studies can identify which parameters require quantitative measurement and how they can best be measured.

It is believed that the behavioral sciences have much to offer in providing appropriate techniques for the collection of qualitative information and in educating engineers and planners in its use. Specific techniques that were cited include those listed previously such as focus groups, in-depth personal surveys, and game simulations.

Whereas the bulk of our discussion on this topic addressed the need for a balance in the use of qualitative and quantitative information, one transportation researcher argued that qualitative information was more work significant than quantitative information. This view was based upon a mistrust of quantitative methods or, perhaps more properly, a recognition of their limitation. It was also linked to a desire to disaggregate the regional planning process closer to individual neighborhoods and population subgroups.


TOPIC 3: PROJECT EVALUATION

The demonstration and the evaluation of innovative transportation actions offer an important opportunity for conducting the needed diagnostic research involving behavioral relationships. The workshop members agreed that, unfortunately, the history of transportation demonstration projects has been disappointing. Demonstration projects have been conceived for a variety of reasons, including political favoritism, and all too often experimental design has been an afterthought. Indeed, some projects have been implemented in such an apparent rush that no thought seems to have been given to evaluation at all, and rich research opportunities were lost.

Another problem with demonstration projects has been a tendency to treat them individually rather than in a building block context. The success of an individual project has been defined not in terms of whether or not the experimental design was properly implemented, but rather in terms of a perception of the suitability of the transportation action being tested. From an experimental standpoint, a demonstration can be successful regardless of whether the transport action being tested seems meritorious based on the demonstration results.

Perhaps more serious than our inability to properly devise and implement demonstration projects has been the general failure of transportation planning professionals to adequately and consistently evaluate the effectiveness of transportation actions and policies. Unless there is blatant evidence to the contrary, the basic assumption seems to be that a transportation action that was implemented on a permanent basis is achieving the intended objective with no significant adverse side effects.

Thus, at present transportation planners are not even using the tools and techniques they already possess for project evaluation, much less using methods from the behavioral sciences. As a first step, the important role of experimentation and routine project evaluation must be established. Once established, the participants agreed, transportation planners should draw heavily upon experiences of the behavioral sciences in experimental and quasi-experimental design.

## TOPIC 4: CITIZEN PARTICIPATION

Perhaps more than any other area discussed in the workshop, citizen participation programs already utilize a number of behavioral science techniques. These include attitude surveys, delphi, and focus groups. These techniques and their potential utility are summarized in Table 7.1. It was noted, however, that these techniques are sometimes not properly applied, and that other promising behavioral science techniques are not used at all. Three reasons were cited for this situation:

1. Despite documentation prepared by agencies such as the Federal Highway Administration, many transportation planners do not have sufficient information and guidance available to select and use behavioral science techniques for citizen participation programs.
2. Many of the techniques require specialized skills and training in the behavioral sciences that cannot be developed simply by the use of manuals and short courses.
3. Finally, there exists in many quarters a lack of commitment to the concept of participatory planning and a consequent reluctance to expend the resources necessary to apply innovative citizen participation techniques.

If a renewed commitment to participatory planning is made and adequate resources and skilled behavioral science professionals are made available, there appear to be a number of promising new behavioral science applications to citizen participation. One which was singled out at the workshop involves the application of organizational development theory, particularly as it relates to small group decision making. The use of organizational development theories and techniques could be extremely useful in establishing stable and enduring mechanisms for citizen participation.

Though the need for long-term mechanisms for citizen participation is recognized, we have been generally unsuccessful in establishing them. In this regard, it was noted at the workshop that

TABLE 7.1

Application of Citizen Involvement Techniques

| Technique | Audience | | | Application of Techniques Areas of Utilization | | | | | | Timing | | |
|---|---|---|---|---|---|---|---|---|---|---|---|---|
| | (1) | (2) | (3) | (4) | (5) | (6) | (7) | (8) | (9) | (10) | (11) | (12) |
| **Techniques using media** | | | | | | | | | | | | |
| 1. Participatory T.V. | X | X | X | | | | | | X | X | X | X |
| 2. Newsletter | | X | X | X | | | | | | X | X | X |
| 3. News releases | | X | X | X | X | | | | | X | X | X |
| 4. Public service announcements | | X | X | X | | | | | | X | X | X |
| 5. Paid advertisement | | X | X | | | | | | | X | X | X |
| **Research techniques** | | | | | | | | | | | | |
| 1. Sample polls | | X | X | | | | X | X | | X | X | X |
| 2. Community profile | | X | | | | X | | | | X | X | X |
| **Political techniques** | | | | | | | | | | | | |
| 1. Citizen referendum | | | X | | X | | | | | X | X | X |
| 2. Lobbying | | | X | | X | | | | | X | X | X |
| **Structure group techniques** | | | | | | | | | | | | |
| 1. Nominal groups | | X | X | | | | X | X | | X | X | X |
| 2. Delphi technique | | X | X | | | | X | X | | X | X | X |
| 3. Charrette | | X | X | X | | | X | X | | X | X | X |
| 4. Workshops | | X | X | X | | | X | X | | X | X | X |
| **Large group meetings** | | | | | | | | | | | | |
| 1. Public hearings | | X | X | X | | X | X | X | | X | X | X |
| 2. Public meetings | | X | | | | X | X | X | | X | X | X |
| **Bureaucratic decentralization techniques** | | | | | | | | | | | | |
| 1. Field office | | X | | | | | X | | | X | X | X |
| 2. Information van | | X | | | | | X | | | X | X | X |
| **Techniques using interveners** | | | | | | | | | | | | |
| 1. Ombudsman | | X | | | | | | | | X | X | X |
| 2. Citizen advisory committees | | X | | | | | | | | X | X | X |
| 3. Advocacy planning | | X | X | | | | X | X | | X | X | X |

(1) Professional
(2) Citizens
(3) Public officials
(4) Public information program of agencies
(5) Citizen groups to influence public agencies
(6) Planners to gather information
(7) Planners to obtain feedback
(8) Planners to evaluate/select alternate
(9) Unusual technique applicable to involvement of a wide cross-section of public, professionals, and public officials in planning process
(10) System planning
(11) Corridor/subarea planning
(12) Project planning

Source: Technical Council Committee 6-Y-7, "Methods for Citizen Involvement," Traffic Engineering, August 1975, p. 12.

there is a critical distinction between confrontation planning (which often occurs) and participatory planning (which occurs much less frequently). Confrontation planning is a short-term, one-shot affair that is conducted in a highly charged adversary atmosphere. This volatile atmosphere is not conducive to effective and meaningful participation regardless of the array techniques, behavioral and otherwise, that are utilized. Participatory planning, on the other hand, should be a continuing exercise that short-circuits the need for confrontation planning. It offers the time and opportunity for reflective and effective participation. However, without an immediate and perhaps controversial issue, it is difficult to generate and maintain broad-based citizen interest. It is in this area that the workshop participants believe the organizational development techniques hold particular promise.

As a final point, it was noted that there may well be a need for post-project evaluation of the citizen participation process to assist in developing and selecting more effective techniques.

TOPIC 5: MORE RESPONSIVE PLANNING PROCESS

The workshop participants agreed that behavioral science techniques could be utilized to make the planning process more responsive to the needs and concerns of decision makers. In some cases this might reduce the scope of required technical analyses, but, more likely, it might refine, reformat, and perhaps redirect technical analysis. Potentially applicable behavioral science techniques identified in the workshop include opinion leader interviews, political science studies (for example, Federal Highway Administration 1976a), and negotiation techniques aimed at achieving consensus.

CONCLUDING COMMENT

No one theory or methodology defines impact assessment. At best, it can be said that guidelines are provided for the identification, prediction, and evaluation of the effects of transportation actions. As more information is accumulated on the interrelationships of the transportation system and the environment, the components of the environment being impacted and the ranges of impacts will be easier to specify. The behavioral sciences can be particularly helpful in developing that theoretical framework. Additionally, the behavioral sciences have identified data collection and measurement techniques as well as research and evaluation designs that are particularly appropriate for transportation impact assessment.

As a final comment, it was concluded at the workshop that there are a number of promising behavioral science techniques that could be applied to urban transportation studies, especially in the area of social and environmental impact assessment. However, these techniques are not a cure-all, and much needs to be done before some can be applied in practice. One clear need, which was evidenced by the workshop discussions, was for transportation planners to increase the specificity of questions for which behavioral science techniques might help provide answers. There is a gulf in terms of training and experience between transportation planners and behavioral science which tends to impede the use of behavioral science techniques in transportation planning. The discussion of this conference represented not a starting point but part of continuing efforts to bridge this gap.

## REFERENCES

Dunlap, R. 1975. Sociological and Social-Psychological Perspectives on Environmental Issues: A Bibliography. Council of Planning Librarians, no. 916.

Federal Highway Administration. 1976a. Effective Citizen Participation in Transportation Planning, vols. 1 and 2. U.S. Department of Transportation. Washington, D.C.

_____. 1976b. Social and Economic Effects of Highways. U.S. Department of Transportation. Washington, D.C.

Finsterbusch, K. 1976. A Methodology for Social Impact Assessments of Highway Locations. Report FHWA-MD-R-76-20, Bureau of Research, Maryland Department of Transportation.

Llewellyn, L., C. Goodman, and G. Hare, eds. 1975. Social Impact Assessment: A Sourcebook for Highway Planners. National Bureau of Standards. Washington, D.C.

Steiber, S. 1976. Evaluation Research: A Bibliographic Overview. Council of Planning Librarians, no. 975.

Struening, E., and M. Guttentag, eds. 1975. Handbook of Evaluation Research. Beverly Hills, Calif.: Sage.

U.S. Department of Transportation. 1975. Environmental Assessment Notebook Series. Washington, D.C.

# Transportation for the Mobility Limited
## Arthur Saltzman and Robert Paaswell

A workshop was held for the purpose of integrating attitudinal and behavioral modeling and measuring techniques into transportation planning for the mobility limited. Planning for these population subgroups is complicated because (1) the groups are highly heterogeneous; (2) federal and state policy in this area is rapidly evolving and changing; (3) a wide range of solutions with tremendous cost variation have been proposed to serve the mobility limited; (4) there are many suppliers of transportation for the mobility limited, ranging from public to private; and (5) a great deal of supply is sponsored or regulated by nontransportation sources (for example, Department of Health, Education and Welfare).

The workshop was to consider all mobility limited persons. However, because elderly and handicapped transportation issues so dominate the current situation, it was difficult to deal with any other groups. In fact, most of our discussion left the elderly aside and concentrated on the handicapped groups, reflecting the salience of the wheelchair accessibility issue. Legislative activity in Congress, rule making in the Department of Transportation (DOT) and the Department of Health, Education and Welfare, and litigation in the courts have caused the accessibility and mobility of handicapped persons to dominate public transportation planning.

The specific issue areas discussed by workshop participants fall into three categories: (1) institutional issues, (2) demand and supply, and (3) design. A review of the development of federal policy on transportation for the elderly and the handicapped allowed the institutional issues to be raised. Basic demand and supply issues were not discussed as extensively as institutional issues but are nonetheless important because they provide a basis for providing solutions. Finally, equipment and facility design issues often appeared to be an issue separate from the previous two, but the linkages between equipment design and demand were recognized. The sections that follow summarize the workshop deliberations in each of these areas. Concluding the workshop report is a review of the behavioral science tools and techniques that are applicable to the issue areas.

INSTITUTIONAL ISSUES

First, we considered how federal laws for the mobility limited had developed. As a result of a number of events, the elderly and the handicapped have become significant pressure groups in the political arena. Recommendations from the White House Conference on Aging (1972) directly affected upcoming urban mass transportation legislation. Section 16 of the Urban Mass Transportation Act, as amended, was one of the first attempts by Congress to influence accessibility of mass transit and to focus attention on mobility for elderly and handicapped persons. Transportation for the handicapped escalated to a major policy problem with the passage of Section 504, Rehabilitation Act of 1973. This act requires that all publicly financed facilities be accessible to the handicapped.

Going beyond legislation, our discussion dealt with how regulations were developed to implement these laws. In general UMTA did not make the transit industry respond to early Congressional mandates until the elderly and the handicapped went to court. This brought up the issue of community participation and pressure groups, and we discussed items such as how to respond to special interest group conflict. Are there techniques that we can use to resolve some of the conflict that developed as a result of ignoring elderly and handicapped group needs? Another issue that surfaced was whether the vocal minorities represented the local handicapped community. Was there reasonable representation of all factions of the handicapped?

A more basic institutional issue is defining the mobility limited and determining the variations in their transportation problems. Lifestyles of the elderly and the handicapped are not homogeneous; tremendous diversity exists within these groups. Transportation planners have tended to view the elderly and the handicapped in a very simplistic and stereotypical way. They have lumped these people together and considered anybody who was elderly, handicapped, young, poor, or old as transportation disadvantaged. More recently, transportation planners, with the assistance of behavioral scientists, have defined these groups based on functional disabilities. However, federal activity in the mid-1970s still identified only elderly and handicapped persons as deserving special attention from the transit industry.

The planning requirements promulgated by UMTA in the Federal Register of April 30, 1976, indicate that special attention must be given to the transportation needs of elderly and handicapped persons. Projects designed to benefit elderly and handicapped persons are required from each urban area as a condition for receiving UMTA capital or operating assistance. The transportation improvement programs (TIPS) submitted to UMTA after September 30, 1976, must include these projects as part of the program's annual elements.

These rules give each locale flexibility in the way it will comply. An area may propose its own technique for serving the elderly, nonambulatory (in wheelchairs), and semiambulatory persons, or it can opt for any one of three suggested minimum levels of efforts:

1. Five percent of Section 5 formula funds allocated to an urban area must be used to serve these groups. Special efforts in planning and implementing projects specifically designed for these groups are required.

2. All buses bought must be wheelchair-accessible until at least one-half of the fleet is accessible, or a substitute service that would result in comparable coverage and service must be provided.

3. A system must be available to ensure that at least ten round trips per week would be provided, if requested, for every nonambulatory or semiambulatory person in the urban area.

The special effort approach (option one) was the one generally taken by most urban areas. This was the situation when UMTA had to respond to Section 504 of the Rehabilitation Act of 1973, requiring all facilities purchased with federal funds to be accessible to nonambulatory persons. UMTA 504 regulations focused on accessible facilities rather than requiring equivalent services for the handicapped to solve their mobility problems. Workshop members discussed the viability of this regulatory approach versus a process-and-guidelines approach, which the Federal Highway Administration often employs.

An associated supply side issue at the workshop was how to allow for a variety of local solutions to accommodate the diverse users and local characteristics, while ensuring that a substantial effort is made to solve the problem.

Finally, the subject of implementing the 504 regulations brought up the issue of resource constraints. Inflationary impact has become a major consideration of every federal activity. If UMTA's 504 regulations are fully implemented, it is likely to have a disastrous effect on the transit industry. Funds that are used for mobility limited groups tend to decrease service for the general population, and, therefore, considerable resistance to the 504 regulations occurs among transit operators. Workshop participants also reviewed future fuel constraints and their possible impacts on serving the mobility limited.

The regulatory process for meeting the intent of the law was developed out of pressure from a small but well-organized lobby.

The concept of accessibility posed by the handicapped was taken literally by DOT and a hardware solution resulted. Many operators or representatives of metropolitan planning organizations (MPO) in the panel did not believe this represented the universe of acceptable solutions. Thus, it was suggested that behavioral scientists perform a research role to describe and interpret the behavior of both the lobby groups and the government groups responsible for developing legislation. This would be derived from processes used in industrial psychology. Of particular interest would be the pressures within a group to arrive at a particular decision (hardware versus software and the like). Behavioral scientists also could develop a process of mediation between the lobbyist and the regulator. The mediator (psychologist, sociologist, or economist) would have to understand the costs associated with the results of any final action.

The prediction by sociologists and social psychologists of the social impact of regulations to assist the elderly also must be carried out. Will improved delivery of transit actually have an impact on the lives of the disadvantaged, and is this impact measurably beneficial? What social factors, other than transportation, must be considered to have the effect that transportation regulations implicitly assume will occur? Sociologists must help define whether transportation is the important key to a higher quality of life that the disadvantaged require. Precisely, are the costs to be incurred for fully accessible systems the best investment for federal capital, or are there alternative investments that would have greater effects? It was felt that social science analysis is necessary, since engineering and economic analyses are so ingrained in institutional decision making as to make it difficult to step back and reassess their policy.

## DEMAND AND SUPPLY

After lamenting the current situation, the group took a retrospective look at how the problem of the mobility limited would be approached if we had it to do all over again. If we had this chance, consideration of basic demand and supply issues would be important. One of the issues was how perceived demand translates into actual demand by population subgroups. Looking to the future, we discussed techniques to determine impacts under changing demographic and socioeconomic conditions.

The demand analysis seemed to lend itself to a structured set of questions that could be raised and evaluated by applied psychologists and sociologists working as a team with engineers and economists. The fundamental problem would be to separate demand analysis from counting numbers of people in a specific category who would ride a particular piece of hardware and to start with a needs analysis. Based on a needs analysis, implementation procedures would become more obvious. Based on the types of systems proposed, the value of investments made for transportation could be determined.

Of particular importance is establishing the role that transportation is to play in the overall quality of life of the transportation disadvantaged. Little real analysis has been done on the range and priority of activities for these groups and the modes of transportation acceptable to them. A number of trade-off analyses would be part of an overall demand analysis to determine the portion of costs the disadvantaged ought to pay to have improved transport. For example, investment in an accessible fixed-route system might preclude investment in coordinated paratransit. The community would be purchasing, primarily, access to work—the predominant role of fixed-route transit. This purchase could be at the expense of more dispersed travel to a broader range of activities. Sociologists must tell us more of the overall daily life of the transportation disadvantaged and provide a better description of their universe. Before demand analysis can be carried out, it must be established whether the varied cohorts of this heterogeneous group have access to a car. Demand analysis can then use behavioral and attitudinal models to link the trip need with the attributes of the alternative modes. Acceptability of the modes based on the importance of the activity, the accessibility of the activity, and the ease or hardship of using the mode will make demand analysis relevant to the needs of these groups.

Again, one point continually emphasized in the workshop was the lobbying strength of the handicapped group for fully accessible public transit. Although it removes the work-trip barrier for the group, this solution does little to meet the larger amount of latent demand of the transportation disadvantaged.

These demand analyses must not start, as is the case now, with a preconceived solution (dial-a-bus for medical trips, lifts on public transit, and the like). Rather we must start with a true needs analysis, then test alternative solutions against their costs and the relative proportion of trip needs (by priority of activity) that must be met. To do this the planning process must stimulate more government-group interaction, with trained social science planners as mediators. Neither group must be permitted the knee-jerk reaction that now passes for disadvantaged planning. Both must understand the extent of social research needed to develop a body of knowledge for disadvantaged travel as great as now exists for travel for the general population.

On the supply side we were interested in how supply attributes affect demand. For example, an operational supply issue is the role of paratransit and conventional transit operators. The need for each of these types of operators was recognized, but we were interested in an assessment of the best service mix.

Coordination issues were also reviewed. Should we coordinate to reap the proposed economic benefits of large-scale operations? What are the benefits of coordination among transit and paratransit operators, and if we do coordinate, what are the best techniques to use?

Finally, combining supply and demand issues, the group discussed the adequacy of programs to solve mobility problems. What solutions are currently being offered, and how well are they solving basic mobility problems? The issue of accessibility versus mobility came up, and it was suggested that behavioral approaches are needed to determine the range of solutions and how, in particular, accessible buses could solve mobility problems.


DESIGN

The development of Transbus provided a convenient vehicle for raising some of these design issues, but, unfortunately, it illustrates a situation where behavioral scientist inputs to the design of a vehicle to advance the state-of-the-art were only sparse. With Transbus, UMTA tried to accommodate too many objectives. Transbus was originally an attempt by the industry and UMTA to design and develop a better and cheaper bus, with only minor concern for accessibility.

Reflecting workshop participants' diversity of background, there were many different perspectives on Transbus, but, in general, the group felt the first major mistake was to add additional design requirements to a bus that was to become the industry standard. Requiring a lower floor and a ramp or lift substantially compromised the ability to design a low-cost vehicle. The second major error made in the development of Transbus was the attempt to put a prototype research and development effort into on-line operation before it was completely tested and proved reliable.

Certainly, behavioral scientists should have had more influence on Transbus design. Perhaps more important was the role that could have been played by behavioral scientists in the agencies that were making the Transbus policy decisions. They could have pointed these agencies toward the right problems. But behavioral scientists in the agencies need management support; only then can human factor analysis be a valuable tool in system design.

The easiest area to identify for behavioral science input is the issue of design. In the design of hardware for buses there are many areas where human factor analysis can be used. Ramps, elevators, seats, and stations must be designed for all users. We need also to look at interfaces: when we design a system it must be with consideration for the total system and not only how to build a better bus. For example, there is little use for a ramp which lets a non-ambulatory person out onto a curb that is not accessible in a wheelchair.

## TECHNIQUES

Behavioral techniques that have potential in this area were discussed in the workshop. These techniques could focus on a number of specific areas of interest that deal with the disadvantaged:

1. Demand analysis—improved use of behavioral and attitudinal models, better understanding of psychometric analysis, development of multidimensional scaling (MDS) techniques, and improved standards for information collection through surveys and panels.
2. Supply analysis—human factors analysis of design, special training programs, and sensitivity training.
3. Institutional issues—the introduction of political science in solutions and improved understanding of behavioral theory applied to institutions and to conflicts between hierarchies of institutions.

In the demand area, the workshop emphasized the long-term problems of the disadvantaged. In particular, would short-term hardware solutions have a real impact on solving long-term mobility problems of the disadvantaged? Further, how are the profiles of the disadvantaged changing as urban form changes, rural areas grow again, and energy and economy of operation become major federal policy issues? We talked about attitude measurement, prediction of behavior from attitudes, and various survey design techniques as the behavioral scientist's input to demand.

On the supply side the workshop was concerned with coordination of service. Interorganizational theory gives considerable insight into the factors that induce and inhibit true cooperation. An additional issue on the supply side is the need for new programs and training for operators and maintenance personnel. Sensitivity training about the mobility limited and those who have special needs is important in that regard.

In reviewing institutional issues we deliberated on whether the political scientist should be considered a behavioral scientist. If political scientists use this title, then it is important for them to analyze the roles of the various participants in the decision-making process.

Behavioral scientists should have some input to the area of conflict resolution. Techniques such as group dynamics, role playing, and role of a skillful intermediary to help resolve conflicts are deemed important. Behavioral scientists who appear as expert witnesses also can have a direct influence on transportation for the mobility limited. Too, behavioral scientists can give advice to lobby groups on how to impact legislation. Finally, they can help develop evaluation techniques to determine whether the implemented solutions are solving transportation problems of the mobility limited.

# Energy Conservation in Transportation
## Carl S. Rappaport and Joseph Margolin

The Arab oil embargo of 1973-74 clearly demonstrated our
dependence on imported petroleum. Since that time our vulner-
ability has worsened as U. S. petroleum imports have increased
from one-third to one-half of total petroleum consumption. This
increasing dependence threatens to constrain our foreign policy objectives, weakens our national security, aggravates our balance of
payments deficit, and intensifies inflationary pressures. The U. S.
government has responded to this large and increasing dependence
by encouraging development of domestic energy sources, promoting
diversion to such plentiful fuels as coal, sponsoring research and
development on new fuels, establishing a strategic petroleum re-
serve, preparing contingency plans, and fostering energy conservation in buildings, industry, utilities, and transportation.

Transportation accounts for over half of the petroleum consumed in the United States. Prior to the embargo, the petroleum
intensity of transportation had been rising, due to increased vehicle-
miles of personal travel and ton-miles of freight transportation per
capita, increased modal energy intensities, shifts toward more
energy-intensive modes, and more use of petroleum relative to
other energy sources.

This report will describe the private and public responses to
the embargo; indicate some of the attitudinal, motivational, and behavioral obstacles to transportation energy conservation policies,
programs, and measures; list some contributions behavioral scientists might make to overcome these obstacles; and suggest specific
applications of behavioral science concepts and techniques to energy
conservation in the transportation sector.

## RESPONSES TO THE EMBARGO

The embargo brought about interesting, but rather minor,
changes in the attitudes and behaviors developed during the era of
increasing energy extravagance. These changes appeared to be related more to the uncertain availability of gasoline and to the incon-

venience of waiting in long lines at service stations than to the increased price of gasoline. Various socioeconomic groups responded
differently, depending on the nature and extent of their discretionary
travel and the availability of alternatives.

During and after the embargo, the federal government adopted
a number of policies to conserve fuel in the transportation sector.
Some of these were intended to increase energy efficiency within
each mode of transportation. Others were intended to shift transportation demand from energy-intensive modes to energy-efficient
ones. Still others were intended to reduce the demand for travel.

Within the area of increasing modal energy efficiencies, the
single most significant conservation measure is the fuel economy
standards program for automobiles and light trucks. Another significant measure is the 55-miles-per-hour speed limit, at which
motor vehicles operate with more fuel efficiency than at higher
speeds. The vehicles-in-use program encourages motorists to operate and to maintain their vehicles and to purchase equipment (for
example, radial tires) to increase fuel efficiency. The voluntary
truck and bus program encourages more fuel-efficient driving,
maintenance, and equipment in the truck and bus industries. Similarly, the air, rail, and maritime industries are taking steps to increase fuel efficiency. Many state and local highway departments
have improved traffic operations to conserve fuel.

Within the area of shifting modal demand, a significant measure is the ride-sharing program to promote the use of carpools
and vanpools, particularly for work trips. Encouraging diversion
of intercity passenger demand from auto or air to rail or bus will
generally increase energy efficiency. At appropriate times and in
appropriate places, diversion of urban passenger demand to transit
will increase energy efficiency. Transportation system management makes more effective use of existing transportation facilities
through low-capital policy measures; frequently, these alleviate
congestion, improve air quality, and promote energy conservation.

To reduce travel demand, measures have included substituting
telecommunications for transportation, promoting land use changes
which permit fewer or shorter trips or both, and lifestyle changes
which reduce dependence on travel.

Using 1985 as the time horizon, the measure with the highest
payoff in terms of fuel conserved is the automotive fuel economy
standards program. The 55-miles-per-hour speed limit and ride-
sharing programs are the measures with the next highest payoffs.

## POLICY OBSTACLES

The obstacles to effective implementation of these high-payoff measures are largely attitudinal, motivational, and behavioral. In the first place, attitudes, motivations, and behaviors developed during the era of increasing energy extravagance are unlikely to change overnight in the absence of clear and incontrovertible evidence as to the nature, extent, and timing of the nation's energy crisis.

Second, the end state of an energy-conserving social, economic, and political system—in both transportation and other energy-using sectors—is generally predictable, relatively clear, and apparently stable. However, the transition from an energy extravagance ethic in an era of cheap and plentiful supply to an energy conservation ethic in an era of expensive and scarce resources will be neither quick nor painless. Unfortunately, the management of unstable transitions is considerably less advanced than that of stable end states.

Third, transportation is a derived, or second-order demand. Almost always, the primary demand is the activity at the destination or the good or service obtained through transportation. Accordingly, the energy used in providing transportation services is a third-order demand, and the conservation of that energy is a fourth-order demand. It is no wonder that many individuals and institutions are uneasy about dealing with this level of abstraction.

Finally, it is easy to confuse contingency with continuing measures. Continuing measures are those which can appropriately be taken now or soon, even in the absence of a contingency such as an embargo. In contrast, contingency measures are those appropriately taken only in the event of a contingency.


## BEHAVIORAL SCIENCES

Behavioral scientists can help to overcome these attitudinal, motivational, and behavioral obstacles in the following ways:

- Designing and administering measurements of attitudes and opinions.
- Observing behavior, analyzing behavior modification, and understanding the linkages among attitudes, motivations, and behaviors.
- Designing and implementing research and evaluation plans and criteria to test or demonstrate alternative energy conservation programs.

- Understanding how and why individuals or firms decide whether, where, and by what mode to transport themselves or their commodities.
- Understanding the role of mobility in the American lifestyle, with particular emphasis on the American love affairs with the single-occupant automobile, light truck, and van and with the single-family, detached home in the suburbs or exurbs.
- Understanding the differences among socioeconomic, demographic, and geographic groups in terms of attitudes, motivations, behaviors, responses, and impacts.
- Understanding the influence of life cycle and roles on attitudes, motivations, and behaviors.

Behavioral scientists can help to overcome these obstacles by developing and updating answers to such questions as the following:

- What are the attitudes of various groups and individuals about the current energy situation? How do they expect it to change in the future?
- How are these attitudes changing through time as a result of actions by energy producers, transportation equipment manufacturers, transportation operators, and federal, state, and local governments?
- What are the motivations of various groups and individuals in their transportation decisions?
- What are the behaviors of various groups and individuals in their transportation decisions?
- What rewards or penalties or both would most effectively modify the behaviors of various groups and individuals in transportation energy-conserving ways?

In addition to helping overcome obstacles to energy conservation in the transportation sector, behavioral scientists can assist in a more positive fashion. Behavioral scientists can provide paradigms, principles, concepts, approaches, and techniques that help to identify, select, plan, design, implement, monitor, and evaluate policies, programs, and measures compatible with current and emerging attitudes, motivations, and behaviors.


BEHAVIORAL APPLICATIONS

This section discusses some of the actual and potential applications of the behavioral sciences to energy conservation in the transportation sector. It is organized along the lines suggested by David Hartgen in Chapter 5.

## Cognitive Structure

Since the embargo awakened our consciousness to the crucial role of energy in the American lifestyle, significant progress has been made in surveys to measure attitudes and changes in attitudes about energy consumption, conservation, efficiency, supply, demand, and price. For example, survey respondents have described their attitudes toward fuel-efficient cars, carpooling, and the 55-miles-per-hour speed limit.

Further research and applications are needed to understand the development of attitudes on complex and emerging issues on which political consensus is in the process of formation and on which there are relatively few unambiguous indications of the nature, extent, and timing of the problem. We need to know more about how people perceive and adapt to changing situations, how they determine whether the changes are permanent or temporary, and how they decide what actions to take in accommodation. We need to understand the asymmetry between rewards and punishments, between incentives and disincentives. For example, congressional and public reactions to proposed energy taxes were very different from those to the proposed energy rebates. On the other hand, the response to exclusive bus and carpool lanes depends in large part on whether or not the lanes were taken away from single-occupant automobiles driving in the same direction.

## Behavior

As in the case of attitudes, surveys have been effectively used to measure actual and planned behavior. For example, survey respondents have described their automobile purchases, their carpooling practices, and their compliance with the 55-miles-per-hour speed limit.

However, further research and applications are needed on effective ways to modify behavior in energy-conserving ways. Recent research in highway safety suggests that instructiveness is an important criterion. It is necessary to inform people of specific actions they can take to conserve fuel rather than merely directing them not to be "fuelish." Personal relevance is also important in behavior modification. The suggested actions must be relevant to the people concerned. Immediacy is important because a person is more likely to modify behavior if informed of suggested actions at an appropriate time and place. Conspicuous modeling is important because people tend to imitate opinion leaders who have modified their behavior in obvious ways. Motivating appeals are important to reach people in ways that motivate them to take actions they would not otherwise take. For example, the big use of small media may be more effective than the small use of big media. In other words, sending out flyers along with driver's license renewals may be more effective than a prime-time television spot.

Further research and applications are also needed on the linkages among attitudes, motivations, and behaviors; on effective ways to reinforce behavioral changes and prevent backsliding; on effective ways to test, monitor, and evaluate measures and responses on a small scale to avoid undesired or unanticipated impacts; and on the differences between behavioral responses to continuing and contingency actions.

## Learning

Further research and applications are needed on the processes by which individuals and institutions learn of changed situations and by which they decide to take actions compatible with the changes. There are time lags between the occurrence and recognition of the changes and between recognition and response. There are also diffusion patterns for recognition and response among groups and individuals. We need to know more about how to facilitate these processes, how to reduce time lags, and how to accelerate diffusion.

## Social Structure

Further research and applications are needed on the pervasive importance of transportation energy use in American lifestyles and on how this relationship will change through time, with changes in fuel prices and availabilities. Also, we need to know more about responses of various socioeconomic and demographic groups to these changes. We need to know more about the kinds of measures and appeals that are likely to be most effective with each. We need to consider equity in the distribution of transportation energy use so that undue burdens are not placed on particular groups.

Further research and applications are also needed on the changes in income, employment, and well-being that will result from the changed energy situation. Fuel prices and availabilities will alter relative wealth and influence positions of regions, groups, and individuals. Boom towns will appear to exploit energy materials, while other areas will suffer relative declines. Behavioral scientists could assist in easing such adaptions.

Finally, further research and applications are needed on effective ways to tailor transportation energy conservation actions to site-specific values, conditions, and institutions. While energy conservation is a national objective, its attainment will require the active involvement of states, metropolitan agencies, and localities. In fact, every conservation measure except the automotive fuel economy standards program will depend in significant part on actions by these units.

## System Design

Further research and applications are needed on human responses to fuel-efficient transportation facilities and vehicles. We need to know more about how consumers respond to smaller, lighter automobiles. We need to know more about the trend toward light trucks and vans which are selling at record levels. We need to know more about how actual and potential travelers react to design features in such modes as carpools, vanpools, urban buses, rapid transit, intercity buses, and railroads.

## Group/Organization

Further research and applications are needed on the formation and maintenance of interest groups in energy and transportation. In view of the pervasiveness of the interactions between transportation and energy, the enormous economic and political stakes involved, and our emotional attachment to particular modes of transportation, there is certain to be intensive and extensive lobbying for support at all levels of government and in the media. We need to know more about the relative influence of producer and consumer groups in both energy and transportation.

We also need to know how to foster the public interest in the context of powerful pressure groups, particularly since many people feel victimized by the petroleum companies, the petroleum-exporting countries, and the federal government. The public interest will undoubtedly best be served by a large number of relatively small actions to conserve energy in transportation, since there clearly is no panacea. Accordingly, the concept of just noticeable differences may help policy makers decide how far and how fast to move.


## AN INTERPRETIVE ASSESSMENT

As the preceding discussion has indicated, there are many more potential than actual applications of behavioral science concepts and techniques to energy conservation in the transportation sector. In order to encourage appropriate applications, transportation policy makers and planners must learn to express current or emerging issues in terms and at times that are meaningful to behavioral scientists. At the same time, behavioral scientists must learn to address these issues in problem-oriented ways which shed light on the responses to and impacts of alternative mixes of policies, programs, and measures. While there are many important applications of the behavioral sciences to the subject of transportation energy conservation, both transportation and behavioral experts must be careful to avoid overpromising what can be delivered and when. We must be aware of both the contributions and the limitations of behavioral science applications to energy conservation in the transportation sector.

During the last few decades, transportation policy development, planning, and evaluation have evolved from a civil and mechanical engineering orientation to embrace a number of concepts from social and behavioral sciences. As long as the major imperative of transportation policy in the United States was infrastructure development of post roads, canals, waterways, railroads, highways, and airports, the engineering orientation was timely and appropriate. As the focus shifted toward resource allocation and management, transportation turned to economics for concepts such as benefits and costs, supply and demand, efficiency and equity, price and income, and growth and employment. Still more recently, as the focus has shifted from transportation facilities to services, it has become increasingly clear that transportation policy development, planning, and evaluation should also look to the behavioral sciences—psychology, sociology, anthropology, political science, and marketing—for useful paradigms, principles, concepts, approaches, and techniques.

One example may clarify this process. During the last decade, mechanical engineers in government and industry developed a seatbelt interlock system to force people to do what was clearly in their own self-interest. The system was a technological success: it saved lives, its economic benefits exceeded its economic costs, and it had no significant adverse income distribution effects. Nevertheless, the system failed because no one investigated or understood the behavioral and political responses to it.

In the November/December 1976 issue of Transportation Research News, the executive committee of the Transportation Research Board published the following list of "The Ten Most Critical Issues in Transportation":

- Financing requirements and alternatives for transportation systems and services
- Energy efficiency in transportation
- Intergovernmental responsibility for transportation systems
- Transportation system maintenance technology and management
- Transportation system performance criteria and design standards
- Effects of transportation regulations
- Improvement of existing nonurban transportation facilities
- Transportation, land use control, and city forms
- Transportation and the environment
- Transportation safety

Each one of these issues involves major energy aspects, whether as trade-offs among conflicting goals or as institutional arrangements and processes for policy evaluation. This is no surprise, considering the pervasive impacts of our apparent abundance of energy together with its historically low prices. Further, these impacts are reflected in attitudes, motivations, behaviors, and habits, which are unlikely to change overnight.

In this context, it is important for transportation policy makers, planners, and managers to ask for assistance from behavioral scientists at appropriate times and in appropriate terms. For example, it may not be enough to know that it is technologically feasible to produce a smaller, more fuel-efficient car that costs less to own and operate in that the present value of gasoline saved during its economic lifetime exceeds its incremental capital cost. It may also be necessary to ask how the automobile companies are likely to market the smaller cars and how consumers are likely to respond. Behavioral scientists are likely to be asked to compare and contrast the viability and social acceptability of alternative policies and programs and to recommend particular ones on these grounds. While this would be a highly desirable and constructive development, both transportation and behavioral specialists must guard against an Orwellian approach to implementing selected policies and programs.

In the context of the transportation planning process, the trend toward disaggregation has clearly demonstrated the need for behavioral paradigms, concepts, and insights. Individual and household decisions about where, when, and how to travel are strongly influenced by attitudes and previous behavior as well as the availability and price of transportation facilities and services.

In the context of transportation evaluation, behavioral scientists can often shed light on whether and why the benefits, costs, and other impacts of a particular transportation policy, program, or project were similar to or different from those anticipated during the planning phase. Responses to new or evolving policies, programs, and projects are often strongly influenced by attitudinal and behavioral factors.

In conclusion, behavioral scientists have a timely opportunity to play a positive role in transportation policy development, planning, and management. This role is to help bring about the effective selection and implementation of desirable and viable public policies. If behavioral scientists are to fulfill this role, transportation and behavioral specialists need to communicate in a common language on appropriate matters and at appropriate times. Transportation specialists will need to inform behavioral specialists of current and emerging issues to which the behavioral sciences may contribute insights. Behavioral specialists will need to address these issues in relevant and timely fashion. This kind of communication is likely to involve an iterative and gradual process.

# Lessons and Instructions:
# A Conference Summary

## Samuel Z. Klausner

### THE CONFERENCE RATIONALE

Transportation is a social activity employing material technology. Transportation, as a social system, could no more be organized and operated without an appreciation of institutionalized social rules than could the technology be developed without engineering principles. Every planner, policy maker, or manager is, implicitly, a social leader, the master of a set of behavioral rules for attaining social goals and for judging the worth of those goals. These social rules, in a fundamental form, have been codified in our cultural sourcebooks dating back, at least, to the Book of Leviticus and Aristotle's Politics. What better teacher of social rules for managing transportation have we than the history of transportation taken in the light of these cultural sourcebooks and tested in the experience of the practitioner? Perhaps the new element in the conference title is the term "science."

The behavioral or the social sciences, as they have evolved in academic settings, have indeed produced knowledge that is not available through common sense, that is more generalizing and abstract than that codified in the cultural sourcebooks or recorded by historians, and that becomes available and is validated through highly rationalized procedures. The behavioral sciences represent an attempt by academic intellectuals in a rationalistic culture to arrive at generalizations about social, psychological, and cultural phenomena. It is hoped that this knowledge may guide our behavior. We may even hope to influence evolving social situations with this knowledge and in the light of our values.

Professionals and technologists draw on these general ideas for guidance in practical human activities. Some have more success than others. The fields of education and of psychotherapy, for

---

I thank Albert G. Crawford for his critique of an earlier draft of this manuscript.

example, consider the psychologist's ideas of personality and of learning in designing their work. The history of the practical efforts of educators and healers is socially distinct from that of psychology. Yet, the human sciences have helped rationalize the practical fields, although it is not clear whether the practical efforts thereby succeed more frequently. The historically recent success of engineering, with its origins in the crafts, in availing itself of the insights of physics and chemistry is a parallel case, but one in which success is more apparent. The problems identified by practitioners are not necessarily those identified by scientists. Special attention is required to apply scientific generalizations to the unique situations of practitioners.

The application of knowledge may be thought of as involving three steps: (1) seeing the relevance of scientific propositions to some practical needs, (2) translating the scientific propositions into practical principles for action, and (3) constructing and implementing procedures consistent with those behavioral principles.

Application is a cultural process. It occurs within social relations such as those between transportation planners and students of behavior. These relations must be such as to provide the occasions and mechanisms for the application of knowledge. The different stages of this process may be led by different actors, each contributing a part to the whole. For purposes of this discussion we will term those who develop the scientific propositions "behavioral scientists," those who translate scientific statements into behavioral rules "research technicians," and those who construct and implement procedures the "behavior program managers."

Our discussion about applying behavioral knowledge might concentrate on the structure of relationships in which the application takes place. Such a social systems analysis would be important for establishing social policies. The conference did not choose this focus. Alternatively, the discussion might be conducted from the perspective of any one of the behavior scientists. The conference would then have considered the place of transportation knowledge within all social knowledge and the introduction of transportation concerns into behavioral science. This was not the conference focus.

An analysis of action from the perspective of the transportation agency, specifically the transportation planner, the policy maker, and the manager, would focus on the social science data available regarding transportation and on programmatic suggestions. This was the focus of the conference.

The programs discussed were not, by and large, transportation programs but were, as the conference title suggests, programs for enabling the transportation manager and the planner to benefit from the contributions of behavioral scientists. The conference papers and workshops ranged over many issues. Nearly all of the issues, however, referred to the substantive contributions of behavioral scientists. This paper, as an interpretive conference summary, will draw the discussion together under three headings: (1) identifying the three types of students of behavior, (2) specifying some of the classes of knowledge professed by each type in relation to transportation, and (3) suggesting some of the arrangements needed for training and supporting these specialists and enabling them to apply their knowledge to transportation problems.


## THE STUDENT OF HUMAN BEHAVIOR AS A TRANSPORTATION ANALYST AND ACTIVIST

### Reasons for Interest in Students of Behavior

Throughout, the conferees projected an ambivalence toward the behavioral scientist in transportation. On the one hand, the behavioral scientist was depicted as potentially powerful: a seer of the unseen in prediction studies, a master of rhetoric in persuading populations to patronize or otherwise support a transit system, and an interpreter of the public will to the authorities. On the other hand, behavioral science was cast in a service role, responding to problems as perceived and defined by others, in this case the transportation authorities. The emerging montage is less one of a priest or a prophet offering fundamental pronouncements about the world than of a magician summoned to assist the authorities in working their will.

Why are transportation managers interested in interviewing and possibly hiring social scientists? In general, behavioral science has become a significant field in societies with culturally and politically pluralistic populations and in which the state bureaucracy has major policy responsibilities. This is true in the present case. More specifically, however, the limits of do-it-yourself behavioral science have been reached by the transportation system. This is because transportation has shifted from an emphasis on major capital investment in facilities to an emphasis on services to varied populations. Transit operators experience this shift through the variety of regulations to which they are subject because of the influence of various publics on legislation, because of public demonstrations of concern with transit operations, even public protests around intended improvements, and because of declines in ridership or increasing restriction of ridership to deprived sectors of the population—among other reasons. As public ownership has increasingly displaced private ownership and as residential patterns have changed in response to the diffusion of the automobile, the social organization of transit has changed. The predicament of the non-driving population and an increasing concern with the ethical obligations of public agencies both conspire to lead transit organizations to self-evaluation and, with that, to an interest in the academic behavioral sciences.

The Three Roles for Students of Behavior

As mentioned above, three types of students of human behavior may be distinguished. They differ in the types of knowledge they control and in the tasks they perform in relation to transportation planning, policy, and management. The conferees discussed sometimes one and sometimes another of these types.

The first type is the academic behavioral scientist. The stress is on "scientist." The behavioral scientist aims to state theories about social events through research. Relevant to the present case is the effort to develop and apply behavioral theories to understanding the movement of people and goods between geographically separated points. As a research methodologist, the behavioral scientist may critique concepts for analyzing a transportation system, for measuring the functioning of transportation, and for testing the validity of measures representing the concepts. The task includes theorizing about personality and culture and about social institutions, such as the economic and political, as well as about the religious and familial, the therapeutic, and the institutions of knowledge and art. In the context of these theories, empirical research methodologies are evolved and appropriate instruments constructed. In the light of theories linking transportation and the organizations it serves, social and environmental impact analyses are conducted with respect to technological, planning, and policy innovations. These analyses become an element in transportation decisions.

The behavioral scientist establishes models for these impact analyses, but, as a more routine matter, the behavioral research technician conducts them as site-specific studies. The behavioral research technician, the second type of student of human behavior, may not be as deeply committed to behavioral theory as the scientist but is a master of techniques for measuring aspects of the social and cultural systems and the traits of individuals. The research technician may apply these talents in monitoring transportation in a locale, in measuring attitudes of travelers, in documenting patronage, or in gathering social accounting data on a transit system.

The behavioral program manager, the third type, neither develops theory nor documents system processes but learns from and exchanges insights with the behavioral scientist and the research technician. The behavioral program manager is a doer, one who effects changes in transportation and in its services to society.

The formal education and preparation of each type of student of behavior shares in certain aspects and differs in others. The behavioral scientist is, ordinarily, a Ph.D. in psychology, sociology, anthropology, political science, or economics, with grounding in areas such as demography, human ecology, human geography, and regional science with a special interest in transportation systems. The technician is trained in social and psychological research, population research methods, mathematical modeling techniques, psychological testing and measurement, and the statistical methods and computer programming ability associated with these operations. The behavioral program manager may not have specialized in behavioral science, but may rather have been educated as a planner or manager. Abilities to negotiate, arbitrate, resolve conflicts, persuade, advocate, and administer personnel are at the heart of the manager's responsibilities. These abilities are enriched by an understanding of behavioral theory and by a command of the system documentation provided by the research technician.

The conference reviewed a number of tasks for students of behavior, organizing them around topical or problem areas—energy, the elderly and the handicapped, and so forth. The following pages will summarize some characteristics of the incumbents, of the type of student of behavior most likely to contribute to each task. The conference itself did not detail these tasks exhaustively. The attempt here will be to present them as illustrations of the types of applications of behavioral science that are possible. The tasks cited by conferees tended to reflect the current activities of students of behavior in the transportation field with the hope of extending those applications to other sites. As the number of behaviorists in transportation increases, these applications will diffuse more widely. In addition, the variety of applications may increase, perhaps exponentially.


The Knowledge Professed

The Behavioral Scientist

The behavioral scientist places transportation issues in their larger societal framework. The issue of the effect on transportation systems of staggered work hours is an example. The behavioral scientist might well go beyond the issue of the impact of such a program on transit systems to the effect of time-staggered journeys to work on the family. Research could include examination of the effect of worker trips on trips by other members of the family and the indirect effect of shifts in family travel on organizations in the community such as retail trade, the delivery of health services, and the management of schools.

The discussion of the mobility-limited, another example, focused on the technical question, posed in a person-machine system frame of reference. The behavioral scientist might reinterpret the question as an economic issue or analyze it in political terms as a study of political movements and the political determination of demand. Another option would be to frame the issue against the underlying processes of social or residential segregation that hamper the access of certain groups to mobility opportunities.

A part of this discussion revolved around the right of individuals to expect and the ability of operators to supply equivalent service to all population categories. A community transit system, short of a dial-a-ride type approach, sacrifices equality of service for some fiscally agreeable average of service. Only the automobile, whether it is owned or rented (including the taxi), approaches equal service to an entire population and may be used as a supplement to public transit to provide equivalent service. Yet, access to an automobile depends on being a driver or on being able to engage a driver and on ability to pay. Equality may also be compromised by restraints that society may place on use in the face of energy accounts or on the state of environmental pollution. Increasingly, public transport is assuming responsibility for the carless. Elderly or handicapped persons tend to be carless because they are not members of a family with a driver or because they are excluded by reason of poverty. By assuming responsibility for them, the transit system both engages in a redistribution of wealth and confirms their right not to be dependent on friends and family. They may elect a less personal dependence on the community. The choice between family and community dependency depends, in part, on the accepted cultural norm. Cash distribution to the elderly and the handicapped, for instance, permits them to purchase taxi transit. It may not be felt to be dignified, however, to accept unearned cash directly from the community. An intrafamilial transfer of cash is less shameful. Yet, to attempt directly to distribute transit service equally is less economically rational.

The behavioral scientist might describe the societal implication of each of these general solutions. The social choice requires a social philosophical judgment. The behavioral scientist might, in that case, indicate the practical implications of various philosophically dictated choices. However, the behavioral scientist cannot substitute for the social philosopher, particularly in a culturally pluralistic society.

The conferees discussed the socially heterogeneous character of the elderly and the handicapped. To describe this heterogeneity and to specify the particular service requirement of each type of elderly or handicapped person, the behavioral scientist draws on knowledge of social structure and personality. Knowledge of the relation of transportation to the social structure permits a specification of the functions of transportation for other social activities. The assessment of the extent to which transportation fulfills such functions, its putative social goals, becomes the appropriate measure of the efficiency of transportation. Ridership and farebox receipts may be but rough indicators of the system's functional success.

The conferees devoted a great deal of time to transportation organization. Concern of transportation leaders has changed from the reduction of congestion to the service of deprived groups, to environmental concerns, and, more recently, to taxpayer revolts. The shift from major capital investment in facilities to emphasis on services reflects these changed social demands. Transportation managers believe they are subjected to conflicting mandates during such times of change. The behavioral scientist might analyze the managers' dilemmas in the light of changing political environments. As the conferees pointed out, the modes of transport enjoy varying types and levels of advocacy from their constituents. Highways have business interests, particularly construction interests, among their advocates. Public transit has more, but less wealthy and powerfully organized, advocates.

Environmental impacts are sometimes described in terms of their physical aspects, such as noise or aesthetic factors. We must also examine the impacts on social activities of these factors. An examination of transportation in relation to other institutions and organizations would be a way of studying these impacts. The impacts of regulatory policies on transportation might also be described by the social scientists.

The conference workshops had much to say about the role of behavioral science in assisting transportation organizations with problems of management. Middle management is integrated less into transportation organization than into industry. Studies of transportation personnel might examine the relationships between the several classes of employees. The labor-management relationship has been crucial for transit systems. One reason offered is that operators have contact more with the public than with their management. Consequently, styles of personnel management in transportation differ from those in industry, where the worker typically does not interact with the public and is more directly supervised

The conferees noted that transportation is controlled by a variety of public and private operators. Further, the regulations imposed on transportation are, sometimes, imposed by nontransport agencies such as the states and the federal government. The influence of various forms of organizational control and the ways that an organization may adapt to control present another area for behavioral science research. Rule making is, for instance, foremost among the procedures used to control transit system management. Research could examine, as the conferees suggested, whether a regulatory approach which promulgates rules, as in the case of UMTA, or the process and guideline approach, as used by FHWA, would better enable a transit authority to adapt to local conditions.

The interface between the transport organization and transport consumers was a constant conference concern. This relation was examined in terms of travel decisions of individuals and organizations and the demographic and socioeconomic factors that influence them. Knowledge of these decisions underlies demand forecasting. Transit management needs such information to identify consumer groups and then to decide what types of services to supply. How does socioeconomic status influence demand? How do individual personality factors influence decisions? What types of rewards affect transportation decisions? What are the levels of demand for various elements in a transportation system?

Energy in transportation is becoming a salient issue. Transportation is a derived, or second-order, demand. The first-order demand is for those social activities facilitated by transportation. The demand for energy emerges as a third-order demand. Thus, models assessing energy demand would include terms representing the social activities and technical characteristics of transportation as these impinge on energy consumption. The behavioral scientist might investigate the use of and influence of communications in marketing, the role of the media, the diffusion of ideas, the establishment of legitimacy of consumption norms, and so forth. How do different groups respond to transportation inconveniences such as those accompanying a gasoline shortage? Responses to shortages vary according to the availability of alternatives or according to whether the travel is discretionary travel, and these, in turn, vary with the social positions of individuals. A number of such situational variables might be investigated.

The effects of policy interventions vary with personality factors as well as with social organizational factors. How does personality influence response to a 55-miles-per-hour speed limit as opposed to other ways of increasing energy efficiency within the mode? How do people react to ride sharing among other strategies for shifting away from energy-intensive activities? How does personality influence interest in substituting telecommunications for travel? How is commitment to a conservation ethic or change in lifestyle related to personality or to cultural and social relations?

## The Research Technician

What are the tasks of the behavioral research technician? Conferees discussed ways of identifying the transport-relevant attributes of a particular population and a particular service area, an activity described as diagnostic research. The research technician would respond here and also would document the state of consumer relations in a particular market, assessing the incentives and disincentives for riders of a local transit system. The research technician might aid in the design of transit facilities. Relying on the person-machine system findings of the behavioral research scientist, the research technician might contribute to the design of ramps, elevators, seats, and stations for a particular community. The research technician would also document economic aspects of transit operations, including a continuing financial audit and energy audit of the system. The research technician, while not functioning as the accountant for the system, could monitor the data generated by the accounting system, shaping the data so that they could be considered in decisions regarding economic trade-offs among alternative community transit systems. The research technician, in a more programmatic sense, might develop a transit system continuing self-evaluation program.

A number of tools are available to the research technician. These include statistical tools, such as those needed to validate demand forecasts, and measuring instruments, such as those for scaling and dimensioning attitudes. The technician commands a knowledge of research design, including various data-gathering strategies such as experiments, fieldwork, surveys, and the methods of data analysis appropriate to these. The research technician would not emphasize the discovery of new variables but would assess particular population parameters for known variables.

## The Behavior Program Manager

The behavior program manager is oriented to action, not action in research but rather in the management of transportation. The manager, too, has conceptual concerns, an interest in issue definition. However, this individual would enter the social relationships of the transportation system, dealing with its other managers, with regulators, employees, and riders, and with transit-affected organizations such as schools, hospitals, industries, zoning commissions, and real estate developers, among others. The knowledge needed here includes practical generalizations from experience. That experience, however, incorporates the vicarious experience of history and of transportation research. The behavior program manager would deal directly with the elderly and the handicapped and other mobility-limited categories. Thus, the issue of wheelchair accessibility, arising around the implementation of Section 504 of the Rehabilitation Act of 1973, would be dealt with through negotiations with the regulatory agency and with those who control the local transit budget. Citizen participation programs might fall in the purview of the behavior program manager. Essentially, the activities would be site-specific. The manager would deal with the local political situation, and analyze local interest group conflicts in a practical sense, and pursue questions such as whether the vocal minorities represent the local handicapped. The behavioral program manager would tailor transit principles to local values and institutions and might even be called as an expert witness in court to advise on the social impacts of some particular innovation.

One of the conference sessions pointed out that the character of the labor force was changing from an older white male labor force that performed well but was alienated from the system to a labor force of young black males who are more aggressive and more assertive about influencing operations. Participation in labor-management negotiations and ongoing relationships would be part of the manager's task. The behavioral program manager would be oriented to optimizing the welfare of the transit organization and the general welfare of the community.

Education is likely to be first among the procedural tools available to the behavioral program manager. Conferees mentioned sensitivity training of operators to help them assist the mobility-limited. Perhaps behavior modification techniques and ideas, in a loose sense, might have application in the marketing of transportation. The manager would also participate in demonstration programs for different elements of transit systems, not so much to evaluate but to assist in the actualization of the demonstration and the implementation of feedback information. Skill in the use of organizational management tools would be urged. Human relations ability to build transit teams would be necessary. Conflict resolution through face-to-face interaction would be routine. Skill at negotiation and arbitration, group dynamics, or role-playing, among other negotiating styles, would be part of the repertoire. Operator selection tests, particularly the interviewing of candidates, illustrate a role in personnel selection. The line between the behavioral program manager and any other transit manager is thin.

## INSTITUTIONALIZING BEHAVIORAL ANALYSIS
## AND ACTION IN TRANSPORTATION

How might these three behavioral roles be institutionalized? The demand for each of them would vary in the several levels of government. The Federal Department of Transportation might well consider a directorate for behavioral science. Aside from the need for a leavening of behavioral scientists in the several offices of the department, there would have to be a location for assembling, a critical mass for both intellectual and organizational reasons. This office would have wider responsibility than that of planning and operation of transport modes. It would develop and examine concepts for national transport policy. The directorate would coordinate behavioral science work in the transportation field in general and in the areas of planning, policy, and management of local authorities in particular. The three types of students of behavior would be represented in the directorate.

Beyond this, behavioral scientists would function either in government or on university faculties. Only the largest local transit systems or state departments of transportation could retain full-time behavioral scientists. Behavioral research technicians and behavior managers, on the other hand, should have positions in all local transportation operating bodies. The behavioral program managers would likely not be full-time behavioral specialists. They might be planners, policy makers, or managers with supplementary behavioral science training.

The education of planners and managers in the study of behavior would probably evolve from appropriate adjustments in the curricula of current transportation and management education programs. These curricula would include materials in the social history of transportation and some of the more general behavioral science tools and analyses. They would, perhaps, cover material on individual personality assessment, person-machine systems, environmental and social impact analysis, and economic demand modeling. Fundamentally, though, the training is in management—in dealing with people in organizations and in being political actors. For the present population of planners and operators, it would be worthwhile to consider educational conferences as a way of providing them with training in behavioral science and the application of this knowledge in transportation planning, policy, and management.

# 8
## CONCLUSION

Even a cursory reading of the papers in this volume indicates a major change in the viewpoint of transportation planners and policy makers in the space of a decade or less.  Until the 1970s, transportation technology, its planning, implementation, operation, and management, was predicated on the provision of supply to satisfy a demand exogenously derived.  Transportation engineers and planners perceived their role primarily as benign providers of an infrastructure service to the manifest demands of travel consumers.

However, the consumers revolted in the 1960s, in particular against the several impacts of urban highway transportation.  Social and environmental considerations, along with perceived arbitrariness in decision making, led to major rejection of highway policy, with the result that the major transport supply deficits, actual and projected, were to go unfulfilled.

The end of the highway movement in urban areas brought a shift in investment to public transportation, a dying technology, and moribund institutions were rejuvenated by a massive federal program, this in the face of overwhelming evidence that conventional mass transit could never satisfy more than 3 to 5 percent of the total urban travel demand.

The other event of the 1970s was the emergence of resource constraints.  Although energy is the most obvious, various other resource limitations have arisen, not the least of which is capital for investment.  This exhaustion has led to the inevitable end of an era of transportation development as a demand-satisfying agent.

Finally, one other event, well developed by Daniel Brand, may be noted.  This is the growth in governmental regulations and requirements.  Since the federal government is the agent for funding up to 90 percent of the state and local activities in transportation, the number of program requirements and the justification to obtain funds have increased exponentially. Hence, the time, energy, and uncertainty in initiating projects have generated delay and unpredictability. In essence, decision making has become diffused and more difficult.

It is within this setting that transportation policy and planning now must operate. It is a model that requires the control of and probably reduction in the demand for travel. Yet transportation has no tools to either plan for or implement demand control. Indeed, such a set of requirements requires the transportation policy maker, the planner, and the system manager to deal with the modification of the behavior of individuals and social groups. The field is not organized or staffed to deal with this predicament.

Out of this background an increased sensitivity to, and an orientation toward, behavioral science and technology has emerged in transportation. The aggregate view of society qua transportation, as measured by socioeconomic descriptors, vehicle miles of travel, functional trip purpose, and manifest destinations, is far too superficial for present needs. In an age in which limited transportation options must be fine tuned within severe constraints, far more basic understanding of individual and group needs must be obtained. Equally, a more sophisticated definition of societal components must also be had if mobility needs are to be met. It is becoming increasingly obvious that descriptors such as race, income, age, and physical condition are inadequate to plan cost-effective transportation adjustments. More specific definition relatable to transport behavior is a basic necessity for this purpose.

Patterns of household behavior, in terms of spatial and temporal structure, are probably fundamental to transportation planning since this class of behavior can define the elasticity of demand on the one hand and the acceptability of constraint policies on the other. It should be noted that the interest in the household is more nearly on the need structure, the temporal pattern of those needs, and the bases upon which the household chooses to satisfy those needs, as well as when or where. Obviously, an operational model of this process, combined with a more general segmentation of the population, can provide a far more predictive and generalizable methodology for trip generation than currently available. It would also provide a basis for aggregation that overcomes most of the problems inherent in currently used zonal definitions.

More importantly, such models of household behavior would provide a far better understanding of individual and social group response to alternative demand control policies, for instance, pricing policies, which may modify certain kinds of behavior but not other kinds. How individuals and groups will respond must depend upon their trade-off calculus within the context of their need structure. Hence, the effectiveness of demand constraint policy options cannot be determined with any precision without a more sophisticated understanding of the behavior of the household.

Although it is not possible to define the structure in detail, some of its characteristics can be. Needs are time varying and may require satisfaction at sites remote from the household. The temporal characteristics of the growth of need are likely to be the trigger for travel. Although the need sets have different frequency properties, their combination defines some time series which have a threshold amplitude determined by personal and social characteristics. It is hypothesized that this combination determines trip generation, distribution, and mode choice, at least for discretionary travel. Hence these personal and social characteristics deriving from need structures must be the basis for stratifying populations. The exact dimensions of the segmentation is not known. However, the methodology for attacking the problem does exist, for example, market segmentation, attitudinal methods, and psychographics, to mention only three. The obvious benefit of this approach is that it should produce far more stable and generalizable categories for transportation planning and policy in particular.

There are, of course, a variety of techniques that can be employed to obtain insight into the response process and hence shorten the time for evolution of policy alternatives. These methods, well developed in the behavioral sciences, involve small group behavior and organizational development principles. These methods, although they generate qualitative data, have been effective in identifying critical values, variables, and perceptions about issues and operations. Further, as was noted in the environmental and social impact analysis workshop, we appear to be moving into a domain in transportation policy and planning where quantitative approaches, certainly alone, may be of limited reliability.

It should also be noted that these small group methods are equally useful in developing quantitative theory and measures. Securing items for attitude batteries is routinely done on small groups, usually of arbitrary composition. Similarly, in conducting item analysis, small groups are used. This is the general procedure in test construction. In essence, there is no reason not to use small groups for both qualitative studies and for developing quantitative measures.

Carrying the process one step further, research and analysis can be done in laboratory settings. Controlled laboratory experiments have been consistently used in the behavioral sciences both to develop and test theory. It is equally useful, and has been employed with increasing sophistication, in the study of social and group processes. Using direct, mediate, and simulation methods, a fairly wide range of social and group processes can be analyzed reliably and highly economically. Such techniques have been used extensively in several fields. Rarely have they been used systematically in transportation. Rather, the orientation has been to conduct massive data collection in highly uncontrolled field studies. One consequence has been an overreliance on inductive inference and data manipulation.

There is a logic in the behavioral sciences, very little different, it may be noted, from the natural sciences. Theory or technology development involves a series of stages from abstract modeling, laboratory studies, prototype development, field testing, and evaluation. This applies to concept development, test construction, or man-machine system design. In applying behavioral science and technology to transportation policy and planning, such a paradigm seems essential for most of the issues discussed in preceding chapters of this book. It does not seem credible that massive energy conservation or demand control strategies can be considered for implementation without systematic analysis of behavioral response. Doing otherwise is likely to lead to social conflict and confrontation. The well-developed behavioral science paradigm is a relatively direct and economic means of both identifying response sets to such alternatives and estimating their acceptance or rejection, among other things.

Finally, the small group technology that exists in the behavioral sciences has direct application in the citizen participation and conflict resolution areas. Work done in this area in the 1960s has provided a variety of tools both for understanding conflict processes and for minimizing their effects. Similarly, organizational development (OD) and small group methods are directly applicable to the development and administration of participatory processes that have the potential for providing constructive transaction between transportation planning and engineering and the social groups impacted by those activities. As has been noted, these techniques have had wide application in the industrial area and should be equally effective in transportation policy and planning.

The issue of transit management is clearly a critical one in light of emerging demands for productivity and operating efficiency. As pointed out in the workshop, transit is unique in that direct contact with the consumer is by a driver who functions outside of direct supervision. In essence, transit operations depend heavily on driver and consumer feedback on performance. In this context, the connection between the major part of the labor force and the overall goals of the institution is indirect and often tenuous.

Interestingly, the one analogous public system having similar labor management relations is the police. That is, the patrol officer operates, for the most part, independent of direct supervision. Consequently, the public's perception of the criminal justice system is often determined by the behavior of the local officer. The police case has been examined in considerable detail by behavioral science methods. Issues in selection, training, and supervision have been studied and behavioral techniques developed in all these areas. Thus, selection, training, and OD methods exist that should be employed in transit, especially at the first-line labor force level.

In the area of social impact, varied questions arise that need to be dealt with. The social consequences, direct and indirect, of major changes in land use are not well understood. There is a tendency to use terms, such as "social cohesiveness," that are difficult to define operationally to say nothing of measuring. There are serious issues of criteria as well as definition. As a consequence, social impact has often been dealt with on a simplistic basis, for example, number of dwelling units taken.

However, varied sociological and psychological studies have been done on response to disaster and dislocation. Some have been descriptive, but others quite operational. These may be useful in transportation impact analysis. Similarly, considerable behavioral science technology has been developed on group processes and on developing group cohesion. Much of this work has relevance to social impact analysis as well as relocation assistance.

A final area that should be mentioned is decision making at the planning and policy level. In these cases decision making goes on under conditions of uncertainty and with imperfect information Also, the technical, experiential, and personality characteristics of decision makers differ depending upon the institutional hierarchy and their location in it. Thus, their decision-making rules differ, or at least the values of weights applied to variables in the decision set differ. What are the variables used in transportation decision making? How, in fact, are the decisions made? It is a tenet of the planning profession that the planning process is to provide a rational basis for decision making. Yet decision makers do not consistently use that rational base. Planners also often perceive the process as an end, that is, a decision that a decision maker should adopt. If decision making does not work that way or is made on exogenous grounds, it is questionable whether the planning process is cost effective. More importantly, policy making may not be cost effective. There is a series of obvious questions about the transportation decision-making process as there is among other public and private systems. Few of these issues have been studied in transportation.

However, given the large number of steps, as well as the diversity of public and private actors, in the decision-making process in transportation, the implications for transportation policy are significant. There is a variety of behavioral and social science work on decision making, ranging from abstract models of the process to choice behavior, style, and personality variables. These approaches offer several rather powerful means for understanding and ultimately improving the transportation policy decision process.

In viewing the status of transportation, it has become extremely clear that this class of infrastructure service has been and is a major force in both qualitative and quantitative organization of the society. It is a transactional system that by its characteristics has determined the spatial extent of, as well as the constraints on, social interchanges. However, transportation engineering and planning have abstracted the functional from the behavioral so that the focus of these activities has been on the mechanics of movement rather than the motivation for it.

It is now clear that transportation policy, planning, operations, and management must provide more direct response to individual and social needs and objectives, as well as economic ones. The significance of issues such as transportation for the elderly and the handicapped and environmental considerations are symptomatic of the unresponsiveness of the transport process. Similarly, energy, economic, and other resource constraints are implying major changes in the ways transportation can be used. These evolving demands on transportation clearly require a far better understanding and integration of individual and group needs, perceptions, information processing, learning, decision making, and choice than is now employed. These are all issues requiring behavioral science and technology as a part of and an adjunct to the policy and planning process.

It is equally clear that the transportation field has been and is increasingly sensitive to the use of behavioral sciences. The basic question is whether or not these fields have the capacity to provide the needed science and technology, that is, to provide method and technique that can fit effectively into the complex sociotechnical system that is transportation. There is little doubt that the behavioral sciences have the capacity to deal with many of the major problems confronting transportation. However, to take advantage of this capacity requires that two major conditions exist. One concerns the location of the behavioral sciences in the organization of the transport process. The least payoff can come from postdecision applications. That is, to use behavioral science and technology as a means of implementing a priori decisions is unlikely to be effective. Work in mode choice behavior is exemplary of this. The basic objective in this area has been to increase transit usage; the original thrust was to employ consumer psychology techniques. However, transportation, being a meta system, is not a utilitarian product in the conventional sense. Consequently, a new basis for understanding mode choice behavior is required. Indeed, this is the essential research and development now in progress.

This exemplifies the point that effective utilization of the behavioral sciences requires that they be integrated into the long-range planning process. This is true simply because behavior relative to transportation is essentially nonmodal. If transportation is perceived as linkage between needs and need satisfiers, it is need and need satisfier attributes that define acceptable transportation systems, not modal properties in isolation. It is at this class of interface that the behavioral sciences can be particularly useful and are probably most needed.

It seems clear from this conference that a wide range of behavioral issues in transportation is manifest. It is recognized by planners, policy makers, and managers, as well as behavioral scientists. The immediate question is how best to integrate behavioral science and technology into the multidisciplinary structure of transportation. Perhaps the next step is a study of how effectively to bring the behavioral sciences into the planning and policy process. Under any circumstances, there is much benefit to be gained by transportation agencies in experimenting with ways to draw on behavioral science and technology more effectively than has been done. Such experimentation seems especially urgent in the face of radical changes in the fundamental requirements for mobility that have occurred, and must continue to occur, through the remainder of this century.

# APPENDIX A
## Behavioral Theory and Technique:
## An Annotated Bibliography of
## Applications to Transportation

ENGINEERING DESIGN

Braunstein, M. L., and O. F. Coleman. "An Information Processing Model of the Aircraft Accident Investigator." Human Factors
9 (1967): 61-70.

Verbal reports elicited from accident investigators and motion
pictures of the investigators' activities during 16 investigations
of light aircraft accidents were used as the empirical basis for a
computer model of the aircraft accident investigator. The model
simulates the major processes apparent in the investigators' reports, including the selection of aircraft and terrain features to
be observed and the generating and testing of kinematics hypotheses. The computer program accepts a description of aircraft damage and gouge marks and generates a series of kinematics hypotheses. The effects of variations in investigator
parameters on the outputs of the model were studied in a series
of 40 simulation runs. A preliminary comparison was made between the output of the model and the conclusions of a human investigator working with the same data.

Bronzoft, A. L., S. B. Dobrow, and T. J. O'Hanlon. "Spatial
Orientation in a Subway System." Environment and Behavior 8
(1976): 575-94.

Uses a problem-solving approach to gather information concerning the ease or difficulty of traveling the New York City subway
system. Subjects are given a destination and asked to get there
as fast and efficiently as they can. They are then interviewed
concerning their strategies and actual performance. An analysis
of their errors is also performed. Conclusions are framed in
terms of the clarity and availability of directions and markings
within the subway system.

Chaney, R. Whole Body Vibration of Standing Subjects. Boeing
Co., BOE-D3-6779, 1965.

Cooper, G. E. "Understanding and Interpreting Pilot Opinions." Aeronautical Engineering Review 16 (1957): 47-52.

Dewar, R. E., and J. Ells. "Comparison of Three Methods for Evaluating Traffic Signs." Sponsored by Committee on Motorist Information Systems, Transportation Research Record 503 (1974): 38-47.

Three experiments were conducted to compare three methods of evaluating traffic sign perception. In the first experiment, subjects were required to classify signs according to type and to identify the meaning of the signs while driving toward them under normal highway traffic conditions at 30 mph (48 kph) and 50 mph (81 kph). The distances at which subjects were able to classify and to identify each sign were measured. Two classes of sign, regulatory and warning, were used, and half of each class had symbolic messages while the other half had verbal messages. The second experiment was a partial replication of the first, with certain modifications. The signs were one-third normal size and the subject drove the vehicle at 17 mph (27 kph). The third experiment was a laboratory study in which verbal reaction time required to classify and identify slides of traffic signs was measured. Signs used in the first two experiments were used as stimuli in the third experiment. The results indicated that the three measures of performance were closely related. Signs were classified at a greater distance than they were identified. Performance was better on symbolic than on verbal signs (except for the reaction time measure), and it was better on warning than on regulatory signs. In addition, performance on individual sign messages was highly correlated across the different measures.

Dewar, R. E., J. G. Ells, and G. Mundy. "Reaction Time as an Index of Traffic Sign Perception." Human Factors 18 (1976): 381-92.

Verbal reaction times to identify and to classify 20 traffic sign messages were measured under three conditions—sign alone, sign plus visual loading task, and sign plus visual loading task plus visual distraction. Similar trends were found in the three experiments: reaction times were smaller for the classification task than for the identification task, smaller for warning than for regulatory signs, and smaller for verbal than for symbolic messages. Comparison of these reaction time data with on-the-road measures of legibility distance revealed significant correlations. The correlational data add credibility to laboratory measures of reaction times as valid indexes of traffic sign perception.

Dewar, R. E. , and H. A. Swanson. "Recognition of Traffic-Control Signs." Sponsored by the Committee on Motorist Information Systems, Highway Research Record, vol. 414, 1972.

The paper includes a review of published and unpublished literature with respect to symbols versus word messages on traffic signs, symbolization philosophies and recognition problems, and education of motorists about meanings of symbols. The paper also reports on a laboratory study and a field study of traffic-sign recognition. The laboratory experiment was conducted to determine the ability of subjects to recognize selected turn-restriction signs under conditions of short exposure. The traffic signs were varied by types of turn restrictions and mode of indicating the sign message, i.e., words, positive and negative symbols, and combinations of these. The experiment made use of a projection tachistoscope. Subjects varied in age, driving skill, and experience. The field study compared the effectiveness of both negative and positive symbols. The effectiveness was measured in relation to the number of motorists disregarding the turn-restriction sign.

Forbes, T. W. "Predicting Attention-Gaining Characteristics of Highway Traffic Signs: Measurement Technique." Human Factors 6 (1964): 371-74.

This report describes an experimental procedure being developed for measuring the probability that a highway traffic sign of given brightness, color, and contrast characteristics can be seen against various day and night background conditions. From the laboratory measurements with this technique, probabilities that a sign will be seen can be determined. Later, field checks with full-scale observations are made to validate the laboratory results.

Forbes, T. W., R. F. Snyder, and R. F. Pain. "A Study of Traffic Sign Requirements II: An Annotated Bibliography." College of Engineering, Michigan State University, Lansing, 1964.

Gordon, D. A. "Experimental Isolation of the Driver's Visual Input." Highway Research Record, vol. 122, 1966.

A technique to determine what features of the road and terrain the driver is responding to is presented in this study. The method involves having the driver guide the car while looking through a device containing a small aperture. By decreasing the visual field, the essential information, whatever it is, cannot be seen at once; i.e., the driver is forced to obtain this information in

separate visual fixations. A continuous film record is made of
the driver's field of view, which is later analyzed to indicate the
center of visual aim and the content of each fixation. The essential information being used is easily identified in each separate
restricted fixation. (This technique may also be used to determine the aircraft pilot's perceptual input and may be applicable,
with modifications, to problems of human console design.) This
approach has advantages over eye camera techniques, which provide a record of fixation position. The eye camera does not
show the contribution of peripheral vision, nor does it provide a
means of distinguishing essential from nonessential information.

Gordon, D. A., and R. M. Michaels. "Static and Dynamic Visual
Fields in Vehicular Guidance." Highway Research Record, vol.
84, 1963.

Two main problems are considered in this paper. The first is
concerned with the mathematical description of the moving ground
plane from the driver's point of view. The environment seen by
the driver involves a perspective transformation of ground position, velocity, and acceleration. The formulas governing these
transformations are developed, and the fields themselves are
plotted. The positional field, which includes the angular coordinates from eye position of points in the driver's environment, is related to linear perspective. The velocity field includes the vectors of angular motion around the driver's eye
while moving along the road. The acceleration field presents
vectors of angular acceleration rather than velocity.

The second problem discussed is the use made by the driver of
the positional, velocity, and acceleration fields. To affect driving, these characteristics have to be registered, and the driver's
sensitivity to them influences their utility. This analysis covers
the condition of steady-state driving, where the vehicle moves
rectilinearly or curvilinearly with constant velocity. Departures
from steady-state driving, in turning, braking, avoidance, and
other maneuvers, will be considered in a subsequent paper.

Harper, R. P., Jr., and G. E. Cooper. "A Revised Pilot Training Rating Scale for the Evaluation of Handling Qualities." Report No. 153, Cornell Aeronautical Labs, Ithaca, N.Y., September 1966.

Harte, D. B. "Estimates of the Length of Guidelines of Highway
Guidelines and Spaces." Human Factors 17 (1975): 455-60.
Driving skills depend greatly upon efficient estimates of length
and distance. The present study found that male and female

subjects between the ages of 16–79 grossly underestimated the length of both the guidelines and the spaces between guidelines used on Massachusetts state highways when tested by memory and under actual driving conditions. It is proposed that this major illusion should be dealt with through driver education or through improvement of highway design.

McCormick, E. J. Human Factors Engineering. New York: McGraw-Hill, 1970.

McDonnell, J. D. "Pilot Rating Techniques for the Estimation and Evaluation of Handling Qualities." AFFDL Technical Report No. 68-76, U.S. Air Force Flight Dynamics Lab, Wright-Patterson Air Force Base, Ohio, December 1968.

McRuer, D. T., D. Graham, E. S. Krendel, and W. Reisener. "Human Pilot Dynamics in Compensatory Systems." AFFDL Technical Report No. 65-15, U.S. Air Force Dynamics Lab, Wright-Patterson Air Force Base, Ohio, July 1965.

McRuer, D. T., and H. R. Jex. "Effects of Task Variables on Pilot Models for Manually Controlled Vehicles." Paper presented at advisory groups for Aerospace Research and Development Specialists Meeting on Stability and Control, September 25, 1966, Cambridge, England.

Rockwell, T. H., and J. M. Snider. "Investigation of Device Sensory Capabilities and Its Effects on the Driving Tasks." RF 2091 Final Report, Research Foundation, The Ohio State University, Columbus, Ohio, July 1969.

Van Cott, H. P., and R. G. Kinkade, eds. Human Engineering Guide to Equipment Design. American Institute for Research, Washington, D.C., 1972.

Walker, R. E., R. C. Nicolay, and C. R. Stearns. "Comparative Accuracy of Recognizing American and International Road Signs." Journal of Applied Psychology 49 (1965): 322-25.

This study investigated the hypothesis that symbol road signs (similar to the international signs) could be more accurately recognized than word road signs (typical of the American signs). The Ss used were 81 college undergraduates. The hypothesis was significantly supported under two conditions. Under one condition, both the symbols and signs were black; in the other, the symbols were black and the signs red. A further phase of the study demonstrated the ease with which the symbol signs were learned. A simple memory test conducted 24 hours after the learning indicated perfect recall of the symbol signs and their meaning. The potential significance of the results and research possibilities was discussed.

## MANAGEMENT

Berger, C. J., L. L. Cummings, and H. G. Heneman. "Expectancy Theory and Operant Conditioning Prediction of Performance under Variable-Ratio and Continuous Schedules of Reinforcement." Organizational Behavior and Human Performance 14 (1975): 227-43.

Directionally different predictions were derived from operant conditioning and expectancy theory and were tested in a 3X5 split-plot repeated measures design. Fifteen female subjects were randomly assigned to three schedule and magnitude of reinforcement conditions (25¢-CRE: 25¢-VR-2: 50¢-VR-2). Expectancy theory constructs also were measured at several points during the experiment. Neither model was clearly superior. When additional pay was contingent upon performance, performance increased significantly. However, response levels and response rates were not significantly different between the three experimental groups. Composite scores derived from an additive expectancy model accounted for significant additional increments in explained variance after controlling for baseline performance and schedule of reinforcement. These results were interpreted as indicating a need to include both environmental and perceptual variables in accounts of work behavior.

Golembiewski, R. R., K. Billingsley, and S. Yeager. "Measuring Change and Persistence in Human Affairs: Types of Change Generated by OD Design." Journal of Applied Behavioral Science 12 (1976): 133-57.

There is a truism about applied research that an inadequate concept of change leads to diminished or misguided applied research. Hence this paper urges distinguishing kinds of change, distinctions that are suggested by experience and also are supported with evidence generated by exotic statistical and computational techniques in which we have been engaged. An immediate payoff of making such distinctions is more definite reliance on existing research findings, whose interpretation is necessarily related to their underlying concept of change. More central still, the goal is to facilitate the design and evaluation of efforts to improve the human condition and the quality of life, especially in organizations. Initially, conceptual clarification of "change" will show that at least three kinds seem distinguishable. Later, data from a study of a successful flexi-time intervention will be used to test these conceptual clarifications. Detailed statistical analysis will support the broad position that a unitary concept of change is inappropriate and may be seriously misleading.

Golembiewski, R. T., R. Hillen, and M. S. Kagno. "A Longitudinal Study of Flexi-Time Effects: Some Consequences of an OD Structural Intervention." Journal of Applied Behavioral Science 10 (1973): 503-32.

This study describes the implementation of a flexible work-hours program and analyzes some of its major effects, using both attitudinal and hard data. It both reports an unusual kind of OD intervention, i.e., a structural one, and discusses specific outcomes of a particular version of a design that is currently being widely applied, though typically on the basis of only anecdotal evidence and without the support of OD values and methods.

The study yields a substantial optimism, but one rooted in caution: both the hard and the soft data indicate that the structural intervention worked, but the data do not tell us how much its obvious and persistent impact was the result of the intervention as a technique and how much it was a function of the culture of the host organization, which had been exposed to a range of activities based on OD values. The researchers believe that much of the impact derived from client acceptance of OD values, which found expression not only in the work-hours design itself but also in the dynamics of the implementation of that design. It is clear at least that flexi-time installations are intimately affected by the culture and values of organizations in which they are located. Hence the emphasis here on caution as well as optimism, inasmuch as definitive comparative research is not yet available.

Golembiewski, R. T., and A. Kiepper. "MARTA: Toward an Effective, Open Giant." Public Administration Review 36 (1976): 46-60.

Hackman, J. R., and C. R. Oldman. "Development of the Job Diagnostic Survey." Journal of Applied Psychology 60 (1975): 159-70.

The properties and uses of the Job Diagnostic Survey (JDS) are described. The JDS is intended (a) to diagnose existing jobs to determine if (and how) they might be redesigned to improve employee motivation and productivity, and (b) to evaluate the effects of job changes on employees. The instrument is based on a specific theory of how job design affects work motivation and provides measures of objective job dimensions, individual psychological states resulting from these dimensions, affective reactions of employees to the job and work setting, and individual growth need strength (interpreted as the readiness of individuals to respond to enriched jobs). Reliability and validity data are summarized for 658 employees on 62 different jobs in seven organizations who have responded to a revised version of the instrument.

Hackman, J. R., C. R. Oldman, R. Jansan, and K. Purdy. "A New Strategy for Job Enrichment." California Management Review 17 (1975): 57-71.

Hamner, W. C., and D. L. Harnett. "Goal Setting, Performance and Satisfaction in an Interdependent Task." Organizational Behavior and Performance 12 (1974): 217-30.

This study was designed to determine the effect that goals have on performance and the effect that performance has on reported levels of satisfaction in a competitively structured task. The results of this study give strong evidence to Lodge's theory (Organizational Behavior and Human Performance, 1969, 566-74) that the most immediate, direct motivational determinant of task performance is the subject's goal, and to Ilgen and Hamstra's theory (Organizational Behavior and Human Performance, 1972, 359-70) that satisfaction with one's performance is a function of the difference between actual performance and performance goals and also a function of the difference between actual performance and performance of a reference person. Satisfaction and performance were found to be strongly related only up to the point where a person exceeds the goal or the reference person's outcome.

Hautaluoma, J. E., and J. F. Gavin. "Effects of Organizational Diagnosis and Intervention on Blue Collar Blues." Journal of Applied Behavioral Science 11 (1975): 475-96.

A small midwestern manufacturing company suffered excessive turnover among its blue-collar workers in 1972. An organizational diagnosis involving interviews and survey questionnaire assessment of all employees revealed some possible reasons. Several interventions of feedback, supervisory skills training, and process observation were conducted by a team of organizational psychologists; the effects of the interventions are discussed in terms of changes in turnover, reduced absenteeism, and more positive attitudes toward work, the company, and supervision.

Ivancevich, J. M. " Changes in Performance in a Management by Objectives Program." Administration Science Quarterly 19 (1974): 563-74.

Jenkins, C. D. , D. A. Nadler, E. E. Lawler, and C. Comman. "Standardized Observation: An Approach to Measuring the Nature of Jobs." Journal of Applied Psychology 60 (1975): 171-81.

In an effort to determine the usefulness of standardized job observations, 35 observers were trained to observe the characteristics of jobs. Employees (N = 448) were observed for two hours and were also interviewed. The observation measures were assessed to determine if they possessed repeatability, homogeneity, and convergence. Of the 19 job dimensions studied, 11 demonstrated repeatability and homogeneity. Six of the dimensions were tested for convergence with the interview data, and four showed moderate convergence. It was concluded that job observations are a potentially useful way to measure the characteristics of jobs, but that they have significant limitations.

Latham, C. P. , and S. B. Kinne. "Improving Job Performance through Training in Goal Setting." Journal of Applied Psychology 59 (1974): 189-91.

Latham, C. P. , and C. A. Yukl. "A Review of Research on the Application of Goal Setting in Organization." Academy of Management Journal 18 (1975): 824-45.

Locke, E. A. , N. Cartledge, and C. S. Knerr. "Studies of the Relationship between Satisfaction, Goal Setting and Performance." Organizational Behavior and Human Performance 5 (1970): 135-58.

Previous research and theory has indicated that goals and intentions are the most immediate motivational determinants of task performance, external incentives affect behavior through their effects on goals, and emotional (affective) reactions are the result of value judgments. The present research was concerned primarily with the problem of how evaluations and emotions lead to goal setting. It was argued that being dissatisfied with one's past performance generates the desire (and goal) to change one's performance, whereas satisfaction with one's performance produces the desire (and goal) to repeat or maintain one's previous performance level. Five experiments were reported in which (a) satisfaction was predicted from value judgments, (b) goal setting was predicted from satisfaction, and (c) performance was predicted from goals. In nearly all cases the correlations were high or significant or both. It was found, however, that in some cases the level of performance that yielded satisfaction in the past was not necessarily that which produced it in the present. In these cases it was the individual's anticipated (rather than past) satisfaction that best predicted subsequent goal setting. The relationship of the present theory to other theories of task motivation is discussed briefly (e.g., Dulany; Miller, Galanter, and Pribram; Porter and Lawler; Ryan; and Vroom).

Oldham, C. R., J. R. Hackman, and J. L. Pearce. "Conditions under Which Employees Respond to Enriched Work." Journal of Applied Psychology 61 (1976): 395-403.

Pedalino, E., and V. V. Gamboa. "Behavior Modification and Absenteeism: Intervention in One Industrial Setting." Journal of Applied Psychology 59 (1974): 694-98.

Behavior modification was used in an attempt to decrease absenteeism in a sample of 215 hourly employees at a manufacturing/distribution facility. Employees in four adjoining plants served as comparison groups. An ABA (baseline, intervention, return to baseline) intervention using a lottery incentive system constituted the experimental design. Absenteeism decreased significantly following the experimental group intervention but did not decrease in any of the four comparison groups. Further, stretching the schedule of reinforcement did not increase the rate of absenteeism. Findings are discussed in light of Lawler and Hackman's 1969 study, which indicated that participation, not the incentive system, decreased absenteeism.

Raia, A. P. "Goal Setting and Self-Control: An Empirical Study." Journal of Management Studies 2 (1965): 32-53.

Robey, D. "Task Design, Work Values and Worker Response: An Experimental Test." Organizational Behavior and Human Performance 12 (1974): 264-73.

Sixty subjects participated in an experiment to test the hypothesis that job satisfaction and performance are affected by the interaction of task design and work values, as suggested by Hulin and Blood (1968). Two routine decision tasks were performed by subjects classified as having either intrinsic work values or extrinsic work values. Findings supported the hypothesis that the interaction between job content and work values affects job satisfaction. Performance data partially support the hypothesis. The job enlargement thesis is thus shown to be not generally valid but rather affected by individual differences of subjects.

Stedry, A. C., and E. Kay. "The Effects of Goal Difficulty in Performance." Behavioral Science 11 (1966): 459-70.

Steers, R. M. "Taskgoal Attributes in Achievement and Supervisory Performance." Organizational Behavior and Performance 13 (1975): 392-403.

This investigation analyzes the relationship between employees' task goals and supervisory performance as moderated by n Achievement among a sample of first-level supervisors working under a formalized goal-setting program. Before need strength levels were taken into account, little consistent relationship was found between the five task-goal attributes and performance. After dividing the subjects into high and low n Ach groups, however, it was found that performance was significantly related to increases in feedback and in goal specificity for high n Ach subjects and to participation in goal setting for low n Ach subjects. Goal difficulty and peer competition were found to be unrelated to performance for both groups. These results are then compared to other studies on the topic and it is concluded that individual difference factors, line n Achievement, must be taken into account in any comprehensive theory of goal setting in organizations.

Umstot, D. D., C. H. Bell, and T. R. Mitchell. "Effects of Job Enrichment and Task Goals on Satisfaction and Productivity: Implications for Job Design." Journal of Applied Psychology 61 (1976): 379-94.

A two-phase research project investigated the effects of job enrichment and goal setting on employee productivity and satisfaction in a well-controlled, simulated job environment. In the first phase, two conditions of goal setting (assigned goals versus no goals) and two conditions of job enrichment (enriched versus unenriched) were established, producing four experimental conditions. The results indicated that job enrichment had a substantial impact on job satisfaction but little effect on productivity. Goal setting, on the other hand, had a major impact on productivity and a less substantial impact on satisfaction. In the second phase (after two days' work), people with unenriched jobs worked under the enrichment conditions and people originally without goals were assigned goals. Again, job enrichment had a positive effect on job satisfaction, while goal setting had a positive effect on performance. These results are discussed in terms of the current theoretical approaches for understanding employee motivation on the job.

Wexley, K. N., and W. F. Numeroff. "Effectiveness of Positive Reinforcement and Goal Setting as Methods of Management Development." Journal of Applied Psychology 60 (1975): 446-50.

Two managerial training programs were evaluated. One program involved role playing together with delayed appraisal sessions and assigned goal setting; the other involved role playing with delayed appraisal sessions, assigned goal setting, and immediate reinforcement via telecoaching. Measures of managerial behavior and subordinate satisfaction were collected 60 days after the completion of training. The results indicated that the training programs were statistically more effective than a control program in improving the consideration and integration skills of managers and reducing the absenteeism of their subordinates, although the programs were not statistically different from each other. The success of both treatments was accomplished without any undesired reduction in the managers' general level of initiating structure or production emphasis. The program involving delayed appraisal sessions and assigned goal setting was most effective in increasing subordinate work satisfaction.

White, S. E., T. R. Mitchell, and C. H. Bell. "Goal Setting, Evaluation Apprehension and Social Cues versus Determinants of Job Performance and Job Satisfaction in a Simulated Organization." Journal of Applied Psychology 62 (1977): 665-73.

A simulated organizational setting involving a routine clerical task was the experimental context for the research. One hundred and four subjects were randomly assigned in a factorial design including two levels of goal setting, two levels of evaluation apprehension, and three types of social cues to investigate the effects of the independent variables on employee productivity and job satisfaction. The results showed that people with assigned goals produced more than people without assigned goals, people with high evaluation apprehension produced more than people with low evaluation apprehension, and people receiving positive social cues produced more than people receiving negative social cues. The independent variables had no main effect on overall job satisfaction but did affect attitudes about job pressure, boredom, and satisfaction with one's performance. These results are discussed in terms of their relevance for current theories of task performance and for applications in organizational settings.

Yukl, C. A., and G. P. Latham. "Consequences of Reinforcement Schedules and Incentives Magnitudes for Employee Performance: Problems Encountered in Industrial Setting." Journal of Applied Psychology 60 (1975): 294-98.

Pay incentives reflecting three schedules of reinforcement were compared in terms of their effects on the productivity of marginal workers (N = 88). In a quasi-experimental design, the following treatments were randomly assigned to work crews: (a) continuous reinforcement—individuals received a $2 bonus for each bag of trees they planted; (b) variable ratio—individuals received a $4 bonus contingent upon planting a bag of trees and correctly guessing the outcome of one coin toss; and (c) variable ratio—individuals received an $8 bonus contingent upon planting a bag of trees and correctly guessing two coin toss outcomes. A fourth, geographically isolated crew served as a control. Productivity was highest in the continuous reinforcement conditions. Problems in applying reinforcement schedules in industry are discussed.

Yukl, C. A., K. N. Wexley, and J. D. Segmmi. "Effectiveness of Pay Incentives under Variable Ratio and Continuous Reinforcement Schedules." Journal of Applied Psychology 56 (1972): 19-23.

The effectiveness of pay incentives under variable ratio and continuous reinforcement schedules was investigated in a simulated job situation. Fifteen Ss worked under three-pay incentive conditions, and production for the three groups was compared in order to test hypotheses derived from instrumentality theory and the operant conditioning literature. The results failed to support instrumentality theory. Pay incentives were more effective in motivating increased production when used with a variable ratio schedule than when used with a continuous reinforcement schedule.


SOCIAL IMPACT

Ebbeson, E. B., and M. Haney. "Flirting with Death: Variables Affecting Risk Taking at Intersections." Journal of Applied Social Psychology 3 (1973): 303-24.

A series of four field studies were conducted to examine how motorists behaved at intersections. In each study, the proportion of drivers who pulled out in front of oncoming cars at varying temporal distances was recorded. In the first study, it was found that the proportion of turns in front of an approaching car was related to the log of the temporal distance between the subjects and the oncoming cars by a normal ogive. The remaining studies examined the effects that the presence of various types of audiences had on this risk-taking function. It was found that being forced to wait in a line of cars before being allowed to turn substantially increased the risks that drivers took, whereas the presence of other cars behind and/or beside the subject's car had no effect on the risk-taking function. A hypothesis explaining these effects in terms of the frustration of being forced to wait was supported while a social facilitation hypothesis was not. It was also discovered that males take more risks than females, a fact that could explain the higher accident rate for males.

Griffeth, R. W., and R. W. Rogers. "Effects of Fear-Arousing Components of Driver Education on Students' Safety Attitudes and Simulator Performance." Journal of Educational Psychology 68 (1976): 501-6.

Despite the importance of driving safety, there is little evidence that traditional driver education courses are effective. A 2X2X2 factorial experiment examined the effects of (a) the noxiousness of an automobile accident, (b) one's probability of being in an accident, and (c) the efficacy of safe-driving practices on 144 high school driver education students. The results disclosed that increments in the noxiousness variable greatly reduced error rates on driving simulators. Additionally, if students behaved negligently, driving performance was improved by increasing either their perception of severity of accidents or their chances of being in one. Advantages of discovering effective variables linked to general psychological theories (i.e., expectancy-value theories) were reviewed and implications for implementing these principles in driver education were discussed.

Hoinville, G. "Evaluating Community Preferences." Environment and Planning 3 (1971): 33-50.

This paper describes a new method of research developed by Social and Community Planning Research during the past 18 months. The aim of the research was to arrive at measurements of community preferences so that priority values could be quantified. The method relies on interviews with groups of people who have differing experiences of the variables under study. During the course of the interview, they are asked to play a priority evaluation game using an electronic device built for that purpose. This approach extends traditional attitude survey measurements by allowing and ensuring that respondents understand the concept of trade-off preferences.

Hutchinson, J. W. , C. S. Cox, and B. R. Moffet. "An Evaluation of the Effectiveness of Televised, Locally Oriented Driver Re-education." Transportation Research Record.

Television, with its ability to reach large audiences, has been used extensively in driver-education efforts but its effectiveness has never been measured. The purpose of this research was to measure the effectiveness of a televised, locally oriented, "candid camera" type of driver reeducation program. The mea-sures of effectiveness included a study of changes in driver errors at eight local intersections and an analysis of changes in accident-involvement rate for 48 local intersections.

The televised program, entitled "Traffic Madness," consisted of an 18-month series of 2- to 3-minute locally oriented traffic safety films, produced by research project staff. These showed local drivers in the process of making errors at both rural and urban locations throughout Lexington-Fayette County, Kentucky. In sequence with each type of driver error shown, the correspond-ing correct driving procedure was illustrated.

Both driver errors and total accidents were significantly reduced 17.4 percent ($p < 0.01$) and 12.5 percent ($p < 0.01$) respectively. Driver errors were counted only during home-from-work rush hour traffic on Tuesdays and Thursdays from 4:00 to 5:30 p.m., whereas the accident study encompassed all hours of the week when out-of-county drivers not exposed to the program made up a proportionately larger percentage of drivers in the sample.

Kobayashi, K. , A. Yoichi, and A. Tani. "A Method for Evaluating Urban Transportation Planning in Terms of User Benefits." Transportation Research 9 (1975): 67-79.

In this paper a methodology is developed for evaluation of societal impacts of urban transportation systems from the user's view-point. The evaluation is performed quantitatively in terms of time, cost, convenience, and comfort. User's preference char-acteristics needed for the evaluation are expressed by utility functions, relative weights, and value functions, which are ob-tained through a specially designed direct questionnaire method.

The validity of the evaluation model was investigated by examining its predictability of route selection, and the result was that 80 percent of route selections were predictable by the authors' evaluation model for the sample data. Although this is a preliminary study, the method was applied to evaluate various transportation plannings of a new town and good results were obtained.

Kole, T. , and F. Watman. "Behavior Modification as a Countermeasure for the Drinking Driver." Behavioral Research in Highway Safety, vol. 2, no. 1, 1971.

A countermeasure program to rehabilitate drinkers who drive is proposed in accordance with a behavior modification paradigm. In the proposed treatment program, an attempt is made to alter the maladaptive behavior, driving after drinking, by manipulating environmental stimuli through the following techniques: (1) selective positive reinforcement, (2) aversive conditioning, (3) modeling, and (4) suggestion-relaxation. The proposed program can vary from a minimum of 10 hours to a maximum of 30 hours depending upon the progress of each individual driver. The program includes the presentation of appropriate didactic materials, the discussion of (and encouragement to use) alternatives to driving after drinking, and three brief follow-up reinforcement sessions. In light of various efforts, federal requirements about new countermeasures include needed evaluations. These efforts demand that consideration be given to both program participants and the community at large.

Parsons, M. "Caution Behavior and Its Conditioning in Driving." Human Factors 18 (1976): 397-408.

If people drove more cautiously, there might be fewer accidents. Caution behavior includes pausing and looking. It is suggested that the precautionary pause based on a longer response latency and reduced force can be conditioned into drivers as avoidance behavior. In laboratory research that can be construed as simulation of driving, latencies were lengthened and forces diminished because of the contingencies of an adversive consequence. Accidents, near-accidents, and verbalizations about them can be viewed as aversive consequences that generate driver avoidance behavior, including the precautionary pause. How might the driving environment, including motivational signs, be designed to exploit this process and thereby contribute to highway safety?

Sommer, R. "Room Density and User Satisfaction." Environment and Behavior 3 (1971): 412-16.

Stokols, D. "The Experience of Crowding in Primary and Secondary Environments." Environment and Behavior 8 (1976) : 49-87.

Tardiff, T. J. "The Effects of Socio-Economic Status on Transportation Attitudes and Behavior." University of California, Graduate School of Social Sciences, Irvine.

The major issues of this study are whether or not there are any noneconomic, nontransportation related variables that are useful in explaining individual transportation attitudes and behavior and that improve existing models of transportation behavior. Five variables, theoretically related to objective measures of socioeconomic status, were selected for investigation: alienation, satisfaction with work, powerlessness, future orientation, and person orientation. These social-psychological variables were included in simple hypotheses involving variables measuring transportation attitudes or behavior and were also added to models similar to existing trip generation and mode choice models. It was observed that many of the variables measuring transportation attitudes or behavior were significantly associated with at least one of the social-psychological variables. Thus, it was concluded that the social-psychological variables are useful in understanding transportation attitudes and behavior. However, none of the social-paychological variables were universally useful in all of the trip generation models stratified by trip purpose. Further, the social-psychological variables failed to improve a mode choice model. Therefore, it was concluded that the social-psychological variables do not appear to be useful additions to the types of disaggregate models used in general planning contexts: trip generation models unstratified by trip purpose and mode choice models.

Taylor, D. H. "Driver's Galvanic Skin Response and the Risk of an Accident." Ergonomic 7 (1964): 439-51.

Galvanic skin responses of 20 drivers were measured in two studies covering a wide range of roads and road conditions. Accident histories were obtained for the roads in one of the studies. It is shown that the level of GSR activity does not depend primarily on the nature of the road or conditions. Consistent sources of variation in the GSR are observed, one of them apparently being the subject's experience of driving. The distribution of GSR per unit distance traveled was found to be similar to the distribution of accidents per unit total distance of vehicle travel (the accident rate). The results support a view that driving is a self-paced task governed by the level of emotional tension or anxiety which the driver wishes to tolerate. The possible effects of this on the distribution of accidents is discussed.


TRAFFIC FLOW

Caldwaller, M. T. "Cognitive Distance in Intraurban Space." In Environmental Knowing, edited by G. T. Moon and R. G. Golledge, pp. 316-24. 1976.

Campbell, D. T., and H. L. Ross. "The Connecticut Crackdown on Speeding." Law Society Review 3 (1968): 33-53.

This paper introduces, in the context of a problem in applied sociology and the sociology of law, a mode of analysis designed to deal with a common class of situations in which research must proceed without the benefit of experimental control. The general methodology expounded here is termed "quasi-experimental analysis." The specific mode of analysis is the "interrupted time-series design." Perhaps its fundamental credo is that lack of control and lack of randomization are damaging to inferences of cause and effect only to the extent that a systematic consideration of alternative explanations reveals some that are plausible. More complete explications of quasi-experimental analysis have appeared elsewhere; this paper merely illustrates its use in a situation where a series of observations has been recorded for periods of time both prior and subsequent to the experience of the specific event to be studied. Such data are quite commonly available, yet they are seldom fully utilized and investigators often confine themselves unnecessarily to much less satisfactory methodologies. The 1955 crackdown on speeding in the State of Connecticut furnishes an apt example of the potentialities of such quasi-experimental analysis.

Carr, S., and D. Schissler. "The City as a Trip." Environment and Behavior 1 (1969): 7-37.

The research upon which this report is based has dealt with a special, though increasingly important, urban experience: the approach to the center of a city on an elevated expressway. The study has attempted to identify the relevant variables in the perception and memory-representation of such a trip. Specifically, we have asked how this representation is related to people's expectations and their patterns of looking and how these in turn are related to the form of environment. Through the use of a behavioral record of eye movements, it has been possible to observe an empirical regularity in the process which begins with the formal properties of the highway environment—the configuration of changing elements and their sequential order—and ends with the construction of a cognitive representation of the trip. A central aspect of that regularity is reflected in the relative dominance of elements looked at and remembered. It is that aspect that is reported here in terms of group data, along with comparisons among subject groups of drivers, passengers, and commuters.

Dewar, R. E. "The Slash Obscures the Symbol on Prohibitive Traffic Signs." Human Factors 18 (1976): 253-58.

The problem of whether drivers should be told what they can do (permissive message) or what they cannot do (prohibitive message) is discussed as it relates to traffic sign symbols. A widely used version of the prohibitive message (symbol surrounded by a red ring with a slash through the symbol) was found to have limited legibility because the slash obscures the symbol. Two experiments examined the glance legibility of 15 symbols under each of four conditions—slash over symbol, slash under symbol, partial slash, and no slash. The results indicated that the glance legibility of traffic sign symbols is better when no slash or a partial slash is used to convey the prohibitive message.

Fergenson, P. E. "The Relationship between Information Processing and Driving Accident and Violation Record." Human Factors 13 (1971): 173-76.

Seventeen subjects matched for driving experience were divided into four groups according to their accident and traffic violation records. They were tested for their ability to process information at a significantly (p. 01) lower rate than nonaccident subjects. Subjects who had many violations, but no accidents, were the best information processors. There was a significant (p. 01) interaction between accident and violation record. These results and their implications are discussed.

Garling, T. "The Structural Analysis of Environmental Perception and Cognition." Environment and Behavior 8 (1976): 385-415.

The author is concerned with people's ability to classify and code the physical environment. Specific structural hypotheses were tested through the application of various models for multidimensional scaling, i.e., categorical and dimensional models. In addition, the author compared the above results to those produced via the semantic differential technique. The author concluded that the multidimensional scaling and cluster analysis based on ratings or sortings as to similarity reveal the basis for the evaluative assessments gauged by the semantic differential technique and that the basis is best conceived of as a categorization process to which the individual contributes his systematized knowledge about his everyday physical environment.

Golledge, R. G., and G. Zannais. "Cognitive Approaches to Spatial Behavior." In Environment and Cognition, edited by I. Ittleson, pp. 61-71. New York: Seminar Press, 1973.

Kameron, J. "Experimental Studies of Environmental Perception." In Environment and Cognition, edited by I. Ettelson, pp. 157-67. New York: Seminar Press, 1973.

The author reviews studies of the perception of complex environments. The discussion is separated into four environmental classifications: architectural forms, cities, highways and streets, and natural settings. The majority of reports deal with the study of specific environmental contexts. In sum, the author suggests (1) that more research should be done to develop a general model of environment perception and (2) that a systems approach rather than a S-R approach be used in the environmental perception research. Finally, the author praises the degree of naturalistic experimentation that has occurred within this area.

Lowenthal, D., and M. Riel. "The Nature of Perceived and Imagined Environments." Environment and Behavior 4 (1972): 189-208.

Via the use of questionnaires, interviews, free association, and the semantic differential techniques, the authors were able to compare and contrast subjects' responses concerning how the nature of environment looks to people in relation to how they believe it looks. They found that some qualities are seen to make a greater consistent impact on those who are merely thinking about environmental concepts, and vice versa. Reveals the importance of field experimentation in relation to laboratory experiments.

Mithal, W. L., and G. V. Barrett. "Individual Differences in Perceptual Information Processing and Their Relation to Automobile Accident Involvement." Journal of Applied Psychology, pp. 229-33, 1976.

A perceptual-information-processing model of driver decision making was used as a framework to select and devise predictors of accident involvement. The predictors of field dependence, selective attention, and complex reaction time significantly related to accident involvement for 75 commercial drivers. Initial, simple, and choice reaction time did not relate to accident rate. The visual measures of field dependence and the auditory measure of selective attention were related to the predicted direction with the field-independent drivers making fewer errors in selective perception. This finding lends support to the importance of the further development of an information-processing model of the driving task. Since evidence is accumulating that stable individual differences in information processing relate to accident involvement, consideration should be given to devising techniques to develop these skills.

Moore, G. T. "The Development of Environmental Knowing: An Overview of an Interactional Constructivist Theory and Some Data on Within-Individual Development Variations." In Psychology and the Built Environment, edited by D. Canter and T. Lee, pp. 185-94. New York: Wiley, 1974.

This paper has two aims: first, to outline some propositions of an interactional-constructivist theory of knowing, and second, to report on one part of a modest experiment based on that theoretical perspective and designed to shed some light on three questions about developmental variations in the ways in which people structure their knowledge of large-scale environments: (1) Are there developmental variations in the same individual with respect to the organization of knowledge of different environments (i.e., "within-individual variations")? (2) If so, can these variations be characterized in structural terms? (3) Are these variations developmentally ordered or do they reflect different styles of representation?

Moscowitz, H., K. Ziedman, and S. Sharma. "Visual Search Behavior While Viewing Driving Scenes under the Influence of Alcohol and Marihuana." Human Factors 18 (1976): 417-32.

Two experiments were performed to determine the effects of alcohol and marihuana on visual scanning patterns in a simulated driving situation. In the first experiment, 27 male heavy drinkers were divided into three groups of nine, defined by three blood alcohol levels produced by alcohol treatment: 0.0%, 0.075%, and 0.15% BACs. Significant changes in visual search behavior, including increased dwell duration, decreased dwell frequency, and increased pursuit duration and frequency were found under alcohol. In the second experiment, 10 male social users of marihuana were tested under both 0 mcg and 200 mcg tetrahydrocannabinol per kilogram bodyweight. Marihuana was found to have no effect on visual search behavior. The results are related to previous studies of alcohol and marihuana effects on information processing.

Robinson, G. H., et al. "Visual Search by Automobile Drivers." Human Factors 14 (1972): 315-23.

Data are presented on the visual search of automobile drivers during two maneuvers: (1) entering a highway after a stop and (2) changing lanes on a multilane highway. Head-movement measurements were used to show patterns and timing of search. The relationships between eye and head movements are discussed.


TRANSPORTATION CHOICE

Anderson, N. H. "Information Integration Theory: A Brief Survey." In Contemporary Developments in Mathematical Psychology, vol. 2, edited by D. H. Krantz, R. C. Atkinson, R. D. Luce, and P. Suppes. San Francisco: Freeman, 1974.

Deslauriers, B. C. "A Behavioral Analysis of Transportation: Some Suggestions for Mass Transit." High Speed Ground Transportation Journal 9 (1975): 13-20.

Behavioral principles are outlined and used to analyze bus riding and car driving. It is concluded that transportation behaviors are chains of responses, consequences (reinforcers and punishers), and discriminative stimuli and that alterations of these components will influence ridership. It is suggested that manipulations such as free transit and exclusive bus lanes will attract the carless more than car drivers. Analysis indicates that systems such as Dial-a-Bus and Park-and-Ride have potential for competing with the car because these systems reduce the delay of reinforcement and the aversive consequences associated with bus riding.

Deslauriers, B. C., and P. B. Everett. "The Effects of Intermittent and Continuous Token Reinforcement in Bus Ridership." Journal of Applied Psychology (in press).

The following conditions were successively instituted on the experimental bus (the 11:00 a.m. to 2:00 p.m. daily operation of a campus bus): baseline, variable ratio 3 token reinforcement (every third passenger, on the average, received a token worth about 10¢ for boarding the bus), continuous token reinforcement (every passenger received a token), variable ratio 3 token reinforcement, and baseline. Compared to the experimental controls, experimental bus ridership increased significantly during token reinforcement manipulations. There was no difference in the effects of variable ratio 3 and continuous token reinforcement. The results suggest that compared to continuous token reinforcement, intermittent token reinforcement may provide a viable and economical approach to increasing bus ridership.

Dobson, R., T. F. Golob, and R. L. Gustafson. "Multidimensional Scaling of Consumer Preferences for a Public Transportation System: An Application of Two Approaches." Socioeconomic Planning Sciences 8 (1974): 23-37.

Consumer attitudes toward a proposed new public transportation system were assessed through the application of two multidimensional scaling models to data on preference choices for system attributes. Carroll's vector model and Kruskal's and Carmone's nonmetric unfolding model were compared on theoretical and empirical levels to determine their utility for exposing the latent structure of attitudes for a public project. While the unfolding model was attractive because of a theoretical property, the vector model was able to uncover latent dimensions for the attitudes that could be related via discriminant analysis to socioeconomic and demographic characteristics of the respondents. The vector model also produced an outcome more closely related to a unidimensional analysis of these data. Therefore, even though both the vector and unfolding models produced plausible geometric representations of the attitudes expected to aid urban transportation planners in designing systems, the vector model produced the more acceptable outcome.

Dobson, R., and J. F. Kehoe. "Disaggregated Behavioral Views of Transportation Attributes." Transportation Research Board 527 (1974): 1-15.

Dobson, R., and M. L. Tischer. "Comparative Analysis of Determinants of Modal Choices by Central Business District Workers." Transportation Research Record 649 (1977): 7-13.

The role of individuals' perceptions and preferences in traveler decision making is a growing and active area of theoretical and empirical research. This study was designed (a) to quantify the

relation between perceived system attributes and modal choice,
(b) to compare the magnitude of this relation to that of the alternative relations of sociodemographic and network time and cost
data and modal choice, and (c) to determine whether the linkage
between perceived system attributes and modal choice is dependent on the relations of sociodemographic and network data to
modal choice. The sample was composed of Los Angeles central business district workers who live within approximately 3.2
kilometers (2 miles) of a freeway that feeds radially downtown.
Models were calibrated for three dependent variable criteria;
there were monthly differences in use for (a) automobile versus
bus, (b) automobile versus car pool, and (c) bus versus car pool.
The multiple coefficients of determination for modal choice as a
function of perceived system attributes were statistically significant at the 0.001 level for all dependent variable criteria. The
coefficients ranged from 0.265 to 0.125, but the analogous coefficients for sociodemographic or planning data ranged from a
low of 0.004 to a high of only 0.054. The effects of perceived
system attributes on the dependent variables were not diminished
by the other types of independent variables. Tests of significance for the individual components of combined models with
these types of data showed the perceived system attribute data
to be significant at beyond the 0.001 level in all cases. However,
sociodemographic and network data space appeared to be influenced by the addition of perceived system attribute data to the
degree of becoming nonsignificant in some cases. The overall
conclusion is that perceived system attributes can be a statistically significant correlate of modal choice over and above any
influence by network or sociodemographic variables or both.

Downs, R. M. "The Cognitive Structure of an Urban Shopping
    Center." Environment and Behavior 2 (1970): 13-39.

The author is concerned with evaluating the viability of a cognitive behavioral approach in the prediction of consumer spatial
behavior. The cognitive behavioral approach views the consumer's behavior as a function of the environmental situation
and the decision-making processes with respect to the environment. This formulation is compared with two other consumer
spatial behavioral approaches: market research models and
location theory formulations. The bulk of the article is concerned with an empirical study based upon the cognitive behavioral approach.

Eash, R. W., A. Swanson, and M. Kaplan. "An Analysis and Evaluation of Alternative Schemes to Increase Auto Occupancy." Transportation Research 8 (1974): 335-41.

The paper describes a portion of the work done at the Chicago Area Transportation Study investigating the fuel saving potential of forming car pools for the work trip on a regional basis. The formation of car pools is viewed in traditional economic theory as an example of consumer behavior and pricing. A simple economic behavior model was formulated and applied to the evaluation of several general pricing schemes to increase car occupancy. Using this model the ability of the pricing schemes (which can be interpreted as the consequences of various fuel allocation programs) to reduce fuel consumption was evaluated.

Everett, P. B. "A Behavioral Science Approach to Transportation System Management."

The paper puts forth the proposition that behavior science can contribute to one of the major tasks of transportation systems management (TSM). It is suggested that the coherent perspective and well-documented successes and findings of applied learning theory can make a significant impact upon the TSM task of managing travel behaviors. The paper then outlines the conceptual basis for this endeavor and reviews in detail completed case studies and experimental applications. The paper concludes by specifying a short- and long-term research and application future for an applied learning theory approach to TSM.

Everett, P. B., B. C. Deslauriers, and T. J. Newson. "Increasing the Effectiveness of Free Transit." Transit Journal (in press).

Everett, P. B., S. C. Hayward, and A. Meyers. "The Effect of a Token Reinforcement Procedure on Bus Ridership." Journal of Applied Behavior Analysis 7 (1974): 1-9.

Tokens, exchangeable for a variety of back-up reinforcers, were delivered for several days to all persons boarding a clearly marked campus bus. This procedure increased ridership to 150% of baseline. The experiment was carried out to demonstrate the applicability of operant techniques to urban transportation problems. In this study, a token reinforcement procedure was introduced in an attempt to increase bus ridership while holding the costs of reinforcers to a minimum and circumventing the problems of individual satiety and preferences and of delivering cumbersome reinforcers. A methodology is establishing a token-exchange procedure in an open-field behavior setting, where the subject population size, geographic location, preferences, age, sex, preferred hours of mobility, etc., are unspecified, is also presented.

Ewing, R. H. "Psychological Theory Applied to Mode Choice Prediction." Transportation 2 (1973): 391-410.

In an effort to improve transit ridership prediction, this manuscript proposes a conceptually unique mode choice model derived from the field of experimental psychology. The psychophysical model, as it is called, differs from earlier modal split models in its substantive use of psychological theory. The result is a modal split model with a sound behavioral foundation.

The psychophysical model is tested using data from the recent demonstration of Dial-a-Bus in Columbia, Maryland, and found to be a marginal predictor of modal split. It is noted, though, that the difference between actual and predicted ridership may be accounted for in a second generation model. This will employ individual rather than aggregate data, incorporate the concept of adaptation-level, and refine the decision-making process.

Foxx, R. M., and D. F. Hake. "Gasoline Conservation: A Procedure for Measuring and Reducing the Driving of College Students." Journal of Applied Behavioral Analysis 10 (1977): 61-74.

The study sought to motivate college students to reduce the number of miles they drove each day and thus save gasoline. Students in two psychology classes were divided by class into two groups. The experimental group was offered various combinations of prizes such as cash, a tour of a mental-health facility, car servicing, and a university parking sticker for reducing driving. The value of the prize received was scaled in terms of percent reduction in driving. The contrast group received no inducements. The condition in which the experimental group's mileage reduction was reinforced was counterbalanced by two baseline conditions. Several special recording procedures were used to reduce and detect the possibility of subjects altering their odometers, the source of the driving data. Experimental subjects reduced their average daily mileage by 20% relative to the initial baseline; the contrast group did not change. During the one-month reinforcement condition, the 12 experimental subjects saved some 170 gallons (worth $102) of gasoline.

Golob, T. F., E. T. Canty, R. L. Gustafson, and J. E. Vitt. "An Analysis of Consumer Preferences for a Public Transportation System." Transportation Research 6 (1972): 81-102.

This paper discusses the structure of a market research study to design an evolutionary public transportation system. This system, the Demand-responsive Jitney (D-J), provides door-to-door service upon user request, similar to the service provided by taxicabs. Users share the vehicle in order to minimize costs, and, in large-scale D-J systems, computers would be used to optimally route and schedule the vehicle fleet in the servicing of the requests. The market research study is one part of the D-J Systems Study conducted by the Transportation Research Department of General Motors Research Laboratories. The objectives of the overall study were to design the D-J system and to evaluate the technical and economic feasibility and political and social acceptance of the system within the environment of a selected case study community. Reports have been published concerning the overall study and various phases of the study (Bauer 1970; Howson and Heathington 1970; and Golob and Gustafson 1971).

Golob, T. F., and W. W. Recker. "Attitude Behavior Models for Public Systems Planning and Design." General Motors Research Laboratories, Report No. GMR-1906.

This exploration of the potential applications of behavioral choice models in the planning of public systems focuses on choice models involving attitudinal variables. The areas of application of these models include environmental design, structures, and general cost-benefit analysis of systems. Methods of scaling preference and perception responses elicited through popular survey instruments are evaluated. Models are then investigated for explaining overall preference or choice of alternatives in terms of perceptions of the characteristics of the alternatives. An empirical example is presented in which policies concerning improvements in public transit bus system can be initially formulated using information obtained from an attitudinal model of urban residents' choice of travel mode for their work and shopping trips.

Hammond, K. R., C. Hursch, and F. J. Todd. "Analyzing the Components of Clinical Inference." Psychological Review 71 (1964): 438-56.

The purpose of this paper is to analyze the components of clinical inference within the framework of Brunswik's lens model by means of multiple-regression analysis. Two parallel studies of clinical psychologists, the performance of Ss in a quasi-clinical task, and the performance of Ss learning a multiple-cue probability task involving neutral stimuli provide the context for the analysis. Special reference is made to the problem of clinical versus statistical prediction. Implications for the interrelation between experimental psychology, cognitive theory, and clinical tests are discussed.

Hartgen, D. T., and C. H. Tanner. "Individual Attitudes and Family Activities: A Behavioral Model of Traveler Mode Choice." High Speed Ground Transportation Journal 4 (1970): 439-67.

This paper presents a behavioral approach to the modeling of mode choice, the process whereby individual travelers choose a travel mode. This process is distinct from the problem of estimating modal split, the aggregate result of individual decisions concerning travel mode. Although a number of models have explained modal split statistically through correlation with demographic and system variables, the individual's mode choice decision, a behavioral process, has not been investigated extensively.

In this paper, the decision process leading to an individual's choice of a particular mode of travel is viewed in the context of his behavior as a member of a household or family. A framework of individual behavior is presented, structured around the needs, attitudes, and preferred activities of individuals and their households. It is hypothesized that in its decision process, the household determines a set of activities required to fulfill the needs of its members, whose actions are then influenced by the specific tasks assigned to them. Travel is viewed as a by-product of the performance of some tasks, occurring not for its own sake but only because it links desired activities to locations where they can take place.

One aspect of the travel decision, choice of mode, is examined in detail. A model of this decision process is formulated, based on the activities engaged in by an individual and his attitudes toward the quality of various attributes of the transportation system. Activities are represented by trips, classified by generalized purpose, auto availability, household type, and household income. Attitudes are represented by the importance placed on each of a set of system attributes by the individual traveler for a given trip and his satisfaction with the existing quality of each attribute, for transit and auto models.

The sensitivity of the model is investigated by applying it to hypothetical improvements in two qualitative system variables. The authors are optimistic that the test results, although preliminary, show promise for the model in estimating the usage on new modes or qualitative improvements to existing modes whose attributes have been described in terms of traveler attitudes.

Johnson, M. "Psychological Variables and Choice between Auto and Transit Travel: A Critical Research Review." Working Paper No. 7509, Institute of Transportation and Traffic Engineering, University of California, Berkeley, 1975.

It is well known, and often lamented, that nearly all travel in American metropolitan areas is by automobile. Comparatively, transit travel is almost negligible. (U.S. Department of Transportation data show that in 1970, 96 percent of urban miles traveled involved an automobile, as compared with only 4 percent for all forms of public transportation.)

The reasons for this overwhelming preference for automobile travel have been much speculated upon and, to a lesser extent, studied. Transportation planners, in analyzing the modal split between automobiles and transit, have emphasized what can be called conventional variables, such as travel times and costs, automobile ownership, income, and urban density. On the other hand, popular explanations of travel preferences—by media pundits, social scientists, and next door neighbors—tend to stress psychological or attitudinal variables, which are relatively independent of the conventional factors cited above. Motivations such as enjoyment of driving and auto ownership and privacy, security, and comfort while traveling are commonly mentioned.

This report is concerned with the problem of evaluating the relative importance of the two types of variables, conventional and psychological, as determinants of auto-transit choice. The report has several objectives: to clarify the distinction between the two types of variables, to indicate why it may be valuable to learn more about the influence of psychological variables on travel behavior, to review and critique existing research on this subject, and to suggest additional research that should be done.

Johnson, R. M. "Pairwise Non-Metric Multidimensional Scaling." Psychometrika 38 (1973): 11-18.

A method of nonmetric multidimensional scaling is described which minimizes pairwise departures from monotonicity. The procedure is relatively simple, both conceptually and computationally. Experience to date suggests that it produces solutions comparable to those of other methods.

Johnson, R. M. "Trade-Off Analysis: The Measurement of Consumer Values." Journal of Marketing Research, vol. 11, 1974.

A method for exploring and quantifying the value system of consumers through conjoint measurement is described. Since it is concerned with value systems of individual consumers, the method is most appropriate for product categories where consumers' desires are heterogeneous and where markets are highly segmented.

Koppelman, F., J. Prashker, and B. Begamery. "Perceptual Maps of Destination Characteristics Based on Similarities Data." Transportation Research Record 649 (1977): 32-37.

Individual travel choice behavior may be characterized by individual perceptions of travel alternatives, individual preferences for the attributes of these alternatives, and the availability of these alternatives. The research reported in this paper was part of a general study of how individuals choose locations for nongrocery shopping trips. It identifies a perceptual space that represents the way individuals perceive shopping locations and evaluates the stability of generality of the perceptual representation across independent sample. The perceptual space developed consists of three dimensions that represent (a) size and variety, (b) price and quality, and (c) environment and parking and is similar for two independent samples of individuals. These results characterize the underlying aspects that individuals use to summarize their perceptions of shopping locations, demonstrate the feasibility of developing perceptual spaces for destination choices, and support the use of perceptual spaces developed for small samples as representative of the population from which they are drawn. The results of the cumulative research of which this is a part indicate that it is feasible to develop choice models based on perceived, rather than on engineering, characterizations of transportation alternatives. Relating travel choices to perceptions provides the ability to evaluate the importance of attributes that are not measurable by direct (engineering) methods.

Levin, I. P. "Comparing Different Models and Response Transformation in an Information Integration Task." Bulletin of Psychometric Science 7 (1976): 78-80.

The role of response transformations was examined in an information integration task in which different models were supported for different response scales. In Experiment 1, one group of subjects made subjective estimates of cost in dollars (cost estimates) for a series of hypothetical trips described by varying levels of gasoline price, gas mileage, and distance, and another group of subjects made comparative ratings of the relative expense of each trip. A multiplicative model was supported for the cost estimates and an additive model was supported for the comparative ratings. In Experiment 2, a single group of subjects made cost estimates and then were asked, in the absence of stimulus values, to convert these judgments to comparative ratings. A multiplicative model was supported for each response mode, indicating a linear response transformation. It was concluded that the different response patterns in Experiment 1 were due to different integration processes for different response requirements rather than a nonlinear response transformation.

Levin, I. P. "Information Integration in Transportation Decisions." In Human Judgement and Decision Processes in Applied Settings, edited by M. F. Kaplan and S. Schwartz, pp. 57-82. New York: Academic Press, 1977.

This paper describes a program of research in which behavioral models are applied to problems in transportation. The research pursues two major goals: applying established behavioral techniques and models to further the understanding of transportation consumer decision processes, and using behavior in new decision-making contexts to further the development of theoretical models. A current major interest in transportation research is investigating factors that determine choice of travel mode. A related problem is determining what combination of service and pricing is required to make public transit an equitable and viable mode of travel. This is of particular interest now that the excessive use of private automobiles is seen as a drain on scarce energy resources. To aid transportation planners, researchers must determine the relative value and importance of specific system attributes to various groups of transportation consumers and must describe how system and user characteristics combine to determine mode choice. These are exactly the types of problems for which the models of information integration theory (Anderson 1974) are ideally suited. Several studies are reported later in which the information integration approach is used to analyze transportation decisions. This approach is thought to overcome many of the problems encountered by the traditional approaches.

Levin, I. P., M. K. Mosell, C. M. Lamka, B. E. Savage, and M. J. Gray. "Measurement of Psychological Factors and Their Role in Travel Behavior." Transportation Research Record 649 (1977): 1-6.

Psychological factors are conceptualized as intervening variables linking system and user characteristics to transportation judg-

ments and decisions. The information integration approach of
experimental psychology was used to measure and assess psychological factors by using simple rating scales and algebraic
models of individual decision processes. Two simulation experiments were conducted to illustrate this approach. In the
first, perceived safety of highway driving was measured on a
bipolar rating scale and shown to vary as a simple algebraic
function of factors, such as driving speed, time of day, weather
conditions, and number of hours of continued driving. Other
judgments involving continued driving time and reducing driving
speed were obtained and shown to be highly related to safety
ratings. This supports the idea that psychological factors such
as safety can be measured objectively and used to understand
and predict traveler behavior. In the second experiment, the
desirability of forming car pools was assessed as a function of
the number of riders in the pool, the sex of each rider, and the
acquaintanceship of the rider and the respondent. The acceptability of a given potential rider was a multiplicative function of
sex and acquaintanceship; sex played an important role when the
rider was a nonacquaintance. The desirability of a given car
pool was an average of the desirability of individual riders, so
that a desirable rider would compensate for undesirable riders.
The implication of such results to policy makers is discussed,
but the need for expanded research is stressed.

Luce, R. D. Individual Choice Behavior. New York: John Wiley
and Sons, 1959.

Michaels, R. M. "Attitudes of Drivers toward Alternative Highways
and Their Relation to Route Choice." Highway Research Record,
vol. 122, 1966.

To determine the factors influencing drivers' choice of alternative routes, a study was conducted in which the attitudes of drivers toward two highways were measured. In addition, traffic
characteristics of the routes were measured and the tension
generated on each was determined using nine test drivers. The
routes employed were 47-mile sections of an expressway-design
toll road and a parallel rural primary highway. Drivers were
sampled entering and exiting on both highways. A summated
rating attitude scale was administered to a sample of 3,259
drivers. Descriptive information was also obtained about the
driver, his trip, and travel habits. The results indicated that
these drivers hold stable attitudes toward the two highways,
which clearly differentiate between them. It appears that direct
measurement of driver attitudes is a better predictor of route

choice than descriptive information about the drivers or their
driving habits. In addition, the results provide a means of
rationalizing the attraction of traffic to an expressway on the
basis of drivers seeking to minimize tension in driving. The
results suggest that total stress incurred in driving is a more
important determinant of route choice than either operating
costs or travel time costs. A model of route choice and attraction of traffic is proposed based on tension generation, which
can be related to travel time data. The results of this research
indicate that drivers evaluate alternative highways in a rational,
though subjective, fashion. Such evaluation, however, appears
quite independent of the usual monetary schemes for rationalizing highway benefits and cost.

Nicolaidis, G. C., and J. N. Sheth. "An Application of Market
Segmentation in Urban Transportation Planning." Publication
No. 2149, General Motors Research Laboratories, Warren,
Mich., 1976.

Norman, K. L. "Attributes in Bus Transportation: Importance
Depends on Trip Purpose." Journal of Applied Psychology 62
(1977): 164-70.

Twenty-four college students judged the probability that they
would ride hypothetical bus systems for a work trip (to or from
a job or school) and for a leisure trip (to or from shopping or
recreation). Bus systems varied in terms of the attributes of
fare, total walking distance to and from the bus stop, number of
intervening stops en route, and time of service during the day.
An information-integration model was used in which the subject's
response is assumed to be a weighted geometric average of the
subjective values of the attributes describing a system. The effect of trip purpose was accounted for by changes in the weight
and subjective value of information. This approach increases
the generality of results by using psychologically meaningful
parameters to specify how the effects of an attribute vary from
one situation to another.

Norman, K. L., and J. J. Louviere. "Integration of Attributes in
Bus Transportation: Two Modeling Approaches." Journal of
Applied Psychology 59 (1974): 753-58.

Judged probability of riding hypothetical bus systems was studied
as a function of fare, frequency of service, and walking distance
to the bus stop. The judgment processes of 20 paid college students were modeled by two different approaches. A policy cap-

turing approach using regression analysis indicated that a linear
model accounted for the data adequately. However, a polynomial
model incorporating both linear and multiplicative components in
the judgment policy provided a better fit. A method of scaling
known as functional measurement served to reject the linear
model and confirmed that a multiplying model was correct.
Functional measurement provided subjective scales for fare,
frequency of service, and proximity to the bus stop. The advantages and limitations of both approaches were discussed.

Recker, W. W., and T. F. Golob. "An Attitudinal Modal Choice
Model." Transportation Research 10 (1976): 299-310.

Explanatory variables in this model of urban residents' mode
choice behavior for home-to-work trip are attitudinal ratings by
survey respondents of descriptive attributes of modes perceived
to be available to them. The model methodology is presented in
three parts: individuals are clustered with respect to homogeneity of their choice constraints; the covariance structure of
attitudinal variables is characterized through development of
latent factors describing respondents' perceptions of choice alternatives; and logit probabilistic choice models are estimated
in terms of subsets of descriptive attribute ratings chosen to
represent latent perception factors. Empirical results from
application of the model in the Ottawa, Ontario/Hull, Quebec
Canadian National Capital Region are extremely encouraging.
Goodness-of-fit summaries indicate model performance better
than that obtained using conventional logit models based upon
perceived time and cost data. Moreover, it is proposed that the
attitudinal models provide valuable insights concerning the importance of factors underlying the choice decision structure of
the sample population.

Romney, A. K., R. N. Shepard, and S. B. Nerlove, eds. Multidimensional Scaling: Theory and Applications in the Behavioral
Sciences, Volume 2. New York: Seminar Press, 1972.

Ross, R. B. "Measuring the Effects of Soft Variables on Travel
Behavior." Traffic Quarterly 29 (1975): 333-46.

Stea, D. "Architecture in the Head: Cognitive Mapping." In Designing for Human Behavior, edited by J. Lang, C. Burnet, W.
Maleski, and D. Vachin. Stroudberg, Pa.: Dowden, Hutchinson
and Ross, 1974.

Stenson, H. "Cognitive Factors in the Use of Transit Systems." Final Report, US-DOT-IL-11-0008, Urban Systems Laboratory, University of Illinois at Chicago Circle, Chicago, 1978.

Two studies of college students' mental representations of certain geographical features of Chicago are reported: (1) a questionnaire study assessing knowledge of the gross geography of the city as well as relative locations of rapid transit routes and termini, and (2) a study of students' distance estimates among all pairs of 20 familiar Chicago landmarks that resulted in the indirect assessment of their mental maps of the city. A theoretical analysis of possible types of mental maps is included.

Both studies indicate a poor perception of the relative locations of major places and areas of Chicago and the existence of systematic distortions of actual distances. Since the respondents in these studies were well educated, we conclude that this may be an even worse problem in the general population. Recommendations are made concerning the correction of these misperceptions to lead to greater use of mass transportation systems.

Stopher, P. R., and A. H. Meyburg. Urban Transportation Modeling and Planning. Lexington, Mass.: Lexington Books, 1975.

Thomas, K. "A Reinterpretation of the 'Attitude' Approach to Transport-Mode Choice and an Exploratory Empirical Test." Environment and Planning A 8 (1976): 783-810.

A theory of cognitive structure is presented that is potentially capable of providing a conceptual framework for the study of transport behavior, and, by making use of this theory and the models derived from it, problematic areas in attitude and attribute research in transportation are discussed. An exploratory empirical study is described that successfully tests some of the relationships inherent in the theory in a transport context. Significant correlations were observed between overall attitude toward use of a travel mode and the products of evaluation and belief strength summed over a short series of perceived outcomes of use of that mode. The content, strength, and associated evaluations of salient beliefs about use of a travel mode were monitored during a period of change in the conditions of the service. Predictable changes in belief structure were observed, demonstrating the sensitivity of the techniques used.

Watson, P. L. "Predictions of Intercity Modal Choice from Disaggregate, Behavioral and Stochastic Models." Highway Research Record 446 (1973): 28-35.

TRAVEL DEMAND

Barker, W. G., and J. J. Roark. "The Role of the Urban Transportation Planner in Public Policy." Southwest Division of the
Association of American Geographers Spring Meeting, April 15,
1978, at Houston, Texas.

Horton, F. E., and J. J. Louviere. "Behavioral Analyses and
Transportation Planning: Inputs to Transit Planning." Transportation 3 (1974): 165-82.

The purpose of this paper is to discuss various types of behavioral data of potential relevance to transit planning. In particular, a distinction is drawn between behavioral information regarding feelings, attitudes, opinions, and the like and more
sophisticated types of data dealing with individuals' intentions to
respond in certain ways given certain configurations of stimuli
(transportation variables). The former is shown to be an important input to incremental planning, i.e., where information
as to system performance is desired. The latter is shown to be
critical to decisions regarding manipulations of transit system
parameters, i.e., where knowledge of the outcome of manipulating system parameters is desired.

A methodological example as to how the first type of data—infor-
mational level data—can be collected and utilized in system planning is presented. Specifically, data collected along the lines of
traditional attitude surveys is collected in an attempt to monitor
changes in public satisfaction with the Iowa City, Iowa, bus system before and after major system innovations. Implications of
the collection and analytical procedures are discussed.

Lee, J. W., D. O. Covault, and G. E. Willeke. "Framework for
Using Social Indicators to Monitor, Evaluate and Improve a Pub-
lic Transport System." Work sponsored by Committee on Social,
Economic and Environmental Factors in Transportation, 1973.

This paper proposes a general framework for using social indicators to monitor, evaluate, and improve a public transportation
system. Discussion of this framework is preceded by a definition of social indicators and an explanation of five of their functions. Some general factors and techniques concerning the
selection, measurement, collection, and storage of social indicators are suggested. The specific approach presents eight
areas of concern. These areas are suggested as performance
criteria for evaluating any public transportation system. Furthermore, important questions are listed and are broken down

by related factors. From this systematic approach, the authors specify four sample indicators. These indicators are then developed for the framework's stages of monitoring, evaluating, and improving public transportation systems. In the final section, one of the sample indicators is applied to the Atlanta Model Cities Shuttle Bus System.

Louviere, J. J., and K. L. Norman. "Applications of Information Processing Theory to the Analysis of Urban Travel Demand." Environment and Behavior 9 (1977): 91-106.

Attempt to develop a set of policy-sensitive models in which variables can be experimentally manipulated in order to determine their likely effects on the trip-making propensity of the public. In each of a set of experiments, subjects were presented a set of hypothetical bus systems described in terms of attributes such as fare, frequency of service, and the like. Subjects rated each system in terms of the subjective likelihood that they would ride the bus system described. Of the bus attributes investigated, fare is the most important. Once fare is set at a particular value, however, subjects judge on the basis of other important attributes, such as proximity to the bus stop. Also, subjective judgments conform to a multiplying model between factors.

Michaels, R. M., and N. S. Weiler. "Transportation Needs of the Mobility Limited." Transportation Center, Northwestern University, Evanston, Ill., 1975.

Nicolaidis, G. C., and R. Dobson. "Disaggregated Perceptions and Preferences in Transportation Planning." Transportation Research 9 (1975): 279-95.

This paper uses preferences and similarity judgments with respect to system characteristics of an integrated innovative urban transport system to better understand the demand for public transportation. This transport system concept embraces dual mode transit, personal rapid transit, and people mover vehicles. A major goal of this study is to identify insights that could be uncovered by segmenting a sample of respondents into homogeneous perceptual groups. Three psychometric models are applied to a set of judgments from a set of respondents. The results from these models are used to cluster individuals into homogeneous population segments on the basis of common pattern of preferences. The patterns of preferences for the various groups are then linked to their socioeconomic characteristics. The analysis provides some useful insights as to the socioeconomic profiles of groups preferring automatic vehicle control, basic transport service, and personal luxury service. These results make it possible to better understand the benefits derived by these user groups from different system alternatives.

Nicolaidis, G. C., M. Wachs, and T. F. Golob. "Evaluation of Alternative Market Segmentations for Transportation Planning." Transportation Research Record 649 (1977): 23-31.

In transportation planning, market segmentation is the division of a total population of travelers into groups (segments) that are relatively homogeneous with respect to certain personal characteristics (the segmentation base). It is desirable that the segments be distinct in terms of travel behavior and their reactions to changes in the travel environment, such as the introduction of new transportation services. This paper describes a comparison of market segmentation using six different bases—two based on demographic variables, two on travel choice constraints, and two on attitudinal variables. The six segmentations were compared with respect to five criteria judged to be important considerations in transportation planning: measurability (data availability), statistical robustness, substantiality (size and importance of the resulting segments), relation to travel behavior, and relation to planning of service options. The comparisons showed that no single segmentation base was superior, according to all criteria, but that the segmentation based on multivariate choice constraints satisfied more of the criteria than did the other segmentation. Segmentations of the traveling population based on attitudes were found to have certain specific uses but to be inferior to choice constraints segmentation for most planning purposes.

O'Farrell, P. N., and J. Markham. "Commuter Perception of Public Transport Work Journeys." Environment and Planning A 6 (1974): 79-100.

Commuter perceptions of certain public transport peak-hour performance characteristics are quantified for samples of car-owning public transport users and car users in six randomly selected areas of the Dublin conurbation. The existence of roadside survey data (for buses) and timetables (for trains) has permitted an analysis of the degree of distorted perception of invehicle times, waiting times, and costs. Results show that the use of objective performance data on public transport modes in urban transportation planning models needs to be questioned, as actual times and costs seldom reflect the subjective images of commuters.

Paine, F., et al. "Consumer Conceived Attributes of Transportation: An Attitude Study." Department of Business Administration, University of Maryland, College Park, 1967.

Ryan, C. R., B. P. Nedevek, and E. A. Beinborn. "An Evaluation of the Feasibility of Social Diagnostic Techniques in Transportation Planning Process." Highway Research Record 410 (1972): 8-23.

An examination is made of the feasibility of using social diagnostic techniques in the transportation planning process. This was done through a survey of values and views of residents located within the general area of the corridor of the northern extension of the Stadium Freeway in Milwaukee. A questionnaire was prepared by a team of engineers and social scientists at the University of Wisconsin-Milwaukee. Results of the survey are presented relative to demographic characteristics, attitudes toward transportation services, attitudes toward nontransportation services, and analysis of freeway support and opposition to the freeway project. Conclusions of the research are such that techniques appear to be feasible and can provide valuable information for the development of transportation plans.

Spear, B. D. "Attitudinal Modeling: Its Role in Travel Demand Forecasting." In Behavioral Travel-Demand Models, edited by P. R. Stopher and A. Meyburg, pp. 87-95. Lexington, Mass.: Lexington Books, 1975.

This chapter will examine some recent research efforts that have attempted to apply attitudinal modeling to travel-demand forecasting. The first three studies, by Nicolaidis (1974), Spear (1974), and Hensher, McLeod, and Stanley (1975), all address the problem of identifying ambiguous attributes of transportation, such as comfort and convenience, and incorporate them into disaggregate travel-demand forecasting models. The studies conducted by General Motors Research Laboratories (Costantino, Dobson, and Canty 1974; Dobson and Kehoe 1974; Dobson and Nicolaidis 1974) investigate the use of attitudes as criteria for identifying groups of trip makers with distinctly different patterns of travel-demand behavior. The chapter concludes by presenting a number of topics for future research in which attitudinal modeling can make a significant contribution to the development of improved travel-demand forecasting models.

Yancey, L. L. "Psychological Factors Affecting Urban Travel: Responses to Crowding in Transit Vehicles." National Technical Information Service, Florida State University, Tallahassee, 1972.

A study based upon a survey of residents of a student housing complex at Florida State University developed and tested a survey instrument that examined psychological responses to crowding in transit vehicles. Using a series of sketches and several psychometric scales, it was noted how psychological stresses due to crowding were measurable phenomena and how significant relationships existed between the level of crowding and level of stress.


## BEHAVIOR CHANGE

Berger, C. J., L. L. Cummings, and H. G. Heneman. "Expectancy Theory and Operant Conditioning Prediction of Performance under Variable-Ratio and Continuous Schedules of Reinforcement." Organizational Behavior and Human Performance 14 (1975): 227-43.

Deslauriers, B. C. "A Behavioral Analysis of Transportation: Some Suggestions for Mass Transit." High Speed Ground Transportation Journal 9 (1975): 13-20.

Deslauriers, B. C., and P. B. Everett. "The Effects of Intermittent and Continuous Token Refinement in Bus Ridership." Journal of Applied Psychology (in press).

Everett, P. B. "A Behavioral Science Approach to Transportation System Management."

Everett, P. B., B. C. Deslauriers, and T. J. Newson. "Increasing the Effectiveness of Free Transit." Transit Journal (in press).

Everett, P. B., S. C. Hayward, and A. Meyers. "The Effect of a Token Reinforcement Procedure on Bus Ridership." Journal of Applied Behavior Analysis 7 (1974): 1-9.

Foxx, R. M., and D. F. Hake. "Gasoline Conservation: A Procedure for Measuring and Reducing the Driving of College Students." Journal of Applied Behavioral Analysis 10 (1977): 61-74.

Golledge, R. G., and G. Zannais. "Cognitive Approaches to Spatial Behavior." In Environment and Cognition, edited by I. Ittleson, pp. 61-71. New York: Seminar Press, 1973.

Griffeth, R. W., and R. W. Rogers. "Effects of Fear-Arousing Components of Driver Education on Students' Safety Attitudes and Simulator Performance." Journal of Educational Psychology 68 (1976): 501-6.

Kole, T., and F. Watman. "Behavior Modification as a Countermeasure for the Drinking Driver." Behavioral Research in Highway Safety, vol. 2, no. 1, 1971.

Pedalino, E., and V. V. Gamboa. "Behavior Modification and Absenteeism: Intervention in One Industrial Setting." Journal of Applied Psychology 59 (1974): 694-98.

Wexley, K. N., and W. F. Numeroff. "Effectiveness of Positive Reinforcement and Goal Setting as Methods of Management Development." Journal of Applied Psychology 60 (1975): 446-50.

Yukl, C. A., and G. P. Latham. "Consequences of Reinforcement Schedules and Incentives Magnitudes for Employee Performance: Problems Encountered in Industrial Setting." Journal of Applied Psychology 60 (1975): 294-98.

Yukl, C. A., K. N. Wexley, and J. D. Segmmi. "Effectiveness of Pay Incentives under Variable Ratio and Continuous Reinforcement Schedules." Journal of Applied Psychology 56 (1972): 19-23.

CHOICE DECISION MAKING

Bronzoft, A. L., S. B. Dobrow, and T. J. O'Hanlon. "Spatial Orientation in a Subway System." Environment and Behavior 8 (1976): 575-94.

Dobson, R., and J. F. Kehoe. "Disaggregated Behavioral Views of Transportation Attributes." Transportation Research Board 527 (1974): 1-15.

Dobson, R., and M. L. Tischer. "Comparative Analysis of Determinants of Modal Choices by Central Business District Workers." Transportation Research Record 649 (1977): 7-13.

Downs, R. M. "The Cognitive Structure of an Urban Shopping Center." Environment and Behavior 2 (1970): 13-39.

Ebbeson, E. B., and M. Haney. "Flirting with Death: Variables Affecting Risk Taking at Intersections." Journal of Applied Social Psychology 3 (1973): 303-24.

Golob, T. F., E. T. Canty, R. L. Gustafson, and J. E. Vitt. "An Analysis of Consumer Preferences for a Public Transportation System." Transportation Research 6 (1972): 81-102.

Golob, T. F., and W. W. Recker. "Attitude Behavior Models for Public Systems Planning and Design." General Motors Research Laboratories, Report No. GMR-1906.

Hammond, K. R., C. Hursch, and F. J. Todd. "Analyzing the Components of Clinical Inference." Psychological Review 71 (1964): 438-56.

Hartgen, D. T., and C. H. Tanner. "Individual Attitudes and Family Activities: A Behavioral Model of Traveler Mode Choice." High Speed Ground Transportation Journal 4 (1970): 439-67.

Johnson, R. M. "Pairwise Non-Metric Multidimensional Scaling." Psychometrika 38 (1973): 11-18.

Johnson, R. M. "Trade-Off Analysis: The Measurement of Consumer Values." Journal of Marketing Research, vol. 11, 1974.

Koppelman, F., J. Prashker, and B. Begamery. "Perceptual Maps of Destination Characteristics Based on Similarities Data." Transportation Research Record 649 (1977): 32-37.

Levin, I. P. "Information Integration in Transportation Decisions." In Human Judgement and Decision Processes in Applied Settings, edited by M. F. Kaplan and S. Schwartz, pp. 57-82. New York: Academic Press, 1977.

Luce, R. D. Individual Choice Behavior. New York: John Wiley and Sons, 1959.

Michaels, R. M. "Attitudes of Drivers toward Alternative Highways and Their Relation to Route Choice." Highway Research Record, vol. 122, 1966.

Michaels, R. M., and N. S. Weiler. "Transportation Needs of the Mobility Limited." Transportation Center, Northwestern University, Evanston, Ill., 1975.

Nicolaidis, G. C., and R. Dobson. "Disaggregated Perceptions and Preferences in Transportation Planning." Transportation Research 9 (1975): 279-95.

Nicolaidis, G. C., and J. N. Sheth. "An Application of Market Segmentation in Urban Transportation Planning." Publication No. 2149, General Motors Research Laboratories, Warren, Mich., 1976.

Nicolaidis, G. C., M. Wachs, and T. F. Golob. "Evaluation of Alternative Market Segmentations for Transportation Planning." Transportation Research Record 649 (1977): 23-31.

Norman, K. L. "Attributes in Bus Transportation: Importance Depends on Trip Purpose." Journal of Applied Psychology 62 (1977): 164-70.

Norman, K. L., and J. J. Louviere. "Integration of Attributes in Bus Transportation: Two Modeling Approaches." Journal of Applied Psychology 59 (1974): 753-58.

Romney, A. K., R. N. Shepard, and S. B. Nerlove, eds. Multidimensional Scaling: Theory and Applications in the Behavioral Sciences, Volume 2. New York: Seminar Press, 1972.

Stopher, P. R., and A. H. Meyburg. Urban Transportation Modeling and Planning. Lexington, Mass.: Lexington Books, 1975.

Watson, P. L. "Predictions of Intercity Modal Choice from Disaggregate, Behavioral and Stochastic Models." Highway Research Record 446 (1973): 28-35.

COGNITION

Anderson, N. H. "Information Integration Theory: A Brief Survey." In Contemporary Developments in Mathematical Psychology, Vol. 2, edited by D. H. Krantz, R. C. Atkinson, R. D. Luce, and P. Suppes. San Francisco: Freeman, 1974.

Caldwaller, M. T. "Cognitive Distance in Intraurban Space." In
  Environmental Knowing, edited by G. T. Moon and R. G.
  Golledge, pp. 316-24. 1976.

Carr, S., and D. Schissler. "The City as a Trip." Environment
  and Behavior 1 (1969): 7-37.

Dewar, R. E. "The Slash Obscures the Symbol on Prohibitive
  Traffic Signs." Human Factors 18 (1976): 253-58.

Dewar, R. E., J. G. Ells, and G. Mundy. "Reaction Time as an
  Index of Traffic Sign Perception." Human Factors 18 (1976):
  381-92.

Dewar, R. E., and H. A. Swanson. "Recognition of Traffic-
  Control Signs." Sponsored by Committee on Motorist Information Systems, Highway Research Record, vol. 414, 1972.

Dobson, R., T. F. Golob, and R. L. Gustafson. "Multidimensional
  Scaling of Consumer Preferences for a Public Transportation
  System: An Application of Two Approaches." Socioeconomic
  Planning Sciences 8 (1974): 23-37.

Ewing, R. H. "Psychological Theory Applied to Mode Choice Prediction." Transportation 2 (1973): 391-410.

Garling, T. "The Structural Analysis of Environmental Perception
  and Cognition." Environment and Behavior 8 (1976): 385-415.

Horton, F. E., and J. J. Louviere. "Behavioral Analyses and
  Transportation Planning: Inputs to Transit Planning." Transportation 3 (1974): 165-82.

Johnson, M. "Psychological Variables and Choice between Auto
  and Transit Travel: A Critical Research Review." Working
  Paper No. 7509, Institute of Transportation and Traffic Engineering, University of California, Berkeley, 1975.

Kameron, J. "Experimental Studies of Environmental Perception."
  In Environment and Cognition, edited by I. Ettelson, pp. 157-67.
  New York: Seminar Press, 1973.

Levin, I. P., M. K. Mosell, C. M. Lamka, B. E. Savage, and
  M. J. Gray. "Measurement of Psychological Factors and Their
  Role in Travel Behavior." Transportation Research Record 649
  (1977): 1-6.

Lowenthal, D., and M. Riel. "The Nature of Perceived and Imagined Environments." Environment and Behavior 4 (1972): 189-208.

Moore, G. T. "The Development of Environmental Knowing: An Overview of an Interactional Constructivist Theory and Some Data on Within-Individual Development Variations." In Psychology and the Built Environment, edited by D. Canter and T. Lee, pp. 185-94, 1974.

Recker, W. W., and T. F. Golob. "An Attitudinal Modal Choice Model." Transportation Research 10 (1976): 299-310.

Sommer, R. "Room Density and User Satisfaction." Environment and Behavior 3 (1971): 412-16.

Spear, B. D. "Attitudinal Modeling: Its Role in Travel Demand Forecasting." In Behavioral Travel-Demand Models, edited by P. R. Stopher and A. Meyburg, pp. 87-95. Lexington, Mass.: Lexington Books, 1975.

Stea, D. "Architecture in the Head: Cognitive Mapping." In Designing for Human Behavior, edited by J. Lang, C. Burnet, W. Maleski, and D. Vachin. Stroudberg, Pa.: Dowden, Hutchinson and Ross, 1974.

Stenson, H. "Cognitive Factors in the Use of Transit Systems." Final Report, US-DOT-IL-11-0008, Urban Systems Laboratory, University of Illinois at Chicago Circle, Chicago, 1978.

Stokols, D. "The Experience of Crowding in Primary and Secondary Environments." Environment and Behavior 8 (1976): 49-87.

Tardiff, T. J. "The Effects of Socio-Economic Status on Transportation Attitudes and Behavior." University of California, Graduate School of Social Sciences, Irvine.

Thomas, K. "A Reinterpretation of the 'Attitude' Approach to Transport-Mode Choice and an Exploratory Empirical Test." Environment and Planning A 8 (1976): 783-810.

Walker, R. E., R. C. Nicolay, and C. R. Stearns. "Comparative Accuracy of Recognizing American and International Road Signs." Journal of Applied Psychology 49 (1965): 322-25.

Yancey, L. L. "Psychological Factors Affecting Urban Travel: Responses to Crowding in Transit Vehicles." National Technical Information Service, Florida State University, Tallahassee, 1972.


EVALUATION

Campbell, D. T., and H. L. Ross. "The Connecticut Crackdown on Speeding." Law Society Review 3 (1968): 33-53.

Dewar, R. E., and J. Ells. "Comparison of Three Methods for Evaluating Traffic Signs." Sponsored by Committee on Motorist Information Systems, Transportation Research Record 503 (1974): 38-47.

Eash, R. W., A. Swanson, and M. Kaplan. "An Analysis and Evaluation of Alternative Schemes to Increase Auto Occupancy." Transportation Research 8 (1974): 335-41.

Hackman, J. R., and C. R. Oldman. "Development of the Job Diagnostic Survey." Journal of Applied Psychology 60 (1975): 159-70.

Hoinville, G. "Evaluating Community Preferences." Environment and Planning 3 (1971): 33-50.

Hutchinson, J. W., C. S. Cox, and B. R. Moffet. "An Evaluation of the Effectiveness of Televised, Locally Oriented Driver Reeducation." Transportation Research Record.

Jenkins, C. D., D. A. Nadler, E. E. Lawler, and C. Comman. "Standardized Observation: An Approach to Measuring the Nature of Jobs." Journal of Applied Psychology 60 (1975): 171-81.

Kobayashi, K., A. Yoichi, and A. Tani. "A Method for Evaluating Urban Transportation Planning in Terms of User Benefits." Transportation Research 9 (1975): 67-79.

Lee, J. W., D. O. Covault, and G. E. Willeke. "Framework for Using Social Indicators to Monitor, Evaluate and Improve a Public Transport System." Work sponsored by Committee on Social, Economic and Environmental Factors in Transportation, 1973.

Ross, R. B. "Measuring the Effects of Soft Variables on Travel Behavior." Traffic Quarterly 29 (1975): 333-46.

Ryan, C. R. , B. P. Nedevek, and E. A. Beinborn. "An Evaluation of the Feasibility of Social Diagnostic Techniques in Transportation Planning Process." Highway Research Record 410 (1972): 8-23.

INFORMATION PROCESSING

Braunstein, M. L. , and O. F. Coleman. "An Information Processing Model of the Aircraft Accident Investigator." Human Factors 9 (1967): 61-70.

Fergenson, P. E. "The Relationship between Information Processing and Driving Accident and Violation Record." Human Factors 13 (1971): 173-76.

Levin, I. P. "Comparing Different Models and Response Transformation in an Information Integration Task." Bulletin of Psychometric Science 7 (1976): 78-80.

Louviere, J. J. , and K. L. Norman. "Applications of Information Processing Theory to the Analysis of Urban Travel Demand." Environment and Behavior 9 (1977): 91-106.

McCormick, E. J. Human Factors Engineering. New York: McGraw-Hill, 1970.

Mehrabian, A. , and J. A. Russell. "A Verbal Measure of Information Rate in Studies in Environmental Psychology." Environment and Behavior 6 (1974): 233-52.

Rockwell, T. H. , and J. M. Snider. "Investigation of Device Sensory Capabilities and Its Effects on the Driving Tasks." RF 2091 Final Report, Research Foundation, The Ohio State University, Columbus, July 1969.

ORGANIZATIONAL DEVELOPMENT

Golembiewski, R. R. , K. Billingsley, and S. Yeager. "Measuring Change and Persistence in Human Affairs: Types of Change Generated by OD Design." Journal of Applied Behavioral Science 12 (1976): 133-57.

Golembiewski, R. T. , R. Hillen, and M. S. Kagno. "A Longitudinal Study of Flexi-Time Effects: Some Consequences of an OD Structural Intervention." Journal of Applied Behavioral Science 10 (1973): 503-32.

Golembiewski, R. T., and A. Kiepper. "MARTA: Toward an Effective, Open Giant." Public Administration Review 36 (1976): 46-60.

Hackman, J. R., C. R. Oldman, R. Jansan, and K. Purdy. "A New Strategy for Job Enrichment." California Management Review 17 (1975): 57-71.

Hamner, W. C., and D. L. Harnett. "Goal Setting, Performance and Satisfaction in an Interdependent Task." Organizational Behavior and Performance 12 (1974): 217-30.

Hautaluoma, J. E., and J. F. Gavin. "Effects of Organizational Diagnosis and Intervention on Blue Collar Blues." Journal of Applied Behavioral Science 11 (1975): 475-96.

Ivancevich, J. M. "Changes in Performance in a Management by Objectives Program." Administration Science Quarterly 19 (1974): 563-74.

Latham, C. P., and S. B. Kinne. "Improving Job Performance through Training in Goal Setting." Journal of Applied Psychology 59 (1974): 189-91.

Lathan, C. P., and C. A. Yukl. "A Review of Research on the Application of Goal Setting in Organization." Academy of Management Journal 18 (1975): 824-45.

Locke, E. A., N. Cartledge, and C. S. Knerr. "Studies of the Relationship between Satisfaction, Goal Setting and Performance." Organizational Behavior and Human Performance 5 (1970): 135-58.

Oldham, C. R., J. R. Hackman, and J. L. Pearce. "Conditions under Which Employees Respond to Enriched Work." Journal of Applied Psychology 61 (1976): 395-403.

Raia, A. P. "Goal Setting and Self-Control: An Empirical Study." Journal of Management Studies 2 (1965): 32-53.

Robey, D. "Task Design, Work Values and Worker Response: An Experimental Test." Organizational Behavior and Human Performance 12 (1974): 264–73.

Stedry, A. C., and E. Kay. "The Effects of Goal Difficulty in Performance." Behavioral Science 11 (1966): 459–70.

Steers, R. M. "Taskgoal Attributes in Achievement and Supervisory Performance." Organizational Behavior and Performance 13 (1975): 392–403.

Umstot, D. D., C. H. Bell, and T. R. Mitchell. "Effects of Job Enrichment and Task Goals on Satisfaction and Productivity: Implications for Job Design." Journal of Applied Psychology 61 (1976): 379–94.

White, S. E., T. R. Mitchell, and C. H. Bell. "Goal Setting, Evaluation Apprehension and Social Cues versus Determinants of Job Performance and Job Satisfaction in a Simulated Organization." Journal of Applied Psychology 62 (1977): 665–73.

## PERCEPTUAL MOTOR PROCESSING

Chaney, R. Whole Body Vibration of Standing Subjects. Boeing Co., BOE-D3-6779, 1965.

Cooper, G. E. "Understanding and Interpreting Pilot Opinions." Aeronautical Engineering Review 16 (1957): 47–52.

Forbes, T. W. "Predicting Attention-Gaining Characteristics of Highway Traffic Signs: Measurement Technique." Human Factors 6 (1964): 371–74.

Forbes, T. W., R. F. Snyder, and R. F. Pain. "A Study of Traffic Sign Requirements II: An Annotated Bibliography." College of Engineering, Michigan State University, Lansing, 1964.

Gordon, D. A. "Experimental Isolation of the Driver's Visual Input." Highway Research Record, vol. 122, 1966.

Gordon, D. A., and R. M. Michaels. "Static and Dynamic Visual Fields in Vehicular Guidance." Highway Research Record, vol. 84, 1963.

Harper, R. P., Jr., and G. E. Cooper. "A Revised Pilot Training Rating Scale for the Evaluation of Handling Qualities." Report No. 153, Cornell Aeronautical Labs, Ithaca, N.Y., September 1966.

Harte, D. B. "Estimates of the Length of Guidelines of Highway Guidelines and Spaces." Human Factors 17 (1975): 455-60.

McDonnell, J. D. "Pilot Rating Techniques for the Estimation and Evaluation of Handling Qualities." AFFDL Technical Report No. 68-76, U.S. Air Force Flight Dynamics Lab, Wright-Patterson Air Force Base, Ohio, December 1968.

McRuer, D. T., D. Graham, E. S. Krendel, and W. Reisener. "Human Pilot Dynamics in Compensatory Systems." AFFDL Technical Report No. 65-15, U.S. Air Force Flight Dynamics Lab, Wright-Patterson Air Force Base, Ohio, July 1965.

McRuer, D. T., and H. R. Jex. "Effects of Task Variables on Pilot Models for Manually Controlled Vehicles." Paper presented at advisory groups for Aerospace Research and Development Specialists Meeting on Stability and Control, September 25, 1966, Cambridge, England.

Moscowitz, H., K. Ziedman, and S. Sharma. "Visual Search Behavior while Viewing Driving Scenes under the Influence of Alcohol and Marihuana." Human Factors 18 (1976): 417-32.

O'Farrell, P. N., and J. Markham. "Commuter Perception of Public Transport Work Journeys." Environment and Planning A 6 (1974): 79-100.

Robinson, G. H., D. J. Erickson, G. L. Thurston, and R. L. Clark. "Visual Search by Automobile Drivers." Human Factors 14 (1972): 315-23.

Taylor, D. H. "Driver's Galvanic Skin Response and the Risk of an Accident." Ergonomic 7 (1964): 439-51.

Van Cott, H. P., and R. G. Kinkade, eds. Human Engineering Guide to Equipment Design. American Institute for Research, Washington, D.C., 1972.

# APPENDIX B
## List of Conference Participants

Ms. Virginia Ainslie
Northeast Ohio Areawide
  Coordinating Agency
1501 Euclid Avenue
Cleveland, Ohio 44115

Dr. Mark Alpert
Department of Marketing
  Administration
University of Texas
Austin, Texas 78712

Mr. Michael Arrow
Greater Hartford Transit
  District
179 Allyn Street
Hartford, Connecticut 06103

Mr. George Aul
Wilber Smith and Associates
40 Hemlock Road
New Haven, Connecticut 06513

Mr. William Barker
North Central Texas Council
  of Government
P. D. COG
Arlington, Texas 76011

Dr. Christian Bourgin
Institute de Recherche de
  Transport
2 Avenue de Generale Malleret-
  Joinville
94114 Arcueil Cedex
France

Mr. Daniel Brand
Charles River Associates
John Hancock Tower
200 Clarendon Street
Boston, Massachusetts 02116

Dr. Werner Brog
Sozialforchung Brog
Hans-Grassel-Weg 1
8000 Munchen 70
West Germany

Dr. Pat Burnett
Department of Geography and
  Transportation Center
Northwestern University
Evanston, Illinois 60201

Mr. Thomas Deen
A. M. Voorhees and Associates
7798 Old Springhouse Road
McLean, Virginia 22102

Mr. Joseph Dumas
Transportation Systems Center
Kendall Square
Cambridge, Massachusetts 02142

Mr. David Dunlap
Baltimore Regional Planning
  Council
701 St. Paul Street
Baltimore, Maryland 21202

Dr. Peter Everett
College of Human Development
Pennsylvania State University
University Park, Pennsylvania
16802

Dr. Gordon J. Fielding,
Director
Institute of Transportation
Studies
University of California
Irvine, California 92717

Mr. Ronald J. Fisher
U.S. Department of Transpor-
tation
Urban Mass Transportation
Administration
2100 Second Street, S. W.
Washington, D.C. 20590

Dr. Lewis Frees, President
Interaction, Inc.
12429 Cedar Road
Cleveland Heights, Ohio 44106

Mr. David Gendell
Federal Highway Administration
400 Seventh Street, S. W.
Washington, D.C. 20590

Mr. David N. Goss
Assistant General Manager
Greater Cleveland RTA
1404 East 9th Street
Cleveland, Ohio 44114

Mr. David Hartgen
New York Department of
Transportation
1220 Washington Avenue
State Campus
Albany, New York 12226

Dr. John Havens
American Institute for Research
22 Hilliard Street
Cambridge, Massachusetts 02138

Dr. Arthur Hawley
Department of Geography
University of North Carolina
Chapel Hill, North Carolina
27514

Mr. Terrell W. Hill
General Development Manager
Chicago Transit Authority
Box 3555
Chicago, Illinois 60654

Mr. Avram Horowitz
General Motors
Research Laboratories
Warren, Michigan 48090

Dr. Slade Hulbert
448 St. Francis Drive
Danville, California 94526

Mr. Larry Jenney
Office of Technology Assessment
U.S. Congress
Washington, D.C. 20510

Mr. Norman Ketola
ARI, Ltd.
137 Newburg Street
Boston, Massachusetts 02116

Mr. Ian Kingham
Transportation Research Board
2101 Constitution Avenue, N. W.
Washington, D.C. 20418

Dr. Samuel Z. Klausner,
Director
Center for Research on the
Acts of Man
3718 Locust Walk
Philadelphia, Pennsylvania 19104

Mr. Ken Koschek
New Jersey Department of
Environmental Protection
Bureau of Air Pollution Control
P. O. Box 2807
Trenton, New Jersey 08625

Ms. Patricia Labaw
R. L. Associates
44 Nassau Street, Suite 200
Princeton, New Jersey 08540

Dr. Bo Lenntorp
Department of Sociology and
Economic Geography
University of Lund
Solvegaten 13
S-22362 Lund, Sweden

Mr. David Lerman
Department of Civil Engineering
Massachusetts Institute of
Technology
77 Massachusetts Avenue
Cambridge, Massachusetts 02139

Dr. Irwin Levin
Psychology Department
University of Iowa
Iowa City, Iowa 52242

Dr. Jordan Louviere
Department of Business
Administration
University of Iowa
Iowa City, iowa 52242

Mr. John Mahoney
Tri-State Regional Planning
Commission
World Trade Center
New York, New York 10048

Dr. Joseph Margolin
205 Thistle Drive
Silver Spring, Maryland 20901

Dr. Richard M. Michaels,
Director
Urban Systems Laboratory
University of Illinois at
Chicago Circle
Box 4348
Chicago, Illinois 60680

Mr. John Obermeier
New Jersey Department of
Transportation

Dr. Robert Paaswell
Department of Civil Engineering
SUNY-Buffalo
Buffalo, New York 14214

Dr. Richard Pain
Bio Technology, Inc.
3027 Rosemary Lane
Falls Church, Virginia 22042

Dr. H. McIlvaine Parsons
Executive Director
Institute for Behavioral
Research, Inc.
2429 Linden Lane
Silver Springs, Maryland 20910

Dr. James Perry
Graduate School of Administration
University of California
Irvine, California 92708

Mr. Michael Powills
Barton-Aschman Associates, Inc.
820 Davis Street
Evanston, Illinois 60201

Mr. Richard Pratt
R. H. Pratt and Co. / Barton-
   Aschman Associates
1730 K Street
Washington, D. C. 20006

Mr. Carl Rappaport
Asst. for Energy Policy Analysis
Office of Intermodal Transpor-
   tation
Energy Policy Division (P-13)
Department of Transportation
400 Seventh Street, S. W.
Washington, D. C. 20590

Dr. Larry Richards
Department of Engineering
School of Engineering and
   Applied Science
University of Virginia
Charlottesville, Virginia 22901

Dr. Arthur Saltzman
Institute of Transportation
   Studies
North Carolina A & T State
   University
Greensboro, North Carolina
   27411

Dr. Paul Shuldiner
Department of Civil Engineering
University of Massachusetts
Amherst, Massachusetts 01003

Mr. Robert Skinner
A. M. Voorhees Associates
7798 Old Springhouse Road
McLean, Virginia 22101

Mr. Robert B. Sleight
Century Research Corporation
4113 Lee Highway
Arlington, Virginia 22207

Mr. D. J. Smith
California State Assembly
   Transportation Committee
State Capital Building, Room 4016
Sacramento, California 95814

Mr. Arthur Sosslau
COMIS Corporation
11141 Georgia Avenue
Weaton, Maryland 20902

Mr. Bruce Spear
Transportation Systems Center
Kendall Square
Cambridge, Massachusetts 02142

Mr. Burton Stephens
Office of Research
Federal Highway Administration
400 Seventh Street, S. W.
Washington, D. C. 20591

Dr. Peter Stopher
Department of Civil Engineering
Northwestern University
Evanston, Illinois 60201

Dr. Antti Talvitie
Department of Civil Engineering
SUNY-Buffalo
Buffalo, New York 14214

Ms. Mary Lynn Tischer
Federal Highway Administration
Department of Transportation
400 Seventh Street, S. W.
Washington, D. C. 20590

Mr. Wayne Torrey
Federal Highway Administration,
    HPP-10
400 Seventh Street, S. W.
Washington, D. C. 20590

Mr. Edward Weiner
U.S. Department of Trans-
    portation
Office of the Secretary, P-33
400 Seventh Street, S. W.
Washington, D. C. 20590

Mr. George Wickstrom
Executive Secretary
Metropolitan Washington
    Council of Government
1225 Connecticut Avenue, N. W.,
    Suite 201
Washington, D. C. 20036

Mr. John Wild
National Transportation Policy
    Study Commission
1750 K Street, N. W., Suite 800
Washington, D. C. 20006

Dr. Gerald Wilde
Department of Psychology
Queens University
Kingston, Ontario
Canada K7L3N6

Dr. William F. Woodman
Department of Sociology and
    Anthropology
Iowa State University
103 East Hall
Ames, Iowa 50011

Dr. Michael York
Department of Psychology
University of New Haven
300 Orange Avenue
West Haven, Connecticut 06516

# ABOUT THE EDITOR

RICHARD M. MICHAELS has been the Director of the Urban Systems Laboratory and Professor of Systems Engineering at the University of Illinois at Chicago Circle since 1974. He was previously the Director of Research of the Transportation Center at Northwestern University in Evanston, Illinois. Prior to his academic career, Dr. Michaels worked for the federal government in research and research management in transportation and urban development.

Dr. Michaels has published widely in the area of human factors, systems engineering, and travel behavior. His work has appeared in transportation journals as well as the psychological literature.

Dr. Michaels holds a B.S. from Bates College and received his M.A. and Ph.D. in experimental and engineering psychology from George Washington University.